D0045915

Proof of Life

ALSO BY DANIEL LEVIN

Nothing but a Circus: Misadventures among the Powerful

Proof of Life

TWENTY DAYS ON THE HUNT

FOR A MISSING PERSON

IN THE MIDDLE EAST

Daniel Levin

ALGONQUIN BOOKS OF CHAPEL HILL   2021

Published by
Algonquin Books of Chapel Hill
Post Office Box 2225
Chapel Hill, North Carolina 27515-2225

a division of
Workman Publishing
225 Varick Street
New York, New York 10014

Library of Congress Cataloging-in-Publication Data

Names: Levin, Daniel, [date]– author.
Title: Proof of life : twenty days on the hunt for a
missing person in the Middle East / Daniel Levin.
Description: Chapel Hill : Algonquin Books of Chapel Hill, 2021. |
Summary: "An account by an armed-conflict mediator searching for
a missing person in Syria over twenty tense days—at the end of which
he will either find 'proof of life' or not"— Provided by publisher.
Identifiers: LCCN 2020048421 | ISBN 9781643750989 (hardcover) |
ISBN 9781643751757 (ebook)
Subjects: LCSH: Blocher, Paul (Missing person) | Missing persons—Syria. |
Disappeared persons' families—Europe. | Syria—History—Civil War, 2011–
Classification: LCC HV6322.3.S97 L48 2021 | DDC 956.9104/232—dc23
LC record available at https://lccn.loc.gov/2020048421

10 9 8 7 6 5 4 3 2 1
First Edition

For Reem and Samar

La plus belle des ruses du diable est de vous
persuader qu'il n'existe pas.

The devil's finest trick is to persuade you
that he does not exist.

—CHARLES BAUDELAIRE,
Le spleen de Paris: Petits poèmes en prose

INTRODUCTION

THIS BOOK TELLS the story of my search for a missing person in Syria over twenty grueling days in 2014. It is a true story. This is not a history book about Syria or a journalistic account of a dreadful war full of horrific atrocities. This is also not a moralizing tale. It is hardly newsworthy to observe that evil exists everywhere, or at least everywhere humans exist, and it is certainly not unique to Syria or the Middle East.

The disappearance of the man at the center of this account did not make the news. At first, it was not even noticed, and then, once discovered, it was ignored by everyone who was in a position to help. It is a story about loss and sadness, about violence and death, about unspeakable cruelty and greed—the daily menu in Syria's devastating war. But it is also a story about courage, strength, and perseverance, about loyalty and wisdom. It is the story of all the monsters I encountered who were driven by their ravenous appetite for power and wealth. But it is also the story of some brave and inspiring souls who helped me selflessly and often at massive personal peril. Their acts of courage and sacrifice were my consolation, especially in those dark moments when the lines between those monsters and my own demons began to blur. Their support was my sustenance when those who should have cared didn't. These individuals—these angels—helped because they had lost everything but still managed to hold on to their humanity, which stood in brutal contrast to those who could have helped but chose not to and who had lost nothing *but* their humanity.

THROUGHOUT THESE TWENTY days in 2014, the pressure was unrelenting. Until the very end, I lived with the incessant feeling that my head was being held underwater. I tried to manage my distress, manipulate my own consciousness. I learned to categorize my fears by the degree to which they paralyzed me and also by the way they affected my focus and my memory. It was my memory in particular, my ability to recall these events and dialogues, that was strangely impacted by intimidation and my sense of danger. I learned that physical threats tended to sharpen my mind and etch the moment in my recollection like an engraved image. Later on, when the particular threat had subsided, I would be overcome by exhaustion, but the memory always remained intact. On the other hand, psychological threats, usually unspoken but menacing, tended to cause an immediate trauma, a momentary blackout that led to a frustrating memory void. These blackouts would last just a few moments, but my thoughts and feelings during these intervals ended up lost forever.

As the stakes grew higher, I became increasingly cognizant of my own isolation. During the frequent stretches that I was by myself, I felt exposed and vulnerable—on the street, in an airport or hotel lobby, in a taxi, and even as I made my way to the toilet in the back of a restaurant. I often had the feeling someone might be following me but resisted turning around to check, because I knew that if I did, I'd eventually stop forging ahead. Sometimes, as the pressure mounted in my loneliest, darkest hours, the nature of this nagging sensation morphed into something more vicious, more violent. In those moments, I felt like I was holding a hand grenade that was missing the pin and would detonate as soon as I dropped it out of the sweaty palm of my hand—killing not only me but also all those around me, whose safety was my responsibility.

DURING THESE THREE weeks, I received a crash course in the art of collecting and cashing chips—doing something of value for someone else in order to receive something of value in return at an opportune moment. As a result, I found myself permanently enmeshed in an intricate, dizzying web of favors and counterfavors. While I navigated these treacherous environments, the sensory overload triggered by adrenaline and fear was exhausting. I found myself being constantly tested, which sharpened my peripheral perception to the point of paranoia. I expended tremendous energy just trying to figure out whether I was manipulating those around me or whether I was the one being manipulated. What kept me minimally sane and aware of my own vulnerabilities was the wisdom of my dear friend Jacques de Pablo Lacoste who used to remind me that if you're sitting around a table playing poker and you don't know who the sucker is . . . chances are, it's you.

I KNEW THAT my sanity and survival, as well as my success, depended on my ability to recall every detail, no matter how incidental it may have seemed in the moment, and so I observed every behavioral nuance around me. Every language accent or piece of clothing could reveal vital information or help me determine whether I was in a safe environment or in a dangerous predicament. Every ritual could provide vital clues— from a handshake or kiss on the cheek to a gesture that might seem innocuous and good natured on its face but could carry a darker, threatening message.

I chronicled everything in a diary and recorded several of the conversations with my phone, which I then transcribed into Swiss German. An Israeli acquaintance who had been an officer in the famed Unit 8200 of the Israeli military's Intelligence Corps advised me, for safety's sake, to transcribe and then immediately delete the recordings. He demonstrated how easy it was to hack into my phone and access its data, including the stored recordings. In my heightened state of alertness, it didn't take much to convince me to follow his recommendation. The Swiss-German twist was something I learned from a Russian friend who had remained close to Vladimir Putin since their days together in Dresden in the late 1980s. Apparently, and to this day I'm not sure whether he meant this tongue in cheek, Swiss German was one of the very few local tongues the KGB had struggled mightily to crack. My friend likened this dialect more to a throat disease than a language.

When I couldn't write in the very instant or hadn't been able to turn on my recording device, I reconstructed the events and conversations in my diary before the end of each day. The transcripts of these notes are rendered word for word in the dialogues throughout this book. Not a word was altered and no conversation was summarized when I was able to deliver it exactly as it had taken place, but I did edit the dialogues to eliminate empty fillers such as "umm," "get it?," "I mean," "you know," and "so" at the beginning of sentences, as well as "like"—*yaani* in Arabic.

I recognize that my own memory can be biased and noisy, and at times I was surprised when, much later, I read my own notes, diaries, and recording transcripts because I had remembered some incidences and exchanges differently. Whenever I could, I tried to reconfirm my recollections with those who had been present. At times, their memories and impressions diverged from mine. In the interest of accuracy and objectivity, I have included these discrepancies in footnotes throughout the book. I have also pointed out in footnotes those instances in which I had to rely on others for information and was unable to verify it independently.

As mentioned, some people helped me greatly and supplied me with crucial bits of information at the peril of being discovered and facing draconian, even fatal, consequences. Most of these individuals and their families are still in harm's way, and I have used pseudonyms and altered certain traits or changed minor details of a few venues in order to prevent the possibility of reverse-engineering their identity or location. Lastly, I had to protect myself by concealing the identities of particular individuals. I did not, however, anonymize a single perpetrator, and I did not alter or embellish the physical appearance of any person. Those descriptions are factual and unvarnished.

The following names, listed in alphabetical order, are pseudonyms: Alex, Aliya, Bassel, Clyde, Fuad, Huby, Jamil, Loubna, Paul, Reem, Saif, Samar, Sami, the Sheikh, and Tatyana. All other individuals are called by their real names, including each person in the postscript.

Proof of Life

ONE

HUBY WAS ALREADY seated at our table when I arrived at Marius et Janette, the Parisian restaurant he had chosen for our meeting. It happened to be the same restaurant where I had taken my wife out for dinner the first time she had visited me in Paris shortly after we met in the mid-1990s, and it was also the restaurant my friend Jacques would insist on whenever we were in Paris together.

As soon as I entered, the headwaiter came up to me, took my coat, and informed me that Maître Mazerius was expecting me. The restaurant was unusually empty for a Tuesday evening, just a few scattered guests. There was that familiar mustiness in the air, enriched by the scent of butter and garlic, which seemed to emanate in equal parts from the kitchen, the wood-paneled walls, and the stuffy waiters.

"Have a seat, Daniel," Huby said with a smile. "It's nice to see you. How long has it been? A year?"

"Yes, that sounds about right," I said. "The last time we met was with Jacques, here in Paris, over dinner in this very restaurant."

"Ah, our friend Jacques, how's he doing?"

Jacques was one of my favorite people and as close to a mentor as I had ever had, a fiercely loyal man of exhilarating intelligence and uncompromising principles.

"Excellent, *en pleine forme*, as he would say. Anyway, in your message you indicated that there is something important you would like to discuss with me. So here I am."

I had received an email from Huby a few days earlier, asking me to meet him in Paris on a life and death matter. Huby had never exhibited any melodramatic tendencies in the past, so I was both worried and intrigued.

"Indeed," Huby said with a solemn look, "more than just important. A man's life hangs in the balance. But first, let's enjoy a delicious dinner. This place has the best fish in town, and I've ordered us both the *loup de mer*. I hope you don't mind."

"Not at all, thanks," I replied, surprised that this life and death matter could wait until we had finished our meal and also a little annoyed at having someone else decide what I should eat. I got over my annoyance once I realized that Huby had also taken the liberty of preordering a Macallan, neat, which the waiter placed before me with a knowing smile.

"Once you hear what I am about to tell you, you'll probably think of our dinner as the Last Supper," Huby said, displaying his penchant for religious references.

"Then why wait?" I asked. "If a man's life hangs in the balance, as you put it, let's get on with it. There is no one within earshot. Tell me what's on your mind. What's going on?"

Huby gave me an odd look and lifted his glass of Macallan, motioning for me to do the same. "Let's drink to life," he said with a sudden expression of sadness.

We sat in silence for a few minutes sipping our whiskeys until the waiter brought the fish to the table and presented it proudly on a silver platter. Huby nodded approvingly.

"Come on, Huby," I insisted as soon as the waiter had disappeared with the fish. "What is it you want to discuss with me?"

"I suggest we enjoy this delightful dinner now, live in the moment. We can go for a long stroll afterward, and I'll fill you in on all the gory details."

For the rest of the meal, Huby chatted about politics, then moved to one of his favorite topics, the deeper messages and meanings hidden in Michelangelo's paintings on the ceiling of the Sistine Chapel. But I was not interested in Huby's musings about Renaissance symbolism and Freemasons. When we finished our meal, Huby ordered us each a cognac. From past experience I knew that for Huby there was no such thing as just one cognac; it would be a while before we left for our walk.

"Tell me, Daniel," Huby said after the waiter served our drinks, "are you still engaged in the Syrian conflict?"

I hadn't seen that one coming. My surprise must have been apparent, because Huby immediately added, "Don't worry, I don't really know what exactly you are doing there. When we first met a couple of years ago, you told me a little bit about your political development work in the Gulf and some other initiatives in the Middle East. I asked Jacques what you have been up to these days, but you know our discreet friend Jacques—silent as the grave, so I haven't been able to squeeze any information out of him. But I did hear that you've recently been busy in the Middle East—you know, Lebanon, Jordan, Syria."

If his clarification had been intended to reassure me, it had the opposite effect. I had never told Huby about my work with a European foundation and select individuals in Syria—code-named Project Bistar— toward a negotiated settlement and our efforts to identify and prepare young, promising Syrians for future leadership roles in a postwar Syria.* Sadly, despite the Syrian regime's initial eagerness and support, the rulers' fear of defection ended up far outweighing their desire for national reconciliation and rebuilding, and once we learned that underhanded measures were being taken to prevent this group of future leaders from

---

* Project Bistar started when our foundation was asked in December 2011 to engage in Syria, where the Arab Spring conflict had exploded in March of that year with tremendous violence after the Ba'athist government of President Bashar al-Assad opened fire on unarmed protesters, which in turn triggered massive demonstrations and the impromptu formation of new opposition groups. The request to assist in mediating between the warring sides had originally come from the government, opposition groups, and organizations within Syrian civil society in the hope of working quietly behind the scenes toward a negotiated settlement and, at a second stage, identifying young, next-generation individuals of the Alawite, Sunni, Druze, and Christian communities with leadership potential. At that time, the Syrian regime was keen to appear open to a negotiated settlement, as its troops and affiliated militias were suffering heavy losses. All that changed with the Russian intervention in the Syrian war in September 2015, when Russian, Iranian, and Hezbollah troops turned the Syrian regime's fortunes around, and its officials in Damascus began to deny that they had ever consented to any mediation efforts or negotiations with the "terrorist" opposition.

leaving and participating in our initiative, our foundation had no choice
but to end it in late 2013—or risk ridicule and contempt for our gulli-
bility and our willingness to take part in what had amounted to nothing
more than a public relations stunt by President Assad and his allies. I
was now trying to concentrate on different matters in other parts of the
world in the hope that my disappointment in this failed initiative would
fade away. Huby's mention of Syria brought it all back with a bang.

"What do you mean?" My throat tightened.

"Well, a friend of mine close to Number One mentioned that you
were well connected in that rather nasty part of the world," Huby
answered with a smirk.

"Your friend just happened to mention this?" I asked, too irritated
to inquire about which friend and which Number One he was referring to. Since this was Huby, it could have been anyone in Washington,
London, Paris, Riyadh, or any other capital city. Over the past two years,
I had witnessed Huby's immediate access to the inner sanctum of several global leaders. He was their trusted and discreet adviser, especially
when it came to procuring petroleum resources, and had played a major
role in securing long-term supplies of Niger-originated uranium for
France and Japan—a role that placed him in the crosshairs of the US
government after President Bush's erroneous claim in his 2003 State of
the Union speech that Saddam Hussein had tried to acquire significant
quantities of uranium from Africa.* In Huby's apartment on Avenue

---

* In January 2003, President George W. Bush stated in his State of the Union speech that "the
British Government has learned that Saddam Hussein recently sought significant quantities
of uranium from Africa." This false statement, made in order to bolster the claim that Saddam
Hussein possessed or was developing weapons of mass destruction, became known as "the Sixteen
Words." Huby had apparently drawn the ire of Vice President Cheney's staff when he contacted the
administration to point out President Bush's mistake and explain that Niger's long-term supply of
uranium was already committed to France and Japan and couldn't possibly have been sold to Iraq.
Huby had also shared his findings with his friend Joseph Wilson, an American diplomat who had
investigated the matter and concluded that Saddam Hussein had not purchased yellowcake uranium
from Niger. Ambassador Wilson was penalized for his public conclusion when the CIA employment
of his wife, Valerie Plame, was leaked through a Washington Post columnist. Ibrahim Mayaki, a
former prime minister of Niger, has corroborated these long-term uranium supply commitments
of Niger for the exclusive benefit of France and Japan to me directly. He also confirmed to me that
he had shared this information with Ambassador Wilson during his trip to Niger in 2002.

Foch in Paris's posh sixteenth arrondissement hung pictures of Huby with presidents in the White House, the Élysée Palace, and the Kremlin.

Huby smiled. "Let's say it was eighty percent happenstance and ten percent intentional coincidence."

"I'll try to ignore the missing ten percent, which probably got lost paying for some commission. We are talking about the Middle East, after all."

"Try to check your Swiss instincts, Daniel. It doesn't always have to add up to one hundred. Anyway, back to my question: Are you still doings things in Syria and the region?"

I took a sip of my cognac and nodded. To my surprise, Huby did not order another round but instead asked immediately for the bill.

"In that case, let's discuss the rest on our walk," Huby said as the waiter placed the bill on the table. "I'll need to oxygenate my gray cells for this chat." Huby pulled out his money clip and placed two hundred euros on the table. The headwaiter handed us our coats and Huby his fedora, and we stepped outside the restaurant.

"Let's go for the long loop, if you don't mind," Huby suggested. "We'll end up at the Trocadéro, with a perfect view of the Eiffel Tower. My daily routine when I am in Paris."

"The Eiffel Tower also looks lovely from where we are standing right now," I said, not really in the mood for a three-mile trek in uncomfortable shoes. "Why don't we talk here?"

"*Crétin!*" Huby chided me with feigned disgust. "You must work for that view, earn it with a crisp, honest walk."

We both laughed as we started to stroll to Avenue Montaigne in the direction of the Champs-Élysées. We walked for a few minutes in silence before Huby began. "I was approached two weeks ago by a close friend. Actually, one of my oldest friends, going all the way back to elementary school." He paused, lost in his thoughts. "Something terrible has happened to my friend. His son has gone missing in Syria," he finally continued. Huby's expression was pained.

For a brief moment, my mind went completely numb. Another missing person in Syria. Very, very few disappearances in Syria had happy endings, and I had just lived through an unnerving ordeal trying to find a kidnapped hostage. Against the backdrop of our foundation's Project Bistar, I had been approached several times in 2013 and 2014 with requests for help in locating hostages and missing people in Syria—aid workers, journalists, military advisers, and the occasional adventure-seeking traveler. These requests came from a variety of corners—governments, families, friends of the missing persons—and for a variety of reasons, though they all were based on the assumption that because of my work in the region and the connections formed while interacting with Project Bistar participants and their political patrons, especially the regime in Damascus, I might know someone who knew someone who knew someone who could help. The classic Levantine arrangement, in other words.

From my own painful experiences, I knew how hard, bordering on the impossible, it would be to find the son of Huby's friend in Syria, let alone finding him alive and negotiating his release. It was considered an accomplishment just to obtain reliable information on the fate or recent location of a missing person; it was a *great* accomplishment to obtain proof of life. I was unaware of any case of a released hostage that did not involve direct or indirect ransom payments or informal barter arrangements. I was still reeling from the bitter disappointment of my own recent failure.

Huby must have sensed that he had struck a nerve, because he did not say another word. We strode in complete silence until we turned left on the Champs-Élysées. Immediately, we were met by that typical Parisian cacophony: impatient drivers beeping their horns, a siren of a speeding police car, and the ubiquitous scooters that sounded like amped-up lawn mowers. The glory days of this elegant avenue between the Place de la Concorde and the Arc de Triomphe seemed long gone; at this moment, the street was particularly gray and grimy.

"Why are you telling me this? Why me?"

"Why you?" he returned the question as he stopped abruptly. "I'll tell you why you. Because I need your help."

I was weary and also irritated by Huby's repetition of my question. In the course of our foundation's work and my attempts at profiling and identifying suitable candidates for future leadership roles, I had become suspicious of people who threw my questions back at me instead of answering them. Too often, it was an attempt to stall for time in order to concoct some fabrication or find an inconspicuous way to hide real intentions.

"What makes you think I can help?" I asked.

"Because I believe you might be equipped to help. Because you know the region well. And because I am desperate. I am out of options. Please hear me out, Daniel. You can always say no. Besides, ever since our trip together to that *espèce de con* on his Virginia plantation, I feel a strong bond between us, a friendship. And friends help each other in times of need."

THE TRIP TO Virginia! That was two years earlier, in the fall of 2012. I was joining Jacques for a dinner in a beautiful Georgetown mansion on the outskirts of Washington, DC. It was the kind of male-dominated gathering I had often experienced as a young boy during my father's diplomatic career, when government officials, ambassadors, and prominent businessmen would congregate at our home for alcohol and cigar-infused soirées. I always marveled at my father's ability to cruise effortlessly among his guests and engage in light yet substantive banter; he had perfected the art of small talk in several languages.

This evening in Georgetown had that same familiar feeling. Among the expected guests were two European ambassadors and a US senator, though Jacques mentioned that there was someone else he really wanted me to meet. As soon as we arrived, he wasted no time introducing me to

Huby—Hubertus Mazerius—whom Jacques described as the only interesting person present.

Well, Huby certainly was colorful. He was a gregarious, larger-than-life character who commanded a strong, charismatic presence in the room despite his average, slightly pudgy stature. He was downing a glass of champagne while devouring the canapés with reckless abandon, giving the impression of a fun-loving bon vivant with a strong hedonistic bent.

As soon as Jacques mentioned to him that I had just returned from a trip to Qatar and the United Arab Emirates, Huby launched into the history of the Gulf and began to regale us in rapid-fire, alternating French and English with entertaining stories of his many years in Dubai and Saudi Arabia. Clearly, he knew the region very well, and he seemed to be on friendly terms with several of its rulers and powerbrokers. Even though Huby dominated the dinner with his booming baritone voice, he managed not to seem immodest.

Later that evening, I mentioned to Huby that Saudi Arabia had always been the one country in the Gulf I found particularly difficult to penetrate, and not for lack of trying. Huby took this as an invitation to talk about the impending power transition in Saudi Arabia with all that was at stake once the horizontal brother-to-brother successions had reached the end of the line. In captivating anecdotes of several Saudi princes, he described how the daggers were coming out for the combustible vertical power transition to the next generation, now that the Sudairi Seven—the powerful sons of King Abdulaziz—were slowly dying out. Huby had the talent of triggering that tingling sensation that comes from being clued in on some juicy conspiracy, even when he was just sharing his analysis on the developments he believed were in store for this volatile region. His anecdotes were highly entertaining but not malicious or gossipy. A born raconteur.

At the end of the evening, Huby invited me to a meeting with an influential political operator who had spent decades at the intersection of the US government and the oil majors. Apparently this person also happened to be a very close friend of the Saudi ambassador in Washington. The meeting was to take place the next day at the gentleman's estate in Virginia, about a ninety-minute drive from Washington. Huby's invitation caught me by surprise. I was about to decline when Jacques pulled me to the side and encouraged me to accept, assuring me that the excursion would, if nothing else, be an interesting and entertaining experience. We agreed that his driver would pick me up at my hotel.

At ten sharp the next morning, a black Mercedes Maybach limousine pulled up in front of my hotel, and the driver stepped out to open the car door.

"Good morning, sir," he said with a warm smile as I got into the limousine. "My name's Clyde. We will now collect Mr. Mazerius."

As we drove through the congested roads to Huby's home, Clyde told me about his childhood growing up as a Black kid in Chicago's South Side, and how he had ended up as Huby's personal driver whenever he visited Washington. We arrived at Huby's house, and Clyde stepped out of the car to ring the doorbell. A minute later, Huby showed up, immaculately dressed and wearing what I later learned was his signature Borsalino classic fedora.

"Off we go, Clyde," Huby said in a chipper mood. "You know the address."

"Yes, sir," Clyde replied. "Traffic's not too bad on the way. We should be there by noon."

Huby turned to me. "Our host is a bit of a good ol' boy. Beneath his southern charm beats the heart of a Dixiecrat who believes that this country has gone from sugar to shit ever since the civil rights movement." I caught Clyde's eyes through the rearview mirror as Huby continued. "His vernacular is a tad country-clubby and requires some getting used to. But he's a clever and smooth operator, incredibly well connected to the upper echelons of both parties. As I told you yesterday evening, he also has excellent ties to the Saudis—not only to their ambassador in DC but also to the big kahunas in Riyadh. I am eager to hear his perspective on the upcoming changes in that region, especially who he thinks will succeed King Abdullah when he kicks the can."

"I'm looking forward to meeting him," I said.

"We're invited for lunch," Huby continued, "which essentially means several stiff cocktails and some lousy food. We can stop for something decent to eat on the way back to DC."

We drove through the beautiful countryside with the sun shining softly, and I marveled at the gorgeous display of fall leaves in their full color spectrum. Just before noon, as Clyde had estimated, we drove up a long driveway lined with dogwood trees that must have looked spectacular in spring. A butler was waiting for us in front of the house and walked up to the car.

"Welcome, gentlemen," he said, opening the door on Huby's side. "May I please take your hat, sir?"

Huby handed him his fedora, and the butler walked us into the house to a large reception room. The walls were covered with hunting rifles and mounted animal heads.

A man in his early seventies entered the room, together with a younger man about half his age. Both were wearing cowboy boots and khaki slacks with blue button-down shirts. A huge silver belt buckle with the words AMERICAN BY BIRTH was adorning the waistline of the younger man.

"I'm Richard," the older man said as we shook hands, "and this is my son George. Welcome to my humble abode."

"Thank you, Richard. Pleased to meet you."

"Call me Dick," he said, leaving me a little puzzled about why he would introduce himself as Richard, just in order to switch it immediately to Dick. "Glad you could make it. Nice to see you again, Huby."

As we made our way to the sitting area, Dick turned to his son and instructed him to arrange for a glass of water to be delivered to our driver, referring to Clyde by that hateful word with the hard *r* at the end as he continued to walk nonchalantly toward the sofa.

I was stunned. Huby turned to me without missing a beat. "We're leaving, Daniel. I apologize for the confusion. I thought we were at a private residence, but it seems that we have landed in a plantation."

Dick looked at Huby with a gaze that oozed abject contempt. "Well, Huby, I suppose I was wrong about you. I didn't have you pegged as someone who loves those fuckin' people." Dick then repeated the slur.

The tension in the room was unbearable. For a few long moments, we all just stared at each other.

"You know, Dick," Huby finally said, "I never really saw an upside to people like you. But you've helped me figure it out. People like you exist so that I can atone for all my sins at once. I thank you for that."

Without another word, Huby turned around and walked to the front door. The butler handed him his hat.

"Thank you," Huby said to the butler. "My condolences."

I followed Huby out the door, and we walked straight to the car. Clyde was about to jump out to open the car doors for us, but Huby signaled for him to remain seated.

We drove down the long driveway and turned onto the main road.

"Where are we heading, sir?" Clyde asked.

"Back to DC, please," Huby said. "We'll drop off Daniel at the hotel, and then I'll head home. I suggest we call it a day."

None of us spoke a word for the next thirty minutes. The leaves that had looked so colorful on the way there now seemed ashen, almost dead.

"I'm very sorry for what happened at Dick's place," Huby finally said with a heavy sadness. "It seems that America's original sin is alive and well."

I could tell from Clyde's gaze in the rearview mirror that he had put it all together. When we arrived at my hotel, Huby turned to me and shook my hand with a faint nod of the head. Before I could get out of the car, Clyde had already opened the door.

"Thank you, Clyde," I said. "It was nice meeting you."

"Nice meeting you, too, sir," Clyde replied. "As I say, being Black is a full-time job in this country." Without another word, he stepped back into the car and drove off with Huby.

Later that evening, I met Jacques for dinner. Still trying to process the events in Virginia, I told him about Dick's ugly slur and about Huby's swift and principled reaction. Jacques listened intently.

"I am glad Huby reacted the way he did," he said after I finished my account. "But never forget that Huby is a very clever, shrewd operator. He plans everything carefully, makes deliberate choices, and leaves nothing to chance."

"What do you mean?" I was confused by Jacques's tempered reaction.

"Well, this was obviously not the first time Huby met this Dick," Jacques said, clearly enjoying the double entendre. "He has known him for years, so he must have been aware of his racist inclinations, right?"

I nodded.

"Chances are," Jacques continued, "this was not the first time he has heard this man utter that despicable word. Yet he has not severed all contacts with this person. Why is that?"

I muttered some feeble reply.

"I am not saying that Huby lacks a moral compass," Jacques said. "He is not a bad guy. But he is not a caballero. Then again, very few people are." Being a caballero—fiercely loyal and protective, willing to sacrifice anything, including his own life, to do the right, honorable thing—was reserved in Jacques's world for the finest, most honorable specimen.

"If Huby knew that there was a good chance Dick would show his ugly side, then why did he orchestrate this road trip?" I asked.

"Huby must have thought this through carefully," Jacques replied with a smile. "He knows that you are very active in the Gulf and the

Middle East, and I may have mentioned to him that you also have some decent contacts here in Washington. I already told you yesterday that Huby is a master networker with incredible relationships worldwide— look up the word *Rolodex* in the dictionary, and you will find a picture of Huby. Now, our friend Huby is keenly aware of Dick's behind-the-scenes influence in US politics, so it was a win-win: either the meeting would go well, in which case you would have reaped the benefits of entering Dick's world, with all the considerable business and political benefits his proximity might entail, or Dick would reveal his ugly side, as he indeed ended up doing, in which case Huby would get a chance to demonstrate his noble, progressive principles. In both scenarios, you would think highly of Huby."

"That's a little cynical," I said, "even for you, Jacques."

"Perhaps," Jacques said. "But I have my reasons. Huby is brilliant at collecting credit chips, and he is just as brilliant at cashing them in once they have reached peak value."

"What could he possibly ever need from *me*?"

Jacques sighed. "Nothing right now and nothing tomorrow. But mark my words: we'll live to see the day when Huby will come call-ing, when he will need something from you. And he will count on the fact that you will remember the honorable stance he took when he con-fronted that ugly man in front of you. Huby did not get this far without being a master manipulator. When I said win-win, I did not mean for you. I meant for Huby."

JACQUES'S PREMONITIONS OF two years ago seemed to have been prescient—the day when Huby would come calling had finally arrived. Had I been able to connect Huby's request to see me with that Virginia trip and the favorable light in which he managed to appear, and had I had the presence of mind to anticipate his request of a favor, I probably would have refused the meeting or at least delayed it until its urgency might have rendered it moot. Huby's interest in the Middle East and the Persian Gulf, together with that ominous "life and death matter" wording in his email, should have alerted me to the possibility that this could well involve a combination of a hostage situation and Syria. I was disappointed in my inability to see it coming, and I hated the fact that I was surprised, so unprepared. It was a rookie mistake.

"Okay, Huby," I said reluctantly as I tried to refocus on our conversation. "Go ahead, tell me more about this person who has gone missing in Syria."

"Well," Huby started hastily, either missing or ignoring the trepidation in my voice. "This young man seems to have entered Syria from Turkey with a Kurdish acquaintance about two months ago. His last Skype call to his father was two days after he arrived in Syria. He said that he planned to go to Aleppo to help out some volunteer doctors, or something along those lines, and that he would be in touch once he reached the city. That was the last time his father heard from him. Since then, no calls, no texts, no emails."

"Has he contacted anyone else?" I asked. "His mother, girlfriend or wife, brother or sister? A friend? His employer?"

"His mother died when he was a young boy, and my friend raised him mostly by himself. He has no siblings. He was in between jobs, trying to figure out what he wanted to do with his life, who he wanted to become. I guess this journey to Syria was part of that—trying to find a purpose, trying to find some meaning in his life."

"What's this person's name?" I asked.

"Paul. Paul Blocher."

I knew of thirteen, possibly fourteen, people who were currently missing in Syria, but this name did not ring a bell. Just a week earlier, I had traveled to Washington to meet a friend who worked at the Justice Department. He had been tasked with coordinating the search for missing American civilians in a number of countries, specifically Iraq, Iran,

Yemen, Afghanistan, and Syria. While each disappearance was tragic and fraught with strong emotional pressures from the families, he found the Syrian cases particularly grueling because of the public executions and their viral disseminations through social media. He shared with me the names of all the Americans and Europeans who were missing in Syria so that we could aggregate and synchronize our information.

He told me about the mother of one particular missing person who called him every day in tears, imploring him to find her son. He had asked his colleagues at the FBI and the CIA for assistance but was coming up empty everywhere. One field officer in southern Lebanon told him that he had heard a rumor about this American's death in the infamous Adra prison in the northeast suburbs of Damascus. The Syrian regime had circulated a list of prisoners who were supposed to be released in the coming weeks as a gesture of goodwill, and this American's name had apparently been taken off the list at the last moment. This was not a good sign, and my friend had to break the news to the missing person's mother. Before placing that dreaded call, he asked me to check with a contact of mine in Damascus—a Syrian military doctor, whom I had met seventeen years earlier at a hotel in Cyprus. Over the years, we had stayed in touch sporadically but rekindled our relationship when it turned out that his nephew was one of the participants designated by the Syrian regime in our foundation's Project Bistar.

I'd called this doctor right then to inquire whether he would be able to obtain some proof of life or death. Half an hour later, he called me back with an answer. He had been able to check the death certificates issued by the Adra prison over the past three months, and the missing American's name was not among them. I thanked him and promised to be in touch again soon, and next time without asking for a favor. My Justice Department friend had listened to the conversation and heaved a sigh of relief. "No bad news—I'll take it," he said as he pulled out his own phone to call the missing person's mother.

I had noticed a consistent emotional pattern to these disappear-ances: in the first phase, the primary sensations are desperation and fear, and every day without good news is devastating. After this initial phase, which usually lasts six to eight weeks, the perspective changes and, with it, the emotions. Now, every day without bad news is a day worth cel-ebrating, a day of hope. Judging by my friend's relief and the mother's cries of joy, which I could hear through his phone, it was clear that this person had been missing for a few months. It was a sad pattern, born out of despair and helplessness.

PAUL BLOCHER WAS not on my friend's list, and I had not come across this name in any other context. None of my contacts in Syria, Lebanon, or Jordan had mentioned him when discussing kidnapped Westerners, and his name had not appeared in the local press. I also did not recall seeing his name in the region's chatty social media, which I checked reg-ularly for more or less reliable tidbits that appeared nowhere else.

"Strange," I said to Huby as we continued to saunter up the Champs-Élysées. "I have not come across the name Paul Blocher."

"His name has not been made public," Huby said. "Paul's father con-cluded that his son's chances of survival would increase if he kept the whole thing private."

"He might not be totally wrong in that regard," I said as I remembered a very recent, excruciating search and negotiation for a missing person and how misguided publicity had made everything so much more dif-ficult and painful—and very dangerous—for those involved. Remaining quiet, especially in the first couple of weeks after a person has gone miss-ing, was critical in order to avoid excessive ransom demands based on the captors' perception that public, prominent calls for a person's release proved the hostage's importance and high value. But there was a fine line between being too passive and working behind the scenes through trusted, private channels to obtain information, negotiate a release, or just convey the impression that while the hostage had little value, there still could be a significant upside to the captors if they agreed to release him.*

We arrived at the top of the Champs-Élysées, and Huby motioned for us to turn at the road circling the Arc de Triomphe. At Avenue Kléber, we turned again, and the barrage of noise faded away almost instantly.

Several times, I sensed that Huby was about to say something, but he stopped himself whenever a person approached us on the sidewalk. Finally, he took a deep breath and started to speak. "As I mentioned in the restaurant, your name came up when I asked another friend for help in locating Paul in Syria. I'm only trying to lend a helping hand to someone I care about deeply as he struggles to find his son. Paul is all my friend has left. He's tried everything and everyone but has hit a wall wherever he turns. The government is of no help. It has no meaningful channels into Syria and has made little effort to look into this through the few contacts it does have. My friend also reached out to the aid groups that are active in Aleppo, including Doctors Without Borders. Nobody has heard of Paul, and it seems that he never arrived in Aleppo. The journalists covering Syria have no idea either. My friend also failed to identify this Kurdish acquaintance his son had mentioned—the one who smuggled him across the border into Syria. In their last call, Paul told his father about someone called Alan, but my friend is not sure whether his son was referring to the person who had taken him into Syria. He does not even know whether this Kurdish fellow is Turkish or Syrian. So basically, we have nothing to go on. It seems that Paul Blocher has vanished into thin air." Huby flicked the fingers of his right hand as he spoke.

---

* Many additional considerations factor into a decision of reaching out privately or semi-publicly to the captors, including the hostage's nationality and profession, the official stance of the hostage's home country and government on "negotiating with terrorists" and ransom payments (as well as the gap between the government's official stance and its actions), the visibility and activism of the hostage's family (parents or spouse), the availability of direct access to the captors to avoid message distortions by commercially minded middlemen, and whether a proxy relationship exists between the captors and a political authority (e.g., Alawi militias and the Syrian regime).

"I'm very sorry," I said. "Your friend must be devastated."

"He is. His hair turned white overnight when he could not locate his son. He barely eats and is unable to sleep. He keeps replaying their last conversation in his head, over and over again, trying to discover little bits of information he might have overlooked. I spoke to him by phone this morning, and he couldn't stop sobbing. He told me that he can no longer remember his son's voice—that it is fading away like the image on an old black-and-white photograph."

Huby spoke the last words with a slight tremble in his voice, betraying emotion that resonated deeply with me. The year 2014 had been a particularly awful one in Syria during a war that has had nothing but particularly awful years. It was a year replete with gruesome murders and executions, including the beheadings of American journalists James Foley and Steven Sotloff, British aid workers David Haines and Alan Henning, American aid worker Peter Kassig, the Lebanese soldiers Ali al-Sayyed and Abbas Medlej, as well as countless Syrians. But in addition to these terrifying deaths, some of which were recorded and made public in appalling, grisly videos, there were other people who had gone missing—people whose names were never made public and who remained anonymous and unspoken for, just like Paul Blocher.*

We continued to walk in silence until we arrived at the Trocadéro. As we stepped in between the two wings of the imposing Palais de Chaillot building, the Eiffel Tower suddenly appeared on the other

---

* Most of these nameless people were volunteer doctors, aid workers, and amateur journalists. There were also some adventurers whose absence often remained unnoticed for days, weeks, or even months because these individuals had in their past exhibited a tendency to disappear from time to time. In addition, their families assumed, usually for good reason, that ill-timed publicity would decrease the likelihood of release or survival of their loved ones. In many instances, the main reason no one ever heard that these unfortunate individuals had disappeared in Syria was that their friends and families were overwhelmed and simply unsure what to do or whom to turn to in these moments of worry and anguish. Several of these missing people were dual citizens—American and Syrian, British and Syrian, or French and Syrian—which complicated matters even further, because their families were told or "gently encouraged" to exhaust all avenues with the Syrian authorities first—a dead end by any other name.

side of the river, full of lights and sparkle. Huby stopped at the top of the steps.

"I come to this spot most evenings when I am in Paris," he said. "The view is still as miraculous to me today as it was the very first time I came here, despite all the tourists and peddlers. It never gets old."

There was something mesmerizing about the Eiffel Tower at night, as if a magic wand had touched this iron colossus and turned it into a tree of glittering dreams. I envied Gustave Eiffel for his secret apartment near the top of the tower, which he used for quiet, undisturbed reflection. No wonder he had refused to sell it, no matter how sky high the offer.

Huby and I stood there for a few minutes before walking down the steps and through the Trocadéro gardens next to the fountain. We turned left as we reached the riverbank.

"I would be immensely grateful, Daniel, if you could try to find out what happened to Paul Blocher," Huby said after we left the crowds behind us. "Anything at all. I cannot tell you how much that would mean to his father. And it would also mean a lot to me."

We reached the Pont de l'Alma, right next to the restaurant where our loop had started over an hour earlier.

"Tell me, Huby," I said, "you have such amazing contacts and friends in the Arab world. Couldn't you get anyone there to help you?"

Huby sighed heavily. "Believe me, I've tried. Turns out that these friendships, which I cultivated with great care over thirty years, are one-way relationships. Hell of a way to find that out, I'd say. But aside from those disappointments, Syria is a black hole, where even the best-connected people strike out."

"I'll talk to a few people and see what I can do," I said. "But please don't get your hopes up, and more important, don't get your friend's hopes up."

"I understand," Huby said despondently. "I wish I did not have to burden you with this. I'm really sorry to trouble you."

"It is not a burden. I'm happy to do what I can; I'm just worried it won't be much. Please give me a few days, and I'll get back to you," I said.

"Thank you, Daniel. Thank you."

Huby embraced me in a bear hug. As he squeezed my arms and rib cage, I picked up on a familiar odor in Huby—a slightly sweetish scent that revealed deep worry and anxiety. It was an unmistakable signal, beyond a person's control, a smell I had always been able to register. The first time I remember noticing such scents in people was when I was ten years old playing soccer with other kids in our neighborhood in Zurich. One boy, who was three years older and about sixty pounds heavier than my puny self, seemed to have it out for me that day. He kept tripping and kicking me, until I had enough and confronted him. But instead of accepting my challenge to fight straight up, he told—or, rather, begged—his buddies to hold him back so that he would not have to kill me. "You guys better not let go of my arms, or I don't know what I'll do to this asshole," he kept shouting louder and louder. "I'm telling you, don't let go of me!" It was clear to all the kids there that he did not want to fight me. Your typical playground bully-coward. However, what really stood out was the strong putrid smell this boy was emitting, as if he had thrown up and rolled around in this own vomit.

The first few times I detected this awful scent, I attributed it to someone not having washed in weeks, but eventually I came to understand that this unpleasant aroma often materialized when a person was terrified and that it had nothing to do with hygiene. I realized, to my own surprise, that I was, quite literally, able to smell fear—in others and eventually also in myself. As I grew older, I began to distinguish the various smells and what they represented, but only many years later, through my own study of martial arts, did I learn about the ancient healing art of Jin Shin Jyutsu and its wisdom in correlating smells with states of disharmonized emotions: Fleshy, with a slight tart and metallic tinge, for extreme sadness, when mourning a loss of a person or broken love.

Rancid, with a sour aftertaste, in cases of deep-seated anger; this particular warning had served me well over the years. Putrid, exposing fear in people such as my childhood soccer bully but also the scent I detected in my own children when I'd wake them from a nightmare they were having. Burnt, slightly bitter, as a telltale signal of fakeness and pretense. And, finally, fragrant, divulging worry and nervousness—that unpleasant, slightly nauseating smell that was present before tests in school and the same scent I noticed years later as a parent when my own children were under pressure and anxious. This was the scent I had just picked up on Huby.

TWO

I REMAINED MOTIONLESS for a few minutes. The pain on Huby's face and the heaviness in his voice both lingered in that spot at the base of the bridge where he had just left me to cross to the left bank of the river. Every time I was pulled into the Syrian conflict, particularly in the context of a search for a missing person, I was confronted with appalling behavior that ranged from callous to vicious. Good intentions were met with contempt and ridicule, and empathy was for wimps.

For a brief moment, I resented Huby for having manipulated me. After all, I didn't owe him anything. There had been no favor I would now be forced to return, and what he was asking for was hardly a minor errand. I considered calling Huby in the morning and telling him that I was unable to help. But there was something in his sorrow that swept away my irritation and the reservations I harbored about helping him.

I needed to clear my mind. I started to walk and realized after a few minutes that I had begun to track the same loop I had just walked with Huby. But instead of uncluttering my thoughts, impressions and memories were flooding through me. I was unable to keep sounds and views, even buildings, from triggering recollections, and as I passed the Harry Winston jewelry store on Avenue Montaigne, I recalled the set of audacious heists that thieves had pulled off in 2007 and 2008. These Paris jobs were straight out of a movie, with the robbers dressed up as women in wigs and female clothing, not unlike a kidnapping in Syria three months earlier, where a hostage had been transported across the country and into Lebanon camouflaged as a woman, while two guards took turns pretending to be the husband.* As I walked past the lavish store, I recognized how readily I would have swapped looking for Paul Blocher in Syria with finding the gang responsible for these Parisian robberies.

By the time I reached the Trocadéro, most of the tourists had cleared out. The only people left were a few peddlers trying to sell neon-lit propellers and electric birds they were flying with remote controls, but they, too, were wrapping up for the day. I sat at the top of the wall facing the Eiffel Tower and contemplated my options for helping Huby locate this missing person. I decided to talk to my Saudi friend Khalid and sent him a text message, asking him whether he was still awake and available for a call.

Khalid al-Marri is a fascinating person. He was born in Medina to a Saudi father and a Syrian mother—like Osama bin Laden, as he liked to remind me. We had met by pure chance about fifteen years earlier in the lounge of a hotel in Doha, when we realized that we were both reading the same book. Khalid is equally well versed in the writings of Nietzsche and Schopenhauer as he is in those of Khalil Gibran and Sayyid Qutb, and he always speaks in perfectly crafted sentences, in which every word has its place and function, and not a single syllable is random or superfluous. Khalid's language is a rare combination of poetic beauty and ruthless efficiency, and listening to him often made me feel inarticulate and inadequate. Sometimes, though, I also felt lectured and nitpicked. He had a habit of spelling out every nuance of his analogies and metaphors. Over time, I realized that Khalid's deliberate, analytical style came from a compulsion to express a thought to its fullest conclusion. Whenever I seemed impatient, he reminded me that speaking truth to power required speaking truth completely, with no exceptions or shortcuts.

---

* I had been tangentially involved in the matter by connecting the victim's parents with the Syrian ambassador to Lebanon, to whom I had been introduced by an American friend in Beirut a year earlier. After initially denying any knowledge of the kidnapping, the ambassador hooked up the pleading parents with an Iranian middleman who established a negotiation channel with the kidnappers.

Khalid had been a close confidant of the Saudi crown prince Abdullah when he was running the country during the long illness of his brother, King Fahd. Apparently Khalid's thoughts and opinions were a little too progressive for the taste of some royals and Wahhabi clerics, but he was always safe behind the protective shield of Crown Prince Abdullah. One day in July 2005, just a few weeks before the death of King Fahd, Khalid was told that Crown Prince Abdullah had ordered him to leave the kingdom within six hours. He never told me what had happened between him and the crown prince, other than to say that if you shoot at the king, you'd better not miss! Never again did he return to Saudi Arabia.

Khalid moved to Qatar and became an influential adviser to the emir, Sheikh Hamad bin Khalifa Al Thani, and to his even more powerful wife, Sheikha Moza bint Nasser. Operating out of his new base in Doha, Khalid acted as a gray eminence to rulers in the Gulf and beyond. In his powerful behind-the-scenes role, he directed some of the major Islamic charities in the region toward more progressive causes such as science-based education and gender equality, still displaying the same tendencies that had not done much to endear him to conservative circles in his native Saudi Arabia and in all likelihood had contributed to his expulsion. Khalid shuttled regularly to Arab capitals and also had direct access to the top levels of all groups in Syria—to the regime in Damascus and its Alawite strongholds in the coastal region around Latakia and Tartus, to the main Sunni centers of power, as well as to the political and religious leaders of the Druze and Christian communities.* He was also able to connect at will with the powerful leaders of the byzantine Lebanese fiefdoms and some of their Iranian handlers. Every

---

* Khalid had always been skeptical about Project Bistar and the likelihood of it having any meaningful impact in Syria. His analysis of why we would ultimately fail proved to be spot-on: the leaders in Damascus would lose their incentive for backing and participating in this nonpartisan initiative as soon as they sensed even the slightest improvement to their political fortunes. But despite his misgivings, Khalid still supported the foundation's efforts.

time I had asked Khalid for help in the past, he had given me a straight
answer—yes or no. If no, it was definitive. If yes, he always delivered.
He never asked for anything in return, and whenever I implored him to
let me finally do something for him he would look at me with his soft,
enigmatic smile and quote Abraham Lincoln: "I will prepare, and some
day my chance will come."

Only once, in late 2004, before his expulsion from Saudi Arabia, did
I have the chance to do something for Khalid. He had been asked by a
senior security officer of the royal court in Riyadh to establish a connection to Qasem Soleimani, the powerful Iranian Revolutionary Guard
general and commander of the elite intelligence Quds Force.* While
Khalid never gave me any details about his relationship with Soleimani,
I knew that they remained in regular contact and felt mutual respect
for each other. Khalid refused the request, and apparently the Saudi
officer didn't take it well, threatening that he would report Khalid to the
US Embassy in Riyadh. He would tell the US ambassador not only that
Khalid was friendly with Soleimani but that he was also a money laun-
derer for the Quds Force, which would immediately land Khalid on the
sanctions list of the US Treasury Department's Office of Foreign Assets
Control (OFAC), even though they both knew that this claim was a total
fabrication.

Khalid called me and asked for my advice. At the time, I knew of
several cases in which individuals had been placed on this OFAC list
without any meaningful, independent investigation and verification,
based solely on an unsubstantiated accusation or vague suspicion. In
fact, a mayor of a southern town in Lebanon, who refused to sell his land
to Hezbollah so that it could build rocket launchers close to Israel at an
elevated, strategic location, saw his life upended when Hezbollah retali-
ated by having anonymous information delivered to the US Embassy in

* Qasem Soleimani was considered the second most powerful person in Iran behind the Supreme
Leader, Ayatollah Khamenei. He was killed in January 2020 in a targeted US drone strike in Baghdad.

Beirut, insinuating that this mayor was a Hezbollah banker and financier. He promptly ended up on the OFAC list as a designated terrorism supporter, which turned his comfortable life into a nightmare. His accounts were frozen, and word got out in Beirut's gossipy society that he had become toxic. Friends and acquaintances stopped returning his calls, and even his favorite restaurant by the city's marina refused to seat him at a table. Only after five years and the expensive intervention of a former White House counsel was he able to get himself removed from the list.

It was crucial to nip the whole thing in the bud before it became a major headache that might take years to resolve. I suggested that we preempt this Saudi security officer and let the US Embassy in Riyadh know in advance that these allegations against Khalid were false and nothing other than a perfidious maneuver to settle a personal score by getting him in trouble with the US authorities. I contacted a friend of my father's, a retired American diplomat who had played a key role in the negotiations of the Panama Canal's return to Panama and had a tremendous network in the US Foreign Service. He agreed to place a call to the embassy in Riyadh. Apparently his call had its intended effect, and the Saudi officer's complaint about Khalid was rejected—quite literally—at the embassy's front gate.

Neither Khalid nor I ever brought up this incident again, but it seemed to have left a lasting impression on him. While our past interactions had always been pleasant and cordial, they had smacked of something more transactional than intimate. After this unpleasant episode, however, his tone and stance toward me changed, as if I had crossed some invisible threshold and been granted entry into a world reserved for his most trusted friends.

Khalid had been one of the two people with the ability to provide me with information on individuals who had disappeared in Syria and Lebanon. The other one was Fouad al-Zayat, a colorful Syrian businessman who was holed up in Beirut's Four Seasons hotel to avoid extradition to Greece in connection with a corruption trial.* Fouad had agreed to help obtain information on a missing journalist after learning that my father had been close to Archbishop Makarios in the early 1960s while serving as a young ambassador to Cyprus during Makarios's presidency. As a Christian in Syria who later made Cyprus his home, Fouad greatly admired Makarios, and the connection to my father was enough for this gregarious man to help me. Fouad was important to my contingency plans in Beirut and always resolute and generous in his assistance, particularly in hardship cases such as kidnappings or political imprisonments in Syria, but his support paled compared to that of Khalid. Without Khalid, the results of our efforts would have been even more meager than they already were. Besides, interacting with Khalid was always a memorable experience, even in his pedantic moments. I never heard a person utter a bad word about him, and over time I got the distinct impression that everyone in his orbit wanted nothing more than to be in his good graces.

I SLID OFF the wall and started to walk down the steps toward the river, passing the crêpe stand where my children, many years ago, had tasted a plain sugar crêpe for the first time. The stand exuded that sweet smell of burnt sugar. They had been fascinated by the gentleman preparing the crêpes and followed every single one of his motions attentively as he sprinkled the sugar on the crêpes, loosened them with a rubber spatula, and then folded them twice to form a triangle. When he handed them to Noa and Ben, the expression on their faces was one of sheer bliss and admiration. I was about to buy a crêpe myself in honor of these happy memories when my phone vibrated. It was a text from Khalid, informing me that he would be available to talk in one hour. I walked back

---

* It was at this makeshift home in Beirut that Fouad had facilitated my interaction with Qasem Soleimani.

to the hotel and waited until it was time to call him. Khalid picked up immediately.

"Lovely to hear from you, Abu Ben," he said in his warm, gentle voice. "I've missed you. Though given the late hour, I assume you're not calling to exchange pleasantries. What's up?"

Straight to the point, as usual. I told Khalid about Paul Blocher and his disappearance in Syria, about the Kurdish handler possibly named Alan, and about Huby's plea to locate him or at least find out what had happened to him.

Khalid sighed. "Oh Daniel, *habibi*," he said softly, "why do you always allow yourself to get dragged into such ugly stories? They almost never end well."

"I'm aware of that," I said. "But I feel like I have to do this. Could you please help me?"

"Of course I will help you. But we both remember the last time you brought something like this to me. There was no reunion with the family, no happy ending."

"I get it, Khalid." I sighed. "I've asked myself why I'm even considering this. Maybe you're right. I should walk away from this. Remember the last time we tried to get proof of life? That experience completely did me in. They had beaten the poor guy half to death."

"If I may offer my counsel, *habibi*, you need to adopt the bed-of-nails principle. It's what gets me through the day in this part of the world. If you stand on just one nail, it hurts. But if you stand on one thousand nails, no single nail stands out, and you feel no pain."

"I see."

"Do you think you can do that?" Khalid asked. "It means that you will have to treat this case as just one of many, even though your relationship with this friend makes the whole thing personal. Do you have the discipline to do that?"

"I can only promise to try my best," I answered.

"You said your friend's name was Huby," Khalid said after a pause. "Is that correct?"

"Yes."

"Huby as in Hubertus Mazerius?"

"Yes."

"I remember him," Khalid said. "King Abdullah thought highly of him during the crown prince years. He is a clever man. Too clever for his own good, perhaps. He was excellent at showing the Saudis that he was a man of principle. They just lapped up his vivid displays of friendship and virtue."

"It's still the same Huby," I said.

Khalid was quiet for a moment. "Please forward me the young man's name in a Skype message. Also, please send me a current picture. If you can, kindly ask your friend to find out which languages the young man speaks and also what his favorite food is. Finally, as you surely remember from our last time, the same drill in order to get proof of life: I need a secure question for the young man, which only he can answer. Just send me the question, and I'll call you back for the answer, so that the two are not in the same message."

"I'll get on that first thing in the morning."

"Good," Khalid said. "I'll see what I can do. I plan to be in Beirut tomorrow, and maybe I'll go to Damascus for a day."

"Thank you, Khalid. Thank you so much."

"Anything for you, *ya ruchi*," Khalid said in his soothing, almost purring voice. "But I hope you told your friend not to get his hopes up."

"I did. He understands."

Khalid exhaled. "Everyone understands until they suffer a tragedy. Until they are hit with the loss of a loved one."

"I know, Khalid. But there is no way to prepare someone for that pain. We learned that the hard way."

"We certainly did," he said. "I will be in touch. Good night."

I sent Paul's name to Khalid by Skype and then switched off all my electronic gadgets. I tried to sleep but gave up after an hour and a half of tossing and turning. I was tempted to go for a walk, perhaps do another one of Huby's Eiffel Tower loops, but my feet ached. I settled for a long, hot shower instead.

At six in the morning, I sent Huby a text message and asked him to call me as soon as he was awake. My phone rang immediately.

"Any news?" Huby asked.

"No news," I answered, "neither good nor bad. Last night I spoke to a friend who is very plugged in when it comes to Syria and the region. If anyone can help, he would be the one." I had decided not to mention Khalid's name to Huby. Khalid preferred it that way, and so did I.

"Thank you for doing this, Daniel," Huby said. "What are the next steps?"

"The next steps are that we need to meet so that I can ask you a few questions. Are you available today?"

"Of course I am," Huby snapped back. "I will be in your hotel in half an hour, if that's not too early."

Twenty minutes later, my room phone rang. It was the concierge, informing me that a Mr. Mazerius was waiting for me in the lobby. I went downstairs immediately.

"Let's find a quiet table to talk," I said as we shook hands. Huby's palms were warm and sweaty.

As we waited for the waiter to serve the coffee, I could see that Huby was nervous, very different from the cool and composed person I had come to know.

"Okay, what do you need from me?" he asked once the waiter retreated.

"Well, it's more from your friend. We need some identifying information for Paul."

"Like what?" Huby was almost hostile in his edginess.

"Huby, I'm just trying to help," I said in an attempt to get him to relax.

"I know, Daniel, I'm sorry. I'm just so anxious. What kind of information do you need?"

"Information such as how many languages Paul speaks, and—"

"Two," Huby replied before I had finished my sentence. "English and French."* Clearly there was no point in trying to calm him down.

"Perhaps you would like to double-check with his father?" I asked.

"There's no need to double-check. I am sure," Huby hissed. "And hopefully also some Arabic by now," he added a little more amiably.

I smiled. If Paul had learned to speak Arabic, it meant that he had not been killed immediately in Syria.

"Okay, thanks," I said. "Just a few more things. Do you happen to know Paul's favorite food?"

"Grilled sardines," he answered without hesitation. "If possible, with fava beans."

I was surprised, not just by the unusual culinary choice but by Huby's intimate familiarity with Paul and his preferences.

"Sardines and fava beans," I repeated. "Don't get that one too often."

We both finished our coffee and paused our conversation while the waiter returned to refill our cups.

"Next thing we'll need is a reasonably current picture of Paul," I resumed. "Do you happen to have one?"

Huby sat silently for a moment before reaching into his breast pocket and pulling out his wallet.

---

* I found out much later that Paul Blocher also spoke German. I am quite certain that Huby didn't mention this during our early-morning conversation in Paris because I took detailed notes while he was speaking. This discrepancy has bothered me ever since. Huby had no reason to withhold this fact, and he otherwise seemed to make every effort imaginable to provide me in great detail with everything I asked for. It is possible, though not very likely, that Huby didn't know about Paul's German proficiency. It is also possible that Huby (mistakenly) thought that a German element in Paul's identity would trigger a negative reaction in me because of my own identity and background. Most likely, though, Huby simply forgot to mention it because of his own state of anxiety and emotional distress. I have never confronted him about this.

"It's not recent," he said as he handed me an old, faded picture of a blond boy with blue eyes. "This is all I have on me. Paul was twelve in this picture. It was taken fifteen years ago. I'll get you something more recent later today."

I took a photo of the picture with my phone, then handed it back to Huby. His eyes were moist as he tucked the picture back in his wallet.

"Do you need anything else?" he asked, struggling now to keep his composure.

"One more thing," I said. "But it can wait if you need a minute."

"No," he said, "let's get this over with. What else do you need?"

"I need a question that only Paul will be able to answer."

"Why do you need that?" Huby asked.

"Because if someone manages to locate him, we will need to be certain that it's Paul."

"I understand," Huby said. "Proof of life." He looked forlorn.

"Precisely," I said.

His gaze was fixed on me, but it felt like he was looking right through me. His eyes were blank. He did not say a word for two minutes. "Whoever finds Paul should ask him about his favorite childhood character," he finally said, enunciating each word slowly as if he was trying to stop himself from crying.

"Thank you. And what is his favorite childhood character?"

"Baloo."

As soon as Huby uttered the name, his shoulders started to shake, first softly, and then with increasing force. He did not make a sound other than an almost imperceptible whimper. But the tears, which he had fought hard to hold back for the past ten minutes, now flowed freely and drenched his face. The waiter came and handed him a few napkins. Huby nodded gratefully.

"Baloo the bear," he continued after drying his eyes. "When Paul was a little boy, I used to read him *The Jungle Book* over and over again.

He could not get enough of it, and he just adored Baloo the bear. For a while, I used to call him Baloo, until he got too old for a *Jungle Book* character."

"I'm so very sorry," I said quietly. "I thought you were just close to Paul's father. I did not realize that you were that close to Paul himself."

"Of course not, how could you?" Huby said. "I hadn't mentioned it last night." He closed his eyes for a moment. "Paul was four when his mother died. His father fell into a terrible depression, a deep hole that he was unable to climb out of for many years. Paul stayed with us for most of that time until his twelfth birthday. We never had children of our own, and Paul became part of us. I took the picture I just showed you on the day I brought him back to his father. So when I told you last night that my friend raised Paul mostly by himself after the death of Paul's mother—well, the non-mostly part took place at our home. Paul was . . . is . . . like a son to my Rose and me. I would never disrespect his father by equating our pain and sorrow with what he is feeling, but it's not far off."

"I'm so sorry."

"Thank you," Huby said quietly. "And please thank your friend for his help."

"I will," I said. I collected my notes and was about to stand up, when Huby placed his hand on my arm.

"One more thing before I leave, if you don't mind," he whispered.

"Sure, what is it?" I had no idea what to expect. Huby's tone and demeanor felt conspiratorial.

"Well, I'm not sure how to put it," he continued in a low, raspy voice. "I'm a little uncomfortable bringing this up, but I have no choice. What about the payment?"

"What are you talking about? What payment?"

"*Your* payment, Daniel. How can I pay you? You'll have expenses, you'll need to be compensated."

There it was, the dreaded money conversation. It had arrived sooner than usual, though to Huby's credit it showed that he was ill at ease asking me for a favor of this magnitude without offering to pay for my efforts. But I couldn't accept any payment, not in any form and irrespective of how creatively it was disguised—not as a fee for my efforts, not as a reimbursement of my expenses, and not even as a gratitude donation to a charity of my choosing.* It was flat-out verboten for me to allow any form of financial consideration to seep into my efforts to find Paul Blocher. I had to have the freedom to be as direct as I needed to be with Huby, free to ask him to behave in a certain way or, more likely, to refrain from behaving in a certain way without having to hear that I was being well compensated for my assistance and should not get it all twisted about who was working for whom. Most important, I needed to be able to walk away from this matter if Huby, Paul Blocher's father, or anyone else disregarded my advice or did anything to jeopardize our efforts. That freedom was only possible without any vested interest whatsoever. Especially a financial interest.

"It's kind of you to offer, Huby," I said. "But I cannot accept any compensation from you. Not for my expenses and not for my time."

"Why not?" Huby probed. "I don't feel right asking you to help me without offering to cover any expenses you might incur. It's the least I can do."

I smiled. "Well, you've offered, so that's settled."

"Come on, Daniel, you know what I mean."

"I'm sorry, Huby, that's the way it'll have to be. No payment, neither direct nor indirect. I have to be in a position to tell anyone who asks and has a right to know that I have received absolutely no compensation in

---

* The most insidious, and unfortunately also the most prevalent, form of payment to locate and negotiate the release of hostages is a "success" fee. Often calculated as a percentage of the ransom payment, it is then grossed up by the requisite fee amount. In many cases, professional middlemen end up sharing this success fee with the hostage's captors.

this matter. That's the only way this can remain a purely humanitarian endeavor, free of any commercial considerations or political interference. Trust me when I tell you that this is in your—in our—best interest."

"Okay, I understand, but what if you have to get on a plane, what if you end up staying in a hotel?" Huby's concern seemed sincere.

"My work for the foundation is taking me to the region any which way, so don't worry about that. Let's just drop this issue, please."

Huby nodded. We stood up and I walked Huby to the hotel entrance. The morning sun was shining straight at us. In the distance, I could see the top of the Eiffel Tower over the rooftops. Traffic was still scarce.

"There's another thing I would like to ask you, if you don't mind," I said as we stepped outside.

"Sure, just please don't make me cry again," Huby answered. We both laughed. A brief moment of levity.

"I asked you last night about your Arab contacts," I said cautiously, "and you explained how useless they have been. But what about your government contacts here in the West, not in the Arab world? You know everyone in DC, in London, here in Paris. Didn't you try to reach out to them for help?"

"Of course I did," Huby said with an exasperated sigh. "It has been an awful, sobering experience. I was told in no uncertain terms that there was nothing anyone could do for me. That Paul had marched into Syria on his own volition, knowing full well how dangerous it was. He was not sent by a newspaper or any other organization. One official even called Paul an adolescent adventurer and added helpfully that this was the price to pay for such woeful stupidity. I almost smacked the guy."

"What a jerk." I knew exactly what Huby was talking about. Had some of those in a position to lend a hand—government officials, current and former diplomats, members of the intelligence community—not displayed such depraved indifference and instead made meaningful efforts to locate those missing persons or at least use their networks to gather valuable information, I would never have been drawn into all these tragic affairs. And had a few selfless, compassionate souls not helped me, even though they were under no obligation to provide support and derived no benefit from it, I would not have made it through those events.

"The crazy part is that many years ago this jerk's boss used to work for me," Huby continued. "But you know yourself how these guys are wired. They're political animals—only as loyal as their options. I thought of raising a huge stink but decided against it. It probably wouldn't have helped us find Paul.

"And the icing on the cake was when one of them warned me that I would be prosecuted if I arranged or made any ransom payment for Paul's release. Apparently the government concluded that all kidnappings in Syria—actually, in the entire Arab world—are committed by terrorists, which renders all payments for the release of the victims illegal."

"How did you respond?"

"I told him that I would view a ransom request as a huge relief, because then at least I would know that Paul was alive, and that breaking some law about negotiating with terrorists was the least of my worries. When he started to repeat his warning, I just got up and left the room. That was the last time I spoke to my government contacts."

Huby promised to send me a current picture of Paul Blocher and implored me to keep him posted. As he walked away from the hotel entrance, his stature shrank and his posture became more stooped with every step until his silhouette resembled that of an old, broken man. I returned to my room and sent Khalid the information and the photo of the image Huby had shown me. I then sent him the security question in a Skype message, and Khalid called me a few minutes later for the answer.

One hour later, I received an email from Huby with a picture of Paul, taken about a month before he entered Syria. He looked very much like the twelve-year-old boy I had seen in the photograph earlier that morning. Shoulder-length blond hair and still those innocent blue eyes. I forwarded the picture to Khalid, who immediately sent a reply confirming receipt and letting me know that he would be in touch in a few days. Only then did I realize how exhausted I was. I fell asleep on the bed, fully clothed, still clutching my cell phone.

THREE

ON THE FLIGHT home to New York two days later, I could not get the picture of Paul Blocher out of my mind, especially those innocent eyes, which displayed none of the toughness necessary to endure a Syrian captivity. If Paul Blocher was still alive, he would have almost certainly been subjected to unspeakable cruelty. A quick death early in his captivity might have actually been his best fate. I was not sure what to wish for.

As soon as I landed at JFK, I received a text message from Khalid, asking me to let him know when I would be able to talk on Skype on a secure Wi-Fi network. I sent him a message once I got home, and at 8 p.m. sharp, he called.

"We may have an interesting lead in the Paul Blocher matter."

"So fast?" I tried to contain my excitement. "That's fantastic."

"I'm not so sure it's fantastic," Khalid replied. "In order for us to have a prayer at finding this young man, or even just at learning what happened to him, we'll have to go through the Sheikh in Beirut."

The Sheikh was one of the most divisive figures in the Middle East. A man as brilliant and as powerful as he was ruthless, a leader who demanded total loyalty and commitment from his followers but who also reciprocated with the same loyalty and commitment to those under his command. I understood from the last time Khalid had helped me that going through the Sheikh meant I would at least get some information on Paul Blocher. If he was still alive, he was being held by fighters who were either in the Sheikh's direct charge or by a group that the Sheikh's men had infiltrated and could access. There were very few places and people in his native Lebanon and in Syria that were beyond the Sheikh's reach.

"What exactly are the next steps?" I asked. "What do you need me to do?"

"Last time, you did not have to deal with the Sheikh directly. I handled that for you," Khalid said. "This time, it looks like you will have the pleasure."

"Why's that?"

"I'm not entirely sure," Khalid replied. "I met with one of his deputies this afternoon, someone called Hussein, whom I've known for years, and mentioned the disappearance of Paul Blocher. I expected a blank look and a shrug of the shoulders. But Hussein seemed to be interested in this matter, asking me for more details, in particular on this Kurdish handler with whom Paul had apparently traveled into Syria. You know, the one possibly called Alan. He also asked me whether Paul was a journalist and whether a newspaper or a television network had sent him to Syria. I assured him that he was not a journalist and that nobody had sent him. When I finished my explanations, Hussein stood up to make a call. He returned about ten minutes later and handed me his phone. The Sheikh was on the line. After exchanging a few pleasantries, the Sheikh asked me how this matter had landed in my lap or, rather, on my back, as he put it. I mentioned your name, and he immediately remembered from our last time. He told me that he would try to help us but that he wanted to discuss it with you directly. So there you have it, *habibi*."

I was quiet for a moment. The Sheikh was feared and admired, despised and lionized. Meeting him was no small matter. I knew from the last experience with Khalid that the Sheikh would not offer any assistance if the missing person was a journalist, but I had no idea why this was such a sticking point for the Sheikh. Khalid's conversation with Hussein brought it all back, and I resolved to ask Khalid about this next time we would see each other, so that I would not lack important information once I came face-to-face with the Sheikh. Though given Khalid's attention to detail, he would probably bring this up on his own as he prepared me for the next steps.

"Is this our only option?" I finally asked. No doubt Khalid would pick up on the trepidation in my voice.

"No, not our *only* option," he replied. "But the most direct option and certainly the fastest one. And when it comes to disappearances in Syria, time is generally not our friend."

I knew he was right. "So what happens next?" I asked.

"Can you be in Istanbul on Tuesday?"

"Yes, I think so."

"Good. Come to the Kempinski right after you land. I'll be waiting there for you. Don't worry about the logistics; I already took care of your room, and a driver will wait for you at the airport. I'll give you all the details when I see you."

"All right, see you on Tuesday. Thank you, Khalid."

"One more thing," he said as I was about to hang up. "Be prepared to fly to Beirut that night. Travel light. You'll be in Beirut for about six to eight hours. Looks like it might be an interesting trip."

"Okay."

"Oh, and please don't mention this to your friend Hubertus," Khalid added. "This is not the time and most certainly not the trip. Good night."

It took me a while to digest everything Khalid had just told me. I knew from my past dealings with Khalid that the Sheikh had access to ironclad sources and information, without distortions by the usual hyperbole and rumor mills so prevalent in the region. He was also known as a profound religious and political thinker, both suspicious and deeply knowledgeable of America and the West. His followers revered him as their commander-in-chief and savior. The prospect of meeting him in person was both exciting and terrifying.

I LANDED IN Istanbul on Tuesday morning. As I walked into the arrivals area, I spotted the driver from the Kempinski hotel, holding up a sign with my initials. The moment I signaled him, he came up to me and told me that Mr. Khalid was expecting me. After about fifty minutes in Istanbul's notorious traffic bottlenecks, we reached the hotel, a gorgeous, former Ottoman imperial palace on the Bosporus. Khalid and I had met there several times before, and I had the sense that he welcomed any occasion to spend time at this beautiful venue. Khalid was seated in the reception area when I arrived and came up to me as I walked through the metal detectors at the hotel entrance.

"Welcome to Istanbul," he said in a jovial mood. "I have already checked you in, so just have your bag sent to your room, and let's sit outside and chat over breakfast."

We walked outside to a beautiful view of the Bosporus, found a quiet table, and ordered some coffee. Even though the wind carried a slight smell of sewage and pollution, reminiscent of the Venetian canals in summer, the panoramic vista of the Üsküdar part of the city on the other side of the waterway was magnificent. Khalid asked the waiter to bring us fresh honey straight off the honeycomb, together with some dates and a few other things to eat.

"I never get tired of this city," Khalid said as he dipped a date into the raw, crystalline honey. "By the way, should you ever find yourself imprisoned in Syria or anywhere else and your guards offer to bring you something to eat, ask for dates. Eating a date a day will allow you to survive any ordeal."

"Thanks, I'll keep that in mind if I'm captured and get a chance to order room service."

Khalid smiled. "Let's get started. We've got a lot of ground to cover, and tonight you are leaving for Beirut."

Even though I had braced myself for this Beirut trip ever since Khalid had mentioned it during our last call, his words still had a dark, ominous ring to them. "Let's do it," I said, trying to sound upbeat, mainly for my own sake.

"So, here's the plan," Khalid continued. "I've booked you on a flight that leaves a little before two a.m. You'll be meeting one of the Sheikh's guys at the airport here in Istanbul on the bottom floor of the business-class departure lounge in the corner near the coffee station. His name is Jamil. Always remember that Jamil is a Ray. Very clever. The Sheikh trusts him." Khalid referred to all security and intelligence officers as "Ray" because of their universal propensity for wearing Ray-Ban sunglasses.

"This Jamil fellow will come all the way to Istanbul to meet me here at the airport and then fly with me back to Beirut?" I asked incredulously. It seemed like overkill to have a chaperone for this two-hour flight.

"That's correct," Khalid said. "The Sheikh wants him to get a feel for you before meeting you himself. If Jamil approves of you, he will take you straight to the Sheikh after you land in Beirut. If he does not approve, you will stay at the airport and return to Istanbul on the early-morning flight."

"So your recommendation was not good enough for the Sheikh?" I asked teasingly.

"Careful, young man." Khalid smiled. "Besides, who says I recommended you?"

We both laughed. The comic relief felt good.

"Anyway." Khalid's serious tone returned. "Jamil will meet you at exactly midnight in the lounge. Even though it is his mission to check you out, you should talk to him freely and naturally and also ask him questions. But remember that he will scrutinize and judge you carefully, as much by your questions as by your answers, like any intelligent Ray would do."

"Got it. I will speak freely yet deliberately." Khalid was showing his penchant for meticulously crafted sentences. He spoke unlike any other person I knew.

"Don't worry, you'll be fine." He signaled the waiter and ordered us some more coffee. "Before I let you rest, there are a few things you should know about Jamil. He's thirty-five years old, from a small Syrian village near Tartus. As he tells it, he lost both of his parents when he was very young, and his uncle brought him to Lebanon."

"What do you mean, 'as he tells it'? Is there another version?" I asked.

"Ah, *habibi*, I am pleased to see that your ears have been sensitized by our Syrian adventures," Khalid said. "It is true that he lost his parents when he was very young, but that's not quite the full story. Jamil's actual father was a French intelligence officer who had met his mother only once. One night, to be precise. Jamil never met his biological father, and if he ever did, he'd probably rip his heart out. Jamil's mother died when he was five. Her brother left Syria a few years later and took Jamil with him to Lebanon, but did not have the means to raise him. Jamil ended up in an orphanage in South Beirut, where the Sheikh found him, or he found the Sheikh, depending on how you look at it. Apparently he stood out at an early age—extremely intelligent and charismatic, and completely fearless. The Sheikh tested him in many ways, and each time Jamil passed with flying colors. I have never heard the Sheikh speak of anyone as warmly as he does of Jamil. He considers Jamil to be the bravest person he knows, someone who does not need an adrenaline-fueled rage to risk his life. The Sheikh likes the saying that strength and courage are not about the size of the dog in the fight—they're about the size of the fight in the dog. That's Jamil. Once, the Sheikh told me that he had never seen anyone who could be as compassionate and as cruel at the same time. Caring and ruthless, soft and hard, yin and yang. Jamil is an extraordinary specimen. You will see for yourself."

Khalid paused for a moment. "Jamil has been through a lot in his young life. In any event, because he is also fluent in English and French, he ended up as the Sheikh's primary liaison officer with foreigners, from intelligence agents to journalists. He once told me that he derives particular pleasure from dealing with foreign journalists, because he extracts more information from them than they do from him, while leaving them with the feeling that they just got the inside scoop—exclusively, of course."

"I understand," I said. "I'll work on the assumption that he'll always be a few steps ahead of me."

Khalid nodded. "Time for you to rest and freshen up. You have a long night ahead of you. I have a few things to deal with here in Istanbul. Why don't we meet later this afternoon at six in this spot and then have a nice dinner at the Tugra restaurant over there in the old palace." He pointed to the stunning building on the side of the hotel. "It's probably the best thing left over from the Ottoman Empire. Certainly the best food."

I retired to the room Khalid had arranged for me. Even though I was tired from the night flight from New York, my mind was racing from Paul Blocher, with his innocent blue eyes, to the Sheikh and his right-hand man, Jamil. I wondered how I had ended up in such a strange situation. I realized that our foundation's efforts to make a difference in Syria with Project Bistar had earned the respect of some of the principal players in the region, including the Sheikh, despite the initiative's ulti-mate failure. There was something about my role that was innocuous and unthreatening enough for them to trust me and grant me access that others might not enjoy. I was not inquisitive like a journalist, not preachy like a diplomat, not patronizing like a UN or EU emissary, and certainly not threatening like a foreign agent. It was the absence of these disqualifying traits rather than any particular skills or assets of my own that had opened a few doors to some remarkable people who usually preferred to remain in the shadows. But if I wanted to find Paul Blocher, those were exactly the people I needed to talk to.

I considered calling Fouad al-Zayat to let him know that I would be in Beirut that night, just in case I ended up requiring an emergency evacuation should the visit with the Sheikh not go as planned. Fouad had excellent connections to most of Beirut's power brokers, including some of the Sheikh's most senior lieutenants, and I knew that he would immediately send his driver, Jihad, with two bodyguards to retrieve me if I was in trouble, as he had done once before when I found myself in a thorny predicament. But I dismissed the idea—Fouad was a very inquisitive person, and he would want to know exactly what brought me to Beirut. If I refused to answer him, or if my information didn't fully satisfy his curiosity, he would investigate on his own, which could expose my entire mission and have disastrous consequences for my safety.

Finally, exhausted by my thoughts, I drifted into a light sleep. When my alarm clock went off an hour later, it took me a moment to figure out where I was and why I was there.

KHALID WAS ALREADY waiting for me when I arrived at our meeting point at six o'clock. He was talking to another gentleman, whom he introduced as Abu Fadl, a senior Saudi intelligence officer. We shook hands and exchanged a few pleasantries, and Abu Fadl left a few minutes later.

"I didn't realize you were still in touch with Saudi intelligence," I said.

"Oh, Abu Fadl is just an old friend," Khalid said, then added with a smirk, "with loads of helpful traits."

"Before we move to the restaurant," Khalid continued as we sat in the chairs at the edge of the water, "I would like to mention a few things that have come up with the Sheikh. Do you remember this fellow called Hussein, the one who handed me the phone in Beirut when I asked about Paul Blocher?"

"Yes," I said. "The Sheikh was on the other line."

"That's right," Khalid said. "Then perhaps you also remember that Hussein asked me whether Paul was a journalist."

"I do." I knew Khalid would not forget to bring this up.

"Well, there is a reason for that. The topic of missing journalists is very sensitive for the Sheikh, and he prefers not to touch it."

"I remember from our last time," I said. "He refused to help us because the missing person was an American journalist. I was never quite sure what he found more objectionable—being American or being a journalist?"

"Without a doubt, being a journalist," Khalid replied. "But I never told you why. The Sheikh is someone who is acutely aware of the power of media. Just like Jamil, whom he taught well, he manipulates journalists with ease and gets the results he seeks either through kindness or through intimidation. He's very charismatic and, when he so chooses, can also be quite charming and not at all scared to engage with journalists on their terms—provided they come to Beirut, of course. Every journalist who meets the Sheikh ends up riveted and seduced. But there was one exception. One journalist whom the Sheikh claimed to dislike, but whom he respected above all others. That journalist was Marie Colvin."*

"Marie Colvin?" I asked in disbelief. "But I knew—"

"I'm aware of that," Khalid cut me off. "When Marie Colvin was killed in Homs, the Sheikh was very upset. He chewed out some people; boy, did he let them have it! He once told me that Colvin saw more with one eye than all the other journalists with two."

"I didn't realize the Sheikh had a relationship with—"

---

* Marie Colvin was an American British journalist who died while covering the siege of Homs in Syria in February 2012. She was recognizable by a black eyepatch that she wore after losing sight in her left eye when she was struck by a grenade blast while reporting on the civil war in Sri Lanka in 2001.

"Nobody did," Khalid interrupted me again.

"But why would it matter to him if Paul was—I mean, is—a journalist?" I asked.

"Because he vowed never again to get involved in a case of a missing journalist. The Sheikh considers the media coverage of the war to be a misleading sideshow. And because he feels that newspaper and television stations take advantage of gung-ho volunteers, who are not seasoned professionals like Marie Colvin. The media companies willingly accept the grave risks these inexperienced individuals are taking when they would not dare dispatch their own correspondents to those dangerous places. There are several of these freelance journalists who have gone missing in Syria, just as they have in other places like Afghanistan or Chechnya. The Sheikh considers the foreign media cowardly and complicit in their deaths. He calls this the media companies' dirty little secret."

"Hmm."

"You should be aware of this in case he brings up the subject of journalists," Khalid said. "Besides, in the end it doesn't really matter, because all of Syria will end up destroyed, with or without good reporting. On that happy note—let's eat!"

Despite Khalid's attempt at levity, I was glum as we headed over to the restaurant. Even the beautiful setting and exquisite food did not remove the heaviness in the air. My chest felt tight, and I could not keep fear and anxiety from enveloping me. I struggled to concentrate as Khalid described Jamil's appearance to me so that I would be able to recognize him and was barely listening as my friend shared a few pointers on the Sheikh's idiosyncrasies and how to navigate around them. Khalid could tell that my mind was elsewhere, and we finished our meal in near silence.* We agreed to meet the next day at the hotel after my return

---

* Khalid later claimed that he had advised me to leave my American iPhone with him in Istanbul and travel to Beirut carrying only my old Nokia phone with the Swiss number, since I would

from Beirut—either in the morning in time for breakfast, in case Jamil decided against taking me to the Sheikh, or in the afternoon if all went according to plan.

---

probably be asked to leave it with one of the Sheikh's men upon arrival in Beirut prior to being taken to the meeting. I have absolutely no recollection of Khalid's advice. In all likelihood, his recollection is the correct one and I had been too preoccupied with my trip to register his valuable counsel. Apparently, Khalid had added playfully that leaving the iPhone behind also had the benefit that my movements couldn't be tracked, though that was not necessarily an advantage, depending on how things would go. Khalid told me that he had attributed my lack of reaction to his lighthearted comment to a diminished sense of humor, especially gallows humor, caused by sleep deprivation and anxiety. Turns out, it was instead a diminished sense of hearing, but he did diagnose the cause correctly. I wish I had heard him and been able to heed his advice.

FOUR

I ARRIVED AT the departure lounge after the security check a few minutes before midnight. The lounge was surprisingly busy for this late hour. As I walked down the stairs to the lower level, I spotted Jamil, who was strategically seated facing the stairs. He stood up as soon as he saw me. I was immediately struck by his fair skin and piercing green eyes. His pleasant features and wavy brown hair did nothing to soften the penetrating gaze of those eyes.

"Why don't we take a seat in the corner by the coffee station, where we were supposed to meet," he said in perfect accent-free English. His voice was soothing, just like his features, in sharp contrast to his blazing stare. I had never seen such fiery eyes; they almost seemed Photoshopped.

We found two seats at the far end of the lounge, and Jamil gestured for me to sit down. "Can I get you coffee or tea or something else?" he asked in equally perfect accent-free French, motioning toward the beverage counter.

"A coffee would be nice," I replied in French, "but, please, let me come with you to get it."

"Oh no," Jamil protested, shifting back to English, "you should stay here and make sure nobody grabs our spot. These are the best seats in the house. Besides, I will be at your disposal for the duration of this trip, so serving you a coffee will start us off on the right foot."

He spoke the last few words in Arabic with a warm smile, without bite or sarcasm, and yet those alert eyes appeared controlling, even threatening.

Jamil returned with two cups of coffee and sat down.

"I will not tell you that Khalid has spoken very highly of you," he said as he handed me my cup of coffee, "because if he hadn't, you and I wouldn't be sitting here together, and you wouldn't meet the Sheikh. So I hope you'll forgive my ill-mannered candor, but it would be inappropriate to start our relationship with an insult to your intelligence."

I was not prepared for such disarming honesty. It had taken Jamil only a few minutes to establish his edge over me, and I worried that if I could not find a way to assert myself, he might conclude that I was not worthy of meeting the Sheikh. I decided to go for broke and match his bluntness. It was a relief that Jamil finally seemed to have settled for English as our language of choice.

"Thank you," I said. "Though I assume you'll still spend the next few hours figuring out whether I have passed muster and deserve to be taken to . . ." I paused, unsure how to refer to the Sheikh, then finally continued, "His Highness." I regretted not having asked Khalid about the proper etiquette in addressing the Sheikh.

Jamil laughed. "That's excellent, my friend. If you keep this up, it will turn out the other way around, and you will be the one concluding that I'm the one who has no business being around the Sheikh. By the way, just refer to him as the Sheikh. All those fancy titles—Your Highness, Your Majesty—we reserve them for those self-crowned rulers in the Gulf with all their kings and princes. Here in the Levant, we prefer more basic ways to address our leaders. Think of us as republicans. 'Sheikh' will do."

"I'll keep that in mind, thanks." It occurred to me that "Sheikh" was also an honorific title but decided to keep that thought to myself.

An attendant approached our seating area to clear our glasses. Jamil raised his left hand and shook his head softly. The attendant stopped dead in his tracks and left immediately. Without uttering a word, Jamil radiated a powerful, natural authority.

"Besides," Jamil continued, "you should know that the Sheikh despises all forms of flattery. Whenever someone addresses him in exaggerated deference or with some superlative, honorific title, he raises his voice and tells the person to stop using the fist of flattery."

"The fist of flattery?" I asked. "I've never heard that term. Usually, it's the sweet sound of flattery, more like a velvet, silken glove than a fist."

"Yes, that's how most people see it," Jamil said. "But in fact flattery prevents us from learning, from growing, because it lulls us into a false sense of achievement and importance. Flattery is far more dangerous than aggression, because it makes us soft and destroys us from the inside. Hence, a fist."

"I understand. A fist it is." I was taken aback by the intensity of our conversation right off the bat. I had never encountered anyone who so radically jettisoned any semblance of small talk. A vague threat seemed to emanate permanently from Jamil, like an unspoken warning that there was no room for error.

"One day, soon after I met the Sheikh," Jamil continued, "he watched me smile when someone told me how smart I was. After the person left, the Sheikh beckoned me to him. 'Remember the lesson I am about to teach you, Jamil,' he chided me in a stern tone. 'If you allow people to flatter and praise you, you will end up speaking to yourself and hearing only your own voice, until one day you will not even bother to listen to that.' It was a lesson I've never forgotten."

"I don't think I will either," I said.

Jamil chuckled. "Good. By the way, you were right. I *will* spend the next few hours checking you out. Just like it was not a stretch to assume that you realized you were here because Khalid had spoken highly of you, it is also not a stretch for me to assume that Khalid told you that this is my job and the main reason I came to Istanbul to pick you up. In addition to making sure your trip is safe and pleasant, of course," he added with a wry smile. Again, Jamil's eyes sparkled menacingly in stark contrast to the rest of his appearance.

"Of course." I fully appreciated what Khalid had told me about Jamil. I had never met a person who could be so warm and so cold at the same time.

Jamil asked for my boarding pass so that he could make sure we were seated next to each other on the flight to Beirut.

"What a coincidence," he said when I handed it to him. "I'll be sitting right next to you. Why don't we make our way to the gate—it's getting late."

We stood up, and my phone rang. It was Huby. I ignored the call but now realized that I had forgotten to record my conversation with Jamil. Before I had entered the lounge, I was about to switch the phone to flight mode so that the recording would not be stopped by an incoming call or text message, but I had been distracted by a loud argument in the reception area between the duty manager and a French passenger who demanded access to the lounge despite not having a ticket that entitled him to this privilege. I was irritated by my own lapse of concentration. Not a promising way to start this journey.

Jamil was observing me this whole time. I got the creepy sensation that he was able to read my thoughts.

"Mobile phones can be more trouble than they're worth," Jamil said as we walked up the stairs toward the entrance of the lounge. "I hope you don't mind, but after we land in Beirut, I would appreciate if you could hand your phone to one of our guys. You'll get it back before you leave."

I nodded. The trip had started.

JAMIL SPOKE VERY little during the flight. I tried to read the newspaper in order to distract myself from whatever lay ahead but could not manage to concentrate. I wondered if Jamil was still mulling over the decision whether to take me to the Sheikh after we landed. After a short time in the air, I saw the beautiful coastal lights of Beirut as the plane approached the runway. Looking down from the starlit sky, the city looked pristine and innocent.

Taxiing to the terminal, I noticed the unusual brightness of two floodlights that were shining on a runway at one remote corner of the airport, giving the sense of an air force base that was preparing for the stealth landing of fighter jets returning from a clandestine mission. Beirut permanently smacked of conspiracies and hidden dangers. Nothing had changed since the first time I had set foot in this city many years earlier.

As the plane reached its parking position and the engines quieted down, Jamil leaned over and whispered that the conversation with the Sheikh would probably be conducted in a mix of Arabic, English, and a little French. Since the Sheikh sometimes used words in a local Arabic dialect spoken in a northeastern suburb of Beirut, Jamil would help me out and translate here or there if he noticed that I was struggling to understand him. But he advised me not to interrupt the Sheikh and just flow with it and that my Arabic would probably be good enough to follow. I was grateful to my Arabic teacher, a Palestinian who had meticulously sensitized me to the rich variety of Arabic dialects throughout the Middle East, particularly in her native Beirut with its myriad slangs and enunciations that varied from neighborhood to neighborhood. I had no idea how Jamil was able to assess my Arabic proficiency since we had exchanged only a few words in that language and Khalid would have certainly informed me if he had told Jamil anything about it, but I had no chance to ask him because just then the doors opened and everyone began to disembark.

The moment Jamil and I stepped out of the plane, a gentleman approached us and motioned toward the door that led down the metal steps to the tarmac. At the bottom of the stairs, a car was waiting for us with a driver and another person, who introduced himself as Hussein.

"Welcome to Beirut," Hussein said. "May I please have your passport?"

We drove on the tarmac under the gangways to a building with a VIP/DIPLOMATS sign. Jamil and I took a seat on the worn-out sofas in one of the waiting rooms while Hussein brought my passport to the security officer.

"Hussein is the person Khalid met with last week," Jamil said quietly. "The one who connected him to the Sheikh on the Paul Blocher matter. He will not be in the meeting with the Sheikh, but you'll see him again when you return to the airport."

I realized that this was the first time Jamil had mentioned Paul. It was also the moment I understood that I would actually be meeting the Sheikh. Somehow I had managed to pass muster with Jamil.

Hussein returned with my passport. "Good to go. Would you mind handing me your mobile phone, please?" he asked in a courteous tone.

Even though Jamil had told me to expect having to surrender my phone, it made me a little queasy. I was now entirely in their hands, without any possibility of communication should something go wrong. Still, I knew that it was established protocol in this kind of an operation, whether in Beirut, Moscow, or Washington. I switched off my iPhone, which I had just turned on after landing a few minutes earlier. Jamil would pick up on even the slightest sign of hesitation, so I handed it to Hussein as nonchalantly as I could—with a disinterested motion and without making eye contact. For a brief moment, I considered holding on to my old Swiss Nokia phone as some kind of insurance policy but quickly dismissed that idea and gave it to Hussein, too. Any metal detector would end up outing my disobedience, thereby jeopardizing the entire mission and possibly my safety. I was grateful that I had remembered to stuff my jacket pocket with a few sheets of paper and a pen so that I could take notes whenever the circumstances allowed for it.

We walked to the other side of the building where a guard saluted as we stepped outside. His demeanor made it clear that Jamil was someone who commanded respect. Another car was waiting, and Jamil and I got inside.

"*Yallah*," he said to the driver. "Let's go."

We drove through the security gate and left the airport. The driver turned on the radio and inserted a CD—Chopin's nocturnes, quite unexpected but apt for this nighttime ride through Beirut.

"It's a short drive, about fifteen minutes," Jamil said. "One more thing before you meet the Sheikh. Don't ask about Paul Blocher. Let him bring it up. He knows that this is why you are here. But he will want to get his own impression of you before broaching the subject. So be patient."

"Thanks for letting me know," I said, hoping to hide my apprehension. Evidently, I would be scrutinized and tested for the entire duration of my visit. I wondered whether I would be blindfolded for this car ride and whether Jamil would be present for the full length of the meeting with the Sheikh.

"I will never leave your side, don't worry," Jamil said, reading my mind. "But it will diminish your standing if I have to correct or defend you in front of him."

As we drove through the deserted streets, I tried to focus on identifying markers of our location, some memorable landmarks. But it was dim, and the buildings and alleys were all gray and interchangeable. We were taking too many turns for me to maintain a sense of direction. I might as well have been blindfolded. As I was fighting the sinking feeling of being at Jamil's mercy, I spotted a small shack selling Lebanese beverages, including *ayran*, the flavorful yogurt drink, and *jallab*, which is made of dates and rose water. Above the shack was a blue neon sign that read FRESH SQUEEZED JEWS. I had to laugh at the typo. Jamil smiled, too.

We arrived at a nondescript building in a residential area and drove into a backyard. The ground was unpaved, and the tires made a crunching sound as the car came to a halt on the dusty gravel. A few emaciated stray cats scampered away from the bright headlights. The yard had a seedy feel to it—not a once-nice place that had fallen on hard times but one that had never been pleasant to begin with. Two armed guards walked up to the car and opened our doors. I was about to step out when Jamil grabbed my arm.

"Another thing," he whispered, "just so that you are not taken by surprise. The Sheikh might try to engage you in a conversation about Jews and Muslims. It could go in any direction, the historic bond between Shia Islam and Judaism, about Jewish influence in the United States, or about Israel. Do not hide the fact that you are Jewish—he has contempt for anyone who does not stand by his roots. Depending on his mood, he might be charming or he might be harsh and aggressive. Try not to draw any conclusions from that. Charming does not mean that he likes you, and aggressive does not mean that he dislikes you. Just be yourself, act naturally. But remember that he will never stop observing you. So relax, it will be fine."

Before I had a chance to thank Jamil for making me feel anything but relaxed, he got out of the car. Only now did it fully hit me that I was about to meet the Sheikh in person. I wondered whether coming here had been a bad mistake and worried that I might lose my balance if my legs buckled. One of the guards stretched his arm into the car, beckoning me.

We walked through a metal detector and into the building toward a dimly lit staircase. I remembered my hesitation before handing over the old Nokia phone to Hussein at the airport. Had prudence not prevailed, my trip would probably have ended this very moment at the metal detector. On each floor were two more armed guards. On the third floor, Jamil signaled for me to step into an apartment. Inside, another guard led us into a sitting area. I was struck by the silence in the building.

None of the guards had spoken a word to Jamil; they treated him with absolute deference.

The damp room was filled with an unpleasant musty odor, as if it had not been aired in years. I tried to ignore the smell, but it was overwhelming. I pondered the possibility that Jamil and the Sheikh had chosen this smelly space deliberately in order to test my concentration and perseverance. I felt extremely self-conscious and worried that my disgust, bordering on nausea, might become conspicuous. I managed to keep my revulsion under wraps but now fretted about overcompensating with forced insouciance. A no-win situation.

An aide brought us tea and some Lebanese pastries soaked in sugary syrup and rose water. Jamil gestured for him to place everything on the table and leave the room. "The Sheikh will be here as soon as he finishes the Fajr prayer," Jamil said when the aide closed the door.

"What about you?" I asked. "No Fajr prayer for you tonight?"

"Careful, my friend," Jamil answered with a tight smile. "You're not out of the woods yet. Besides, I am counting on a one-day prayer dispensation for bringing you here."

Despite the quip, Jamil's eyes were issuing a clear warning. No more sass until I left Beirut.

Jamil noticed my distress, and his expression softened. "Relax, don't worry. It's okay to mess around with me, but I wouldn't recommend it with the Sheikh. Joking with him is like riding a motorcycle through rush-hour Beirut while blindfolded—theoretically possible but not a great idea."

I smiled.

Thirty minutes later, the door opened and four armed guards entered the room, followed by the Sheikh. He was shorter and older than I had envisaged him based on his pictures. Jamil and I stood up immediately. The Sheikh motioned for two of the guards to leave. The others stayed in the room, one by the door and one behind the Sheikh.

"*Assalamu alaikum*," the Sheikh said as he shook my hand.

"*Wa alaika assalam*," I replied.

"Thank you for coming here," the Sheikh said as we sat down. His Arabic had the rapid-fire, abrupt cadence of South Beirut. "I hope the trip was not too inconvenient and that Jamil has treated you well."

"Very well, thank you."

The Sheikh looked at Jamil, then at me, then again at Jamil. He did not speak for over a minute. Had he seen something in me that he didn't like? Finally, he turned back to me and nodded faintly.

"So, by your name, you come from a line of priests, correct?" the Sheikh asked.

I was completely taken by surprise. "Excuse me?"

"Levin comes from Levi, Jacob's third son," the Sheikh said. "From the tribe of Levi come the Levites, who served in your Temple, correct?"

"Yes," I answered, unsure where this was heading, "though, to be precise, it was the Levites' job to serve the Kohen, the priest."

As soon as I spoke those words, I was mortified that I had just corrected the Sheikh, who remained silent. Jamil did not help matters when he leaned over to me and whispered, "Nobody likes a know-it-all."

"Yes, assistants to the priests," the Sheikh said after a long, agonizing pause. "But remember that the first Cohen—Aaron, brother of Moses—was a Levite, too. Besides, assistants are really the ones in charge. To the gatekeepers all the power. Right, Jamil?"

I could not suppress a smile but did not dare look in Jamil's direction.

"Isn't it interesting how you Jews fail to recognize the threat of the eagle?" the Sheikh continued his interrogation.

"I'm sorry?" I had no idea what the Sheikh was talking about. His questions seemed to come out of the blue, without any context. I was unable to figure out their pattern and purpose, other than perhaps to keep me off-balance—in which case, they had certainly achieved their goal. I was certain that I was failing whatever test he was administering.

I was feeling slightly nauseated and this time not because of the mildewy stench in the room.

"Isn't it obvious?" the Sheikh asked rhetorically. "The eagle was the dominant symbol of the Romans, a symbol of power and strength. The Nazis used the eagle. Come to think of it, even the Greek god Zeus had an eagle. What do they all have in common?"

"They all tried to destroy the Jews," Jamil jumped in helpfully.

"Precisely," the Sheikh said with a nod in Jamil's direction. "The Romans and the Germans tried to exterminate the Jews physically; the Greeks, from the inside, spiritually, with an opposing ideology."

The Sheikh paused and looked out the window. The darkness had started to fade, and the faint light was announcing a striking predawn over the rooftops of South Beirut. I waited for him to continue.

"But the most interesting thing," he said, resuming his foray into Jewish history, "is that you have not noticed the biggest threat of all."

I was not sure whether he expected me to say something. Since I had no idea what he was referring to, I kept quiet.

"America," he continued. "The biggest threat to the Jews comes from America. And if you knew your history, you would have recognized the eagle, the American eagle. That was your warning."

"I see the eagle," I said carefully, "but how is America a threat to the Jews? In no country have they been so accepted, so successful."

"Precisely," the Sheikh said. "In this case, the threat comes from assimilation. The Jews are losing their identity, dwindling away, becoming Americans. In a few generations, that is all they will be. Americans. No longer Jews. And, once again, you Jews will have missed the omen of the eagle."*

---

* When I later recounted this exchange to Khalid, he told me that he had heard the Sheikh mention the eagle as a symbol of existential threat to *all* believers, irrespective of their particular religion. He said that the Sheikh regarded the eagle as a token of the physical world's dominance over the spiritual world, of brute force over faith. He had never heard the Sheikh mention the eagle symbolism specifically in the context of the Jewish people. Had the Sheikh mentioned the Jews just

The room suddenly felt dark and heavy, and the mustiness was suffo-cating. I tried to relax my shoulders and focus on my breathing to keep it from becoming labored.

The Sheikh watched me carefully and paused for a moment. I was unsure whether his pause was intended to put me at ease or to make me feel even more uncomfortable. "So all we Arabs have to do," he finally said, "is sit back and wait for you Jews to erase yourselves out of history. The rockets that we deploy from time to time are just a sideshow, a little gift to the journalists. Our useful idiots in the media."

I remembered what Khalid had told me about the Sheikh's disdain for journalists, with the exception of Marie Colvin. I was praying the Sheikh would finally move on to the purpose of our meeting.

"For two thousand years, since the destruction of their Second Temple, Jews have been the people of the book," the Sheikh carried on, dashing my hopes that the conversation would transition to Paul Blocher. "All the persecutions throughout the centuries, the Spanish Inquisition, the Russian pogroms, even the German concentration camps—none of those managed to change that. Jews remained the most learned people, admired for their knowledge. So how delicious it is that now, with their own state and with all the power and status they have obtained in America, that they have finally become stupid like the rest of us. Such a divine sense of humor, it almost makes you believe in God!"

"You don't believe in God?" The words shot out of my mouth before I could stop them. I was incredulous at the Sheikh's inconceivable state-ment. This was a man, after all, who was revered as a religious authority as much as a political leader.

"Well, that depends, my friend," he answered, smiling a little too

---

in passing, I might have doubted my own recollection of this conversation, in particular as I was unable to record it or take notes. But I am certain that the Sheikh mentioned the Jews and the eagle emblem repeatedly, and I distinctly recall being surprised by the lack of vitriol and hatred in the way he pronounced *yahud* and *alyahudi* when referring to the Jews over and over.

triumphantly for the occasion. "Which god do you mean? The god who created *me* or the god whom *I* created?"

I did not know how to respond. The Sheikh had thrown me completely off-balance. Now he waited, leaving me no option other than to answer his question. I had the sudden sensation of being in a vacuum—weightless, in total silence and in a place that was neither light nor dark. I knew that I had to choose my words carefully yet found no path to a clear thought. Only when Jamil tapped me gently on the thigh did I snap out of this hypnotic state of tortuous paralysis.

"I had always assumed that as a man of faith you would be guided by the god who created *you*," I finally said. "But the very fact that you are asking which god I mean leads me to believe that you are referring to the god whom you created."

The Sheikh nodded. "That's a good answer. Am I a man of faith? Who knows . . ."

I could not believe what I was hearing. What the Sheikh was saying would have been considered blasphemous by his own followers. The mere fact that I was sitting in a room opposite this highly controversial and elusive man already strained credulity, but to have a discussion about his belief in God—who created whom?—was flat-out insane. I glanced furtively at Jamil, who seemed to be holding his breath.

"It is not easy to maintain faith in God when one has lost faith in the human race," the Sheikh continued, pulling me back into our exchange. "Let's not forget, we are supposed to be his reflection. God created such an amazing system, almost perfect, and gave us humans free will. Unlike animals, we can choose. Actually, even unlike angels, who are constrained because they know the consequences of their actions. At our best, we humans are greater than angels, because we use our free will to overcome temptation and sinful instincts. But at our worst, oh, at our worst, we are lower than animals. And in this part of the world, my friend, you will see humans at their worst. Their absolute worst."

Suddenly, without a warning, the Sheikh stood up. I shot up, too, as did Jamil. The Sheikh looked at me, then at Jamil. Brusquely, he turned around and left the room, followed by his two armed guards. I was devastated, convinced that I had done or said something that had displeased this man. Not a word about Paul Blocher. I had come to Beirut for naught. By now, the sun was shining through the window, and I assumed that Jamil would take me back to the airport.

"Was that it?" I asked. "Did I say something to offend him?"

Jamil laughed. "Not at all. In fact, he was in rare form. But he had to speak to one of his commanders. He'll be back, don't worry."

"Why didn't he say so?" I asked, both relieved and annoyed.

"Because, as you may have noticed by now, he doesn't want you to feel too comfortable." Jamil was still laughing. "It's easier to stay awake when one is anxious. By the way, you can take a seat. He could be a while."

I sat down and crossed my legs. Immediately, Jamil motioned for me to uncross them.

"After his soliloquy on God, I wouldn't think this would bother him," I said, confused that my crossed legs might still be perceived as a disrespectful posture because they symbolized the Christian cross. "Besides, I thought that Saddam Hussein was the only one who really felt insulted by visitors crossing their legs, and even he probably reacted more for show than because it really hurt his feelings. I'm terribly sorry, I just didn't expect the Sheikh to care."

"It's okay for him not to care, but not okay for you," Jamil said gravely. "Just like it's okay for him to ask you which god you mean, but it's not okay for you to ask him that same question. Crossing your legs is more offensive culturally than religiously, because you end up pointing your foot and the sole of your shoe at the other person. That insult is much less forgivable than any cross or star of David."

Once again, I was on thin ice. "I see," I said. "I'll keep it all in mind."

I knew that every single detail of the exchange with the Sheikh mattered and desperately wanted to write everything down, but I could not afford the risk of upsetting Jamil. Instead, I ran through our conversation over and over in my mind, hoping to etch the Sheikh's words into my memory. It felt like cramming for a test in high school. After a few minutes, a guard entered the room with some fresh coffee and dates. Khalid's advice about the lifesaving power of dates for a person in captivity popped into my head, sending a shiver down my spine. Jamil and I sat there in silence, sipping coffee and nibbling on dates.*

TWENTY MINUTES LATER, the door opened, and the Sheikh entered behind two guards.

"So tell me, my friend," the Sheikh said as he nodded almost imperceptibly at Jamil, "do you think a nation has the right to defend itself with violent means—means that some call terrorism—if it finds itself threatened?"

This was my nightmare. I felt an instant cold sweat run down between my shoulder blades and could taste a salty flavor on my tongue. I prayed that I wouldn't emit that putrid smell—my own fear marker. I wrapped my right hand around the index finger of my left hand in an attempt to calm myself down. My thoughts returned into focus. As with the Sheikh's previous questions, this one, too, had come out of nowhere and without any connection to the last thing we had discussed. I had no idea whether he was referring to the war in Syria, his battles with Israel, his conflict with America, or the power plays in Lebanon. I knew that I could not reply with a question of my own, but a blanket no could be

---

* There is a block of about ten minutes after the Sheikh had left the room and I was alone with Jamil that I cannot account for. I vaguely recall Jamil asking me about my children, but I cannot be sure and also do not recall whether I responded. Countless times, I have tried to reconstruct those moments, but I keep drawing a blank. I attribute this temporary amnesia to the high mental and emotional stress I was under, possibly even exacerbated by Jamil's mention of my family.

interpreted as a challenge to the Sheikh's political identity while a yes would sound like I was pandering. I reminded myself of Jamil's advice and decided to speak my mind.

"Not necessarily," I said. "I don't believe that the end always justifies the means."

"I agree," the Sheikh said after an agonizingly long time. "Not necessarily and not always. But sometimes. Can you live with that wording?"

"I may have to, considering my circumstances here," I replied, instantly regretting my words.

"Well, you certainly get high marks for honesty and courage," he said genially, then added, "though not necessarily for cleverness."

I decided to hold my own in the face of his challenge to my intelligence and risked a question. "If I may, Sheikh, doesn't the answer depend on whether all other means have been exhausted?"

"In theory, yes," the Sheikh answered. "But it is rare that violence is the first resort. We are not those ignorant, depraved Daash mercenaries, blinded by hate and failure. The world tends to forget conveniently that we have tried more peaceful ways to protect our rights and preserve our dignity. And what happened? Nobody paid attention to us, nobody listened to our plight. But when the rockets started to fly, when the bodies started to pile up, then the world suddenly did pay attention. All of a sudden, we were being heard, loud and clear. Of course, then everyone called us savages, called us uncivilized brutes. Uncivilized! Just because we are not as wealthy and as powerful and as advanced as America or Israel or Europe does not mean we are not civilized!"

The Sheikh had worked himself into a frenzy. I was in a precarious situation. Once more, honesty appeared to be the less hazardous route.

"I don't believe that being civilized has anything to do with power or wealth," I said. "Being civilized means being considerate and understanding of an opposing point of view. It means not belittling empathy and compassion, viewing them as a strength, not as a weakness."

I held my breath as the Sheikh stared at me. "Perhaps you are right," he said. "But in our struggle, empathy is a sentiment we cannot afford. A luxury. It is *your* side that punishes reasonableness and rewards extremism. Come to think of it, you know what this reminds me of?"

I shook my head, dreading what might come next. The sweat was trickling down my spine and had reached the edge of my pants, not a particularly pleasant sensation. I squeezed my index finger a little tighter.

"It reminds me of the struggle of Black people in America."

"How so?" I asked, once again rattled by his abrupt change of pace and topic. It felt like I was being forced to run a series of sprints but without sufficient time to catch my breath in between each one.

"Think about it," the Sheikh said. "When Martin Luther King demanded that Black people should be treated with the same dignity as everybody else, he was attacked and abused as an extremist. So along came Malcolm X, who said: 'To hell with that! By any means necessary!' And what happened? The white establishment condemned him: 'Hey, Malcolm X, you're so extreme, why can't you be more like Martin Luther King?' The same Martin Luther King they had just disparaged. Do you understand?"

I nodded.

"That is usually how we end up with violence. Even against our fellow Arabs, our brothers and sisters, and our cousins."

My discomfort must have shown, because the Sheikh looked me up and down, then said: "Feel free to speak candidly. I prefer an honest question to blind approval."

"In that case, if you allow," I said deferentially. "Since you mentioned violence against your brothers and sisters, why is it that this entire region is so beset by war? Why are Arabs killing Arabs with such viciousness and hate? There are no words to reflect the pain and suffering in Syria. And there is no end in sight. Why are Arabs doing this to fellow Arabs?"

"It's a good question," the Sheikh answered, "yet a misleading one. Come to think of it, this, too, reminds me of how people talk about the Black population in America." He paused. "You look confused."

"Well," I admitted, "I didn't expect you to be such a keen observer of America and its politics, and certainly not of its society and the civil rights movement. You are not exactly known as a friend of the United States."

The Sheikh smiled. "Americans misunderstand me. They think I hate the United States on religious grounds. But America is a religious country, and I respect that. In fact, in many ways it's more religious than Lebanon, this cesspool of sin. More fundamentalist, even, and that's saying something coming from me. My hatred doesn't have anything to do with religion."

"It doesn't?"

"No, it doesn't," the Sheikh replied. "You see, my friend, most societies and countries are like ours here. They are dysfunctional because they are tribal at their core. But America is different. The reason America is exceptional has nothing to do with its power. No, my friend, the reason for America's exceptionalism is that it is *not* tribal. It is a melting pot of many cultures, many ethnicities and religions. And if this American experiment succeeds, then all of us who thrive in tribal conflict in this part of the world, all of us who cannot get out of our own way, all of us who cannot evolve, then all of us have lost. *That* is why I am rooting for America to fail. And that, my friend, is hatred."

I tried to process the Sheikh's stupendous words. I felt myself drift off into complete stillness and weightlessness, into that vacuum I had felt earlier when the Sheikh had talked about god. I focused my breathing on my lower abdomen as I willed myself out of this state of limbo.

"You asked me why we Arabs are killing our fellow Arabs," the Sheikh continued. "What I am trying to explain to you is that it's worth having a look at your beloved America to answer this question—specifically, how white Americans like to talk about Black Americans. Think about it: white Americans tend to point to so-called Black-on-Black crime, as if Black people just don't have it in their DNA to be peaceful and law-abiding citizens. It's that same prejudice I hear when you ask me about Arab-on-Arab warfare and killings. You see, just like white Americans are missing the point about their Black compatriots, you are doing the same when it comes to us Arabs. People kill in their neighborhoods. In America, the vast majority of Blacks are killed by Blacks. The vast majority of whites are killed by whites. It's no different here in the Arab world. The real question is: Why is this such a shitty neighborhood? Which brings us full circle back to the tribal issue."

I did my best not to laugh at the Sheikh's colorful language but could not fully suppress it. I sensed Jamil rustling next to me and tried not to look at him. The Sheikh had a serious expression on his face.

"This is not a laughing matter," he said in a stern voice. "Ever since our movement became a force in the region, we have been defending ourselves—yes, by any means necessary! Just like Brother Malcolm. But we have also been trying to end some of the fighting among our brothers, trying to put out these huge fires, these infernos."

"You cannot be an arsonist and a firefighter at the same time," I ventured, faster than I should have.

"Why not?" the Sheikh shot back, glaring at me with eyes that looked like they were firing lightning bolts. "I most certainly can. The real question is whether I *should*. And to that, I say, Why not! The Saudis do it with their export of Wahhabism while claiming to fight terrorism, and the whole world has accepted, even embraced, it. So why not when we do it? And then the Saudis even add insult to injury by supplying the oil to fan the fires they ignite, while the Americans treat them as their bosom friends. I suppose the lesson to be learned here for an Arab is that you should only be an arsonist if you can also supply the oil to fuel the flames. And you still wonder why we call America the Great Satan!"

Before I could come up with an answer, the Sheikh stood up. "This meeting is over. I know that you have come to see me because of the son of your friend's friend who has gone missing in Syria. You have waited patiently for me to address this matter."

My heart was pounding. The conversation with the Sheikh had been so intense and intimidating that I had almost forgotten about Paul Blocher, but it all came back in a flash. Could it be that I would get the information I was here for after all?

"Based on our sources, this person did indeed enter Syria from Turkey," the Sheikh began in a flat, businesslike tone. "He had a Kurdish handler called Alan—a Syrian Kurd from a small village near Kobane. He is the one who brought the person you are looking for across the border. Khalid mentioned to me that you might already be aware of this. But what you might not know is that at some point in his journey there was a third person with them. A Syrian fellow from Hama. His name is Anas. He was seen with them in a place called Manbij. This Syrian is the key to finding the person you are looking for."

"How can I find this Anas?" I asked.

"It won't be easy. Jamil has access to all the information. He will get you what he can before you leave. I pray that you will find your friend's friend's son and that he will still be alive, *insha'Allah*," the Sheikh said, enunciating each syllable—if Allah wills it—slowly and deliberately.

"Thank you," I said. "Thank you so much."

"Don't thank me yet," the Sheikh answered ominously. "Have a safe journey." As he turned around and walked toward the door, which the guards had already opened, he added, "One more thing: Anas is not a good person. Do not forget that."

The Sheikh left, and the guards followed him, closing the door behind them. I found myself again alone with Jamil. I was exhausted and fell back into my seat, completely drained. The room went dark, like an elevator shaft. I wanted to rub my eyes but was unable to lift my arms. I could not even muster the energy to speak.

"You look so dejected, Daniel," Jamil said softly. "Don't be. I will fill you in on everything we know, and hopefully you will be able to find Mr. Blocher."

"I don't get it, Jamil," I said. "Did you have this information all along, or did you find it all out from the Sheikh today?"

Jamil didn't answer immediately. "Hussein and I were the ones tasked by the Sheikh to get the information after he had the conversation with Khalid last week."

"So you could have just filled me in when we met in Istanbul?" I asked, increasingly irritated that I had been forced to fly to Beirut for no apparent reason.

Jamil shook his head in mock disappointment. "By now I would have expected you to have a better sense of how things work around here."

"What do you mean?"

"The question was not whether we were able to find out something about Blocher's disappearance," Jamil said.

"It wasn't?" I was confused. "Then what was the question?"

"The question was whether we would share that information with you. And, if we did, whether we would give it to you for free or whether we would ask for something in return."

"I see." Now I was annoyed at myself for having disregarded everything I already knew about how things were done in the Middle East.

"And as you have just learned firsthand," Jamil continued, "those are questions neither Hussein nor I are in a position to answer. Only the Sheikh makes that decision. And he provides you with what you are looking for only if he approves of you."

"I hope he did, at least enough to give me the information."

"It was unclear for a while," Jamil said with a serious expression. "He gave me the thumbs-up or, rather, the nod only when he came back into the room the second time. I suppose he was trying to figure out whether your candor outweighed your carelessness."

I felt a strong urge to lash out at Jamil's insult, which seemed so gratuitous after such a draining night, but decided instead to ignore his barb. Still, I had to admire the Sheikh's silent nod at Jamil—so much communication among these men seemed to take place through subtle body language and hushed signals. "What happens now?" I asked.

"What happens now is that I will give you some information as I take you back to the airport," Jamil said. "But if you are up for it, I would like to show you something and introduce you to a friend on the way there. We have some time to kill before your flight."

For the first time since I had arrived in Beirut, I looked at my watch. It was nine-thirty in the morning. We had been in the building for about five hours. Jamil stood up, walked to the door, and knocked twice. A guard opened the door from the outside.

"Shall we?" Jamil proposed. "Let's get out of here and find a nice place to have some breakfast. Unless you prefer to stick to dates, of course."

"Breakfast sounds lovely," I said as I followed him out of the room and down the stairs behind the two guards who showed us out.

In the courtyard, the same driver was waiting in the car. Jamil told him where to take us, and we were on our way, though not before the driver popped his Chopin CD back into the player. I was struck by how different the area looked compared to when we had arrived in the dark. The neighborhood was bustling now, and traffic was slow and blaring. Gridlock on Beirut's roads never developed gradually; the stillness of dawn would suddenly explode into the city's noisy and dusty chaos. I sensed a bad headache come on in my temples and prayed that it wouldn't develop into a debilitating migraine. Almost instantly, I had that oppressive, threatening feeling I always felt in this part of Beirut, as if violence and terror were about to erupt. Unlike the upscale beach and marina area with its expensive restaurants and luxury stores, these

southern quarters felt like hostile territory, where every ⸱
potential enemy—although as the assassination of Lebanese pr⸱
minister Hariri in 2005 near the beautiful St. George Hotel showed, the
uplifting feeling of the Corniche and its posh neighborhood was just
a fleeting illusion in this city. I shut my eyes for a moment to ease this
sensory overload.

We drove for about twenty minutes through narrow streets between
rundown apartment blocks, where laundry in all colors hung to dry on
the balconies. Jamil tapped on the driver's shoulder, motioning for him
to stop in front of a small kiosk.

"Come, let's eat," he said.

"Here?" I asked incredulously. After last night's ordeal, I felt entitled
to a lavish meal.

"I know, it doesn't look like much," Jamil said. "But the *za'atar
man'ouche* is the best in the country. Trust me. Besides, I'd like you to
meet the guy who runs this place."

We got out of the car and walked across a dusty path. As we approached
the kiosk, a short man with a gaunt face and deep-set, bloodshot eyes
stepped in front of the counter and barked at two customers who were
sitting at the only table, ordering them to leave. He then walked toward
Jamil with open arms and kissed him on both cheeks.

"Daniel, this is Bassel. Bassel, this is my friend Daniel."

"Pleased to meet you," I said to Bassel as we shook hands.

"A friend of Jamil's is my friend, too," Bassel said in a low voice.
"Welcome to my five-star restaurant. What can I get you?"

"We've had a long night, so let's start with some strong coffee," Jamil
jumped in. "And I have sung the praises of your *za'atar man'ouche*. So
how about some of that and some fresh fruit?"

"Coming right up." Bassel disappeared before I could get a word in.

"Seems like a nice guy," I said to Jamil. "What's the deal with the red
eyes?"

"Bassel has been through a lot," Jamil said. "He's a special person. And as good as his food is, his true talents lie elsewhere."

"They do? Where?"

"Bassel hails from one of the oldest and most prominent families in Damascus. He is a descendant of Shukri al-Quwatli, the first Syrian president after independence. However, he's exceptional for his brain more than his pedigree. He's a brilliant computer expert, invaluable to the regime. He built all their firewalls and monitoring systems. More than once, top tech companies tried to poach him—Google and SAP both offered generous packages to relocate him and his entire family, but the regime made it crystal clear that they would never let him go. He's too important to them, and he knows too many secrets. At the same time, his brilliance also led to his downfall."

"Why? What happened?"

"Bassel and his team regularly monitored and hacked members of the opposition and people suspected of being, shall we say, slightly deficient in the loyalty department. Well, one day he hacked into the email of a major Sunni businessman and found out that this guy kept extensive files on some powerful people, especially the Makhlouf brothers. Of course he reported these findings to his superiors."

"So where's the problem?" I asked. "I would assume they'd be pleased with him for catching someone who was keeping tabs on the president's powerful cousins."

"In a normal country, you'd be right," Jamil said wryly. "But this is Syria. Nothing is normal in Syria. The problem was that this Sunni businessman was one of Ali Mamlouk's best friends."

"Ali Mamlouk, the head of intelligence?"

Just that moment, Bassel showed up with our coffee and some sesame seed cookies.

"Yes, that one," Jamil answered after Bassel had left again to finish preparing our breakfast. "The same Ali Mamlouk who has been placed on everyone's sanctions list as a top war criminal, who also happens to be the same Ali Mamlouk who remained tight with his buddies in the CIA, the MI6, and especially those French DGSE pricks. It's the same old story, right?"

I nodded. I knew that Jamil was right about Western hypocrisy. When a prominent, well-known Westerner went missing in Syria, a senior official from the missing person's government would usually call Mamlouk and ask for help, especially if there was reason to believe that the poor soul was being held by the Syrian regime or one of the militias under the regime's command. And while they were asking Mamlouk for help, the same governments would publicly blast him for his war crimes. Mamlouk would always respond, in the sweetest tone imaginable for such a butcher, that he had no knowledge of the missing person but that he would of course be more than happy to inquire with the authorities on his side—as if he wasn't the ultimate authority in Syria when it came to kidnapping people and throwing them into jail. I almost expected to see a celestial halo appear above his head whenever he pulled off this saintly act.

The strangest part of dealing with murderers such as Mamlouk was everyone's irrational, nonsensical expectation that he would behave honorably and empathetically and that he would assist in freeing people he himself had thrown into his own dungeons, where they ended up rotting away for years, sometimes even decades. In the company of his henchmen, Mamlouk would mercilessly mock these desperate, absurd requests by Western officials. Then, without fail, a few days later he or one of his deputies would call back and claim to possess ironclad evidence that the missing person was being held by those despicable terrorists in the country—a catch-all term that seemed to include anyone who was opposed to the Syrian regime.

To top it off, Mamlouk would add for good measure that perhaps the time had come for the West to drop its support for the rebels and join

President Assad in his righteous fight against these abominable terror-ists. After all, Syria and the West were on the same side in this clash of civilizations, as he liked to pontificate, sometimes sprinkling a Samuel Huntington quote into the conversation for good measure. Twice already I had experienced this ridiculous, cruel charade in the cases of an aid worker and a journalist who had disappeared in Syria, and at the time I had incontrovertible proof that the two missing men were being held by people under Mamlouk's direct command. I would have loved to pick Jamil's brain for some more information about Mamlouk but did not want to distract him from Bassel's story.

Jamil dipped a cookie into the coffee and savored it on his tongue. He motioned for me to do the same, then swallowed the remnants of his coffee-soaked sesame seed confection.

"Apparently," he went on, "this Sunni businessman was actually spying on the Makhloufs and some other powerful folks at the express orders of Ali Mamlouk—something poor Bassel was of course com-pletely unaware of, or he would not have reported it to Mamlouk's deputy. It's like Himmler keeping files on Hitler—these spooks just can't help themselves. In any event, it started a shitstorm, as you can imagine. Turns out, hacking into the email of a person who is spying on the presi-dent's cousins, and then reporting this spying to the head of intelligence who had ordered this spying to begin with—well, let's just say it was a bit of a downer as far as Bassel's career was concerned. So he decided to lie low for a while."

"By running a kiosk in Beirut?" I asked.

"Oh, it's not just any kiosk," Jamil said. "This is where many key play-ers meet, especially security people. Many a secret has been shared at this very table. Bassel has his ears everywhere—just because he is no longer in Syria does not mean he is not plugged in, no pun intended."

As if on cue, Bassel was back with two huge platters.

"One *za'atar man'ouche*," he said as he placed the first platter on the table. "And one *labneh man'ouche*," he added with a grin. "I couldn't help myself. It would be wrong to let Daniel leave Beirut without having tasted both. What happened to your Arab hospitality, Jamil?"

We all laughed. "Dig in," Jamil said as he helped himself.

The food was delicious. The *za'atar* tasted earthy—wild thyme with a subtle minty fragrance. The creamy, smooth *labneh* completed it perfectly. I complimented Bassel on his cooking skills.

"Oh, thank you," he said, visibly pleased. "It's a nice little hobby, useful to fill the time until I get back in the game."

"We didn't just come here for your tasty *za'atar* pizza," Jamil said a little abruptly. "Daniel is in Beirut for a particular purpose. I would be grateful if you could help."

Jamil's words took me completely by surprise. He had not indicated that this pit stop was intended as anything other than breakfast and an introduction to a friend. The casual smoothness with which Jamil navigated his surroundings stood in strong contrast to my own exhausted, breathless state of mind.

"Sure," Bassel said. "Silly me, I thought you came here because you missed me! So how can I help?"

"We need to locate someone," Jamil said. "A Syrian whom I believe you know."

"Who is it?" Bassel asked.

"Anas," Jamil replied quietly.

"Which Anas?" Bassel asked in a weary voice.

"You know which Anas," Jamil said sharply. "Anas from Hama. Abu Sayid."

Bassel's look betrayed great discomfort. I instantly picked up a putrid whiff coming from his direction. All of a sudden, this man was very scared. "Captagon Anas? Seriously? *That* Anas?" he asked. His voice was almost quivering.

"Yes," Jamil said. "*That* Anas."

I perked up the moment I heard Bassel utter "Captagon." Captagon was the drug that was fueling the war in Syria. These little white enormously addictive pills were generating the cash to buy weapons and arm militias on all sides of the conflict. Syria had turned into a massive manufacturing lab for this nasty amphetamine, which had become one of the country's most lucrative export products. I knew from a friend in Riyadh that Saudi Arabia in particular was facing an epidemic of Captagon addicts. And apparently the fighters in Syria were also popping these pills like crazy, which put them in a state of delirious aggression and made them devoid of fear. The fact that this Anas fellow was associated with Captagon was not good news. I remembered the Sheikh's parting warning.

I could tell from Bassel's slumped shoulders and his bloodshot, now droopy eyes that he wished he had not been dragged into this matter. He looked at me and sighed. "Anas is a bad person," he said. "This is not someone you should even want to locate, let alone meet. He contaminates everyone who comes in contact with him. Around him, there is nothing but misery and suffering. Why do you need to find him?"

Before I could answer, Jamil spoke. "Daniel needs to find someone who we believe was with Anas on his way to Aleppo."

Bassel glared at Jamil. "That someone had better be worth the search."

"He is," I said.

"Well, I've heard that Anas is shuttling between Syria, Amman, and Dubai," Bassel said. "One of my colleagues in Damascus—sorry, one of my former colleagues—has been tracking his phone, and I can ask him where Anas is these days, if you would like me to do that."

"I would greatly appreciate it," I said. "Thank you."

"Being associated with Anas is generally not a good thing," Bassel said. "I hope the person you are looking for is fine. Most people who are involved with Anas end up either dirty . . . or dead.

"One more thing," he continued. "I feel bad piling on the bad news, but I think you should know that Anas is rumored to be trading in more than just Captagon."

I was dreading the next piece of information, but I also knew that I needed to have it. Jamil sensed my unease. "Just hear him out," he said gently. "With some luck, it won't be the worst-case scenario."

"If luck is my only strategy, I'm in deep shit," I said.

"*We're* in deep shit," Jamil corrected me. "We're in this together."

I knew that he was just trying to make me feel better, but his esprit de corps still felt good.

"What else is there?" I asked Bassel.

Before Bassel could respond, a group of three young men approached the kiosk. Jamil's posture stiffened immediately, and his eyes narrowed into tight slits. He whispered something to Bassel, then turned around and pointed to our driver who was waiting in the car. Right away, the driver jumped out of the car and rushed over to the three men, cutting off their path to the kiosk. One of the three shouted a profanity at the driver and demanded that he step aside. In an amazingly swift motion, the driver grabbed the man by his throat and squeezed so hard that he dropped to his knees. The other two men froze in shock. The driver then said something that I could not make out from where we were sitting, and the three men scampered away. The whole scene had taken less than thirty seconds, and when it was over the driver got back in the car as if nothing had happened. It was another reminder of where I was.

Jamil's posture relaxed, and his eyes regained their full shape. "You were saying, Bassel?" He was calm as he touched Bassel's forearm. "You mentioned that Anas is trading in something other than Captagon. What is it?"

"I've heard that he's also involved in the people trade," Bassel answered.

"What do you mean?" I asked.

"Well, trading people for cash, or for drugs, or for guns, or for diesel. For whatever has any kind of value."

"Where did you hear that?" Jamil asked Bassel.

"Anas's name came up in connection with some of the journalists who were captured," Bassel said. I could tell from Jamil's intense demeanor and erect posture that this new information had struck a nerve. "Apparently," Bassel continued, "some of the journalists were traded back and forth, sometimes from the Damascus Shabbiha militias to the Nusra fighters, sometimes from Nusra to the Shabbiha, depending on who had captured them in the first place. Sometimes from Nusra onward to the crazies at Suqour al-Sham or even to Daash. We even tracked some trades from the Alawi Shabbiha to the Shabbiha gangs in Aleppo."

"What's the difference?" I asked.

"Originally, the Shabbiha militias were Alawis from the coast," Jamil said. "From Latakia or Tartus, where I come from. But the ones in Aleppo are from Sunni tribes in that area. A different beast, literally and figuratively, if you get my drift. Though, come to think of it, not really that different."

Bassel nodded approvingly. "That's correct. We were tracking certain dealers and traders, including Anas, and realized that some Western journalists had become part of the trade bait. In fact, it was rare for them to be held for a long time by the same group that had captured them."

I was feeling worse and worse as I imagined Paul Blocher being traded from one Syrian group to another, each one as vicious as the other. By now, I had lost my appetite.

"Thank you, Bassel," Jamil said as he got up. He must have sensed my unease.

"My pleasure," Bassel said. "Good luck finding your person. I'll reach out to my colleague in Damascus and ask him to check out Anas and his recent movements. I'll keep you posted."

"I really appreciate it," I said as we shook hands. "And thank you for the delicious food and coffee. I hope we can meet again and just eat."

As Jamil and I walked toward the car, Bassel ran up to us. "One more thing."

"What is it, Bassel?" I detected a trace of impatience in Jamil's voice.

"I have also heard that Anas got involved in the trade of young girls to the Gulf," Bassel said. "Actually, 'trade' is just a euphemism for 'pimping.' I've no idea whether it's true, but apparently there's a ring selling young Syrian girls, many of them orphans, to men in the Gulf. Mainly in the Emirates and Saudi Arabia."

"This is just getting better and better," I muttered under my breath. Jamil gave me a stern look. I had to get my act together.

"Thanks for that information, Bassel," Jamil said. "Please forgive Daniel. He's had a long night. I'd be grateful if you could let me know as soon as you hear back from your contact in Damascus."

"I will," Bassel said, then added, turning to me, "I am really sorry to be the harbinger of bad news. Maybe all this means nothing at all, and the person you are looking for is in a safe place and no longer with Anas. But I thought you should know whatever there is to know."

"Thanks," was all I could muster as I got into the car. My shirt was drenched from the late morning heat. I felt completely worn out and unable to absorb any more information.

"Where to?" our driver asked.

"Take us to the green house," Jamil said. "Daniel could use an uplifting experience before his flight." Despite his scolding glance a few moments earlier, his tone was now kind and caring.

Bassel waved as we drove off. His eyes looked weary, as if any fire in them had been extinguished long ago. I was too drained to speak, even too exhausted to ask Jamil what the green house was.

"Don't be so dejected," Jamil said once Bassel was out of sight. "If you want to find your friend's son, you will have to talk to many different people and gather as much information as you can. Put on your big-boy pants. Nobody will serve you this information on a silver platter."

"I know," I said. "I'm only trying to process what Bassel just told us about this Anas fellow. There's quite a lot to digest."

"Listen, Daniel," Jamil said, "here's what the Sheikh once told me: people come into our lives for one of four reasons—to add, to subtract, to multiply, or to divide. It's basic math, pretty simple and linear. The difficulty is trying to figure out which one is which. Bassel was just trying to add, to give us information."

"I know." The sun was shining straight into my eyes, and I was struggling to keep them open. The fatigue didn't help either.

"Please also keep that in mind when you meet some of the more sinister characters," Jamil continued. "Even a rotten soul like Anas and his gangster pals can be helpful to your quest. They, too, can be here to add. So why not think positive? In the end, everything will be okay."

"What if it's not okay?" I asked, still squinting.

"Then it's not yet the end."

As WE DROVE through the heavy Beirut traffic, impressions of the city and the conversations with the Sheikh, Jamil, and now Bassel flooded my brain. I had a few hours left before my flight back to Istanbul. All I wanted to do was rest and have some quiet time to gather my thoughts after the last ten hours.

"Here we are," Jamil said as we pulled into a courtyard in a residential area. We seemed to be close to the building where I had met the Sheikh. A few children ran up to the car as Jamil stepped out. A boy, no older than five, hugged his leg.

"*Kifak, habibi?*" Jamil asked in a gentle voice as he lifted the child in the air. "How are you? Have you been a good boy?" His Arabic was now soft and melodious, more Syrian than Lebanese.

The boy nodded with a huge grin on his face. Jamil tried to put him back on the ground, but the boy slung his arms around Jamil's neck and did not let go. Tears of happiness were streaming down his face. A young girl, a little older than the boy, came running out of the house and flung herself at Jamil, almost knocking the boy to the ground.

"I missed you, *habibti*," Jamil said to the girl as he hugged her. "Have you been a good girl?"

As the girl nodded, Jamil lowered them both, then grabbed each with one hand and swung them around in circles. They squealed in delight, and every time Jamil tried to stop, they held on to his arms and asked for another round. Eventually, Jamil put them down gently.

"I'm dizzy," he said as they still held on to him in a tight embrace. "Now, please show your good manners and say hello to our visitor, Mr. Daniel. He has come here all the way from America."

The girl let go of Jamil and came up to me with an outstretched arm. "*Tasha rafna*," she said with a sweet smile, looking straight in my eyes. "Pleased to meet you, Mr. Daniel."

"Pleased to meet you, too," I said. "What is your name?"

The girl looked at Jamil, who nodded approvingly. "Aliya," she said.

"Pleased to meet you, Miss Aliya," I said.

Aliya giggled and ran back to Jamil, who was prodding the boy to come to me. Jamil finally took him by the hand and brought him over.

"*Tasha rafna*, Mr. Daniel," the boy said in a timid whisper, looking at his feet.

"Pleased to meet you, too," I replied. "And what is your name?"

"Sami," he answered bashfully while hiding behind Jamil's legs.

"Sami and Aliya are orphans," Jamil said, switching back into English as we walked toward the entrance of the building. "They lost their parents in an explosion in Daraya, on the outskirts of Damascus. A roadside bomb. It ripped through the front of the car, both parents died on the spot. By some miracle, the two children suffered only minor injuries. Physically, on the outside, that is. But psychologically, on the inside, they suffered massive traumas. Their father was decapitated by the shrapnel, and their mother was ripped to shreds. Literally. The two children held on to each other for dear life and cried for weeks on end. That was the state they were in when they arrived here, at the green house. This was six months ago. They have come a long way, but still wake up every night with nightmares, screaming. I try to see them whenever I can. All they have is each other."

"And you," I said.

Jamil smiled. "Yes, and me."

We entered the building into a corridor with pink walls, which were covered with drawings and paintings by the children. Some of the paintings were yellowed—they must have been hanging there for years, even decades. Aliya pointed at one of the drawings and at Sami in order to let me know that her little brother had made it. Sami beamed, then immediately blushed and covered his face with his hands. Jamil gently removed Sami's hands and looked at him approvingly. He gave Aliya a thumbs-up, evidently proud that she had chosen to promote her brother instead of herself.

We entered a large room, and the kids followed us, eyeing me curiously like some kind of visitor from another planet. The couple in charge came to greet us and invited us to have a seat. They must not have been expecting guests, because the woman hurried to adjust her headscarf that was perched loosely on her shoulders, covering just the back of her head. She seemed nervous, and as she fidgeted with the scarf it kept sliding back to reveal her hairline and a pair of sunglasses on top of her head. Jamil quickly let go of Aliya and Jamil, reached over, and in one swift motion removed the woman's sunglasses, pulled the headscarf to an inch above her eyebrows, and pinned the sunglasses back on her head on top of the headscarf to keep it in place. Jamil's intervention had lasted barely two seconds, and his hands never touched her hair or her face. The woman nodded and cast her eyes down. A young boy immediately showed up and served us coffee. Aliya and Sami were again clutching Jamil's hands, refusing to let go.

"All the children here are orphans," Jamil explained. "Most are from Syria, though some are from Lebanon. Almost every child has a similar story to tell as Sami and Aliya. If you could feel all the heartbreak of these beautiful, innocent souls, your faith in mankind would be shattered forever. But this place is special. It has given these children a future, some hope."

Jamil suddenly choked up and left to play with the children in the room, dragging Aliya and Sami, who were still holding on to his legs, with him. It was a side of Jamil I had not expected. For the first time since we met at the airport lounge in Istanbul, his eyes lost their piercing glare, and he completely let himself go with the children. His shirt had come loose, and the two top buttons opened as Sami kept tugging at it. Every time he tried to tuck the shirt back in his pants and close the buttons, another child tackled him, until he was finally knocked over. Once Jamil was on the ground, the children took turns tickling him. As he laughed and rolled from side to side, he took care not to crush the children that were all over him.

After twenty minutes, Jamil told the kids that he had to leave but that he would be back in the evening before bedtime to say good night. I stood up and thanked the hosts for the coffee.

As we walked across the courtyard to the car, Aliya let go of Jamil's hand and held mine. It was hard to keep myself from tearing up. At the car, Jamil told both kids to say goodbye to their visitor the way he had taught them.

"Goodbye, Mr. Daniel," Aliya said with a smile. "Please come visit us again."

"I will," I said. "Goodbye Aliya. It was lovely to meet you."

Jamil prodded Sami, who said softly, "Goodbye, Mr. Daniel." After Jamil prodded him again, he added, "Thank you for coming to our home."

Both children gave Jamil a tight hug, and Sami started to sob uncontrollably. He only stopped when Aliya took his hand and promised him that Jamil would be back later in the day.

I got in the car with a heavy heart. Jamil told the driver to head to the airport. I got the sense that he, too, was struggling to regain his composure.

"This house has a special place in my heart," Jamil said after we had been driving for a few minutes. "The Sheikh started this orphanage decades ago and named it the green house because green is the color worn by those who make it to paradise. It was the favorite color of the prophet Muhammad. And in some ways, this place has become paradise for these children, assuming paradise is a relative concept, of course. Because this generation of children is damned. They will never recover the childhood that was stolen from them." Jamil fell silent, lost in his thoughts. "The green house also happens to be where my uncle dumped me twenty-eight years ago," he added, "two years after my mother died."

I had suspected as much. "What happened to your father?" I asked, even though Khalid had warned me that this might be a sore point. I saw the hardness return in Jamil's eyes.

"My father died for me thirty-six years ago," he said coldly. "Nine months before I was born, to be precise."

As WE APPROACHED the airport, traffic ground to a halt at a large roundabout. A barricade was blocking our lane at a security checkpoint, and three armed men walked up to the car, gesticulating for our driver to move to the side of the road. The leader of the three men was a freakish giant with enormous, bulging muscles, like some monstrous cyclops straight out of Greek mythology. This colossus was armed with an automatic weapon and a pistol in his hip holster. He yelled at our driver and pointed the weapon at his face. Jamil calmly instructed the driver to do exactly as told. The armed giant looked at me, then barked at us to lower our windows. His face was just inches away from mine. His hairline was so low that it practically led straight into his unibrow. "Get out of the car, all of you!" he shouted as he aimed his weapon at my face. "Now!"

"Just do as he says," Jamil said quietly, "and let me handle everything."

"*Sho hadha?*" Jamil hissed at the thuggish figure as he got out of the car. "What the hell do you think you are doing?"

As soon as the man saw Jamil, an incredible transformation took place. His shoulders slumped, and he stumbled backward with his hands raised toward us, as if trying to ward off an evil spirit. "I'm so sorry, boss, I'm so sorry," he kept repeating. "Please forgive me, boss. I did not see you. I did not know it was you. I'm so sorry."

"This is how you treat drivers on the road?" Jamil scolded him. "Do you want everyone to hate us? What were you thinking? Oh yeah, that's right—you were *not* thinking! Imbecile!"

"I'm so sorry, boss," the man repeated over and over, suddenly sweating profusely. "Please forgive me. Can I please escort you? Are you heading to the airport, boss?"

"Where we are heading is none of your business," Jamil answered acidly. "I will deal with you later. And don't you let me catch you on my way back! Crawl back under your rock and stay there until I call for you."

The man was so crestfallen, I actually felt bad for him, even though he had just threatened me with a loaded weapon. We got back in the car, and Jamil tapped on the driver's shoulders. "*Yallah!*" he barked. "Let's get out of here."

"I apologize for that," Jamil said as we drove away. "That guy has been an idiot his whole life. I can't believe they gave him a gun. Big muscles, but nothing between the ears. It seems that Darwin got that one wrong!"

I laughed so hard I started to hiccup. All the tension of the past twelve hours came pouring out of me. The driver gave me a curious look in the rearview mirror. We drove to the same airport gate that we had left at night. As we approached, the driver spoke into his phone, "We're here."

The gate opened, and Hussein came out of the guard's hut and got into the front seat next to the driver.

"Nice to see you again." He addressed me in a friendly, casual tone. "I hope your visit has been fruitful."

"Very fruitful, thanks," I said. Jamil was quiet.

"Glad to hear," Hussein said. "Here are your phones."

I had completely forgotten about my two phones. "Thank you."

We drove up to the side building with the sign VIP/DIPLOMATS. "Feel free to tip the driver," Hussein said. "He will remember this, and you never know when a loyal, motivated driver comes in handy."

I gave the driver a hundred dollars. He pocketed the money with a smile. "Have a safe trip," he said in accent-free English.

"May I please have your passport?" Hussein asked as we walked into the building. "The same procedure as last night, Mr. Daniel," he added with a grin as he took off.

"Hussein gets on my nerves with his *Dinner for One* line," Jamil said. "If you want a friend for life, you should answer, 'The same procedure as every night, Hussein.' I have no idea why he keeps quoting that line."

"It's all right, it's a classic," I said. "Why not, if it makes him happy." There was something ludicrous about Hussein's reference to this British comedy sketch from the early sixties, given my current circumstances. It used to play on television in Switzerland every New Year's Eve through-out my childhood—a long time ago, and in every respect far away from this moment at the airport in Beirut.

Hussein returned a few minutes later with my passport and the boarding pass.

"We should get going," he said. "Preboarding will start soon. And I'd like to get you there for the pre-preboarding."

"Time for me to say goodbye," Jamil said. "I will be in touch with Khalid after I hear back from Bassel. I expect our paths to cross again, perhaps on a happier occasion."

"I was hoping you would escort me back to Istanbul," I said in an attempt to add some lightheartedness to the situation. Jamil ignored my comment. "Thank you for everything, Jamil," I added quickly. "Please give Aliya and Sami a hug from me. And please convey my gratitude to the Sheikh. It was kind of him to help—or to let you help me."

"You can thank Khalid for that," Jamil said. "He saved the Sheikh's backside many years ago when the Saudi king wanted to intimidate his Shia citizens by setting an example with the Sheikh. Without Khalid, it would not have ended well for the Sheikh. So Khalid has unlimited credit on the Sheikh's ledger."

"I didn't know that."*

"It's not exactly public knowledge," Jamil said. "But be sure to remain under Khalid's wings for the duration of this expedition. Others who venture into this space end up having a much darker experience," he added ominously. I considered giving Jamil a hug in recognition of the long night we had spent together. I never got a chance. Without another word, he left the room.

"Shall we?" Hussein asked.

We walked to the door leading to the tarmac, where the same car that had picked up Jamil and me on our arrival was now waiting for us with its engine running. We drove on the tarmac under the gangways

---

* Khalid has remained steadfast in his refusal to share any information about this episode. From the little I could squeeze out of other sources, one of King Fahd's brothers wanted to prove his grit and qualification for a leadership position by getting tough on some Shia leaders in Saudi Arabia. The Sheikh made some comments at the time condemning this crackdown, and his comments were aired on Saudi TV and not particularly well received in the royal court. All this seemed to have taken place in the early 1990s, just as the Sheikh was beginning to leave his mark on Lebanese politics and a few years before the stroke suffered by King Fahd in 1995 that put Crown Prince Abdullah in charge. I was unable to find out whether the Sheikh had been in Saudi Arabia at the time and exactly what Khalid had done to protect him, but it must have been significant enough to leave Khalid perpetually in the Sheikh's good graces.

to the bottom of the metal stairs that led to the front door of my plane. Hussein walked up the stairs with me.

"This is where I say goodbye," he said. "It was nice to meet you. Please give my best regards to Khalid when you see him. He talks of you like his son, so I assume he will be waiting for you in Istanbul, right?"

"That's the plan," I said. "Thanks for all your help."

"My pleasure," Hussein said. "*Twusal bel salameh*, have a safe flight."

I handed the flight attendant my boarding pass. The plane was still empty, and she informed me that boarding would start in about ten minutes. I took my seat and closed my eyes.

I woke up to the light touch of the same flight attendant. "Sir, we have started our descent to Istanbul. Can I bring you anything to drink before we land?"

I had fallen into a deep sleep and missed the entire boarding and takeoff, as well as most of the flight. I had a massive headache and asked for a cup of coffee.

It was late afternoon when the plane landed in Istanbul, just in time for the terrible end-of-the-day gridlock on the way to the city center. Under normal circumstances, I would have tried to avoid the airport's crowded bottleneck spots, but after the night I had just experienced in Beirut, the throng of people felt soothing. The same driver from the Kempinski was waiting for me in the arrivals area. "I hope you had a pleasant trip," he said. "Mr. Khalid is expecting you in the hotel."

Traffic was awful, and it took us an hour to make our way to the hotel. Khalid was sitting in the same place near the lobby entrance where he had greeted me a day earlier. He smiled when he saw me.

"Welcome back. Do you need to freshen up, or shall we go outside and sit at our usual spot by the water? It is a beautiful evening."

"I think I'm beyond freshening up," I said. "If you don't object, I could use a drink."

Khalid laughed. "Let's go. I can't wait to hear all about your trip."

We found our chairs from the previous evening, and ordered our drinks—jasmine tea for Khalid, and a Macallan for me. It was wonderful to relax in the cushioned chair and taste the delicious sting of whiskey in my throat. I was finally able to decompress and felt the tension of the past eighteen hours drain away. A flock of seagulls flew over us with that distinct cawing sound. The previous day's foul smell of sewage and pollution had evaporated, and all I wished for was to relax and not think of anything stressful for a few hours. Yet I knew that I had to bring Khalid up to speed, even though he was waiting patiently and not bombarding me with questions.

I filled him in on the trip to Beirut, from meeting Jamil in the lounge in Istanbul, to the Sheikh, Bassel and the information about Anas, all the way to the stop at the green house and the unpleasant roadblock on the way back to the airport. Khalid listened intently.

"Well, I'd say your trip went better than expected," he said when I finished my account.

"I can't tell," I said. "I feel like I've received a lot of information, yet I find myself starting out from a negative position. Before I can locate Paul, I need to track down this Anas fellow, who, by all accounts, seems to be a pretty nasty guy."

"I understand your trepidation," Khalid said. "But you've actually accomplished a lot. Jamil called me after you took off and told me that he was expecting some information from Bassel in the coming days. The Sheikh approved of you and has asked Hussein to travel to Damascus to speak to Bassel's colleague himself. The phone lines are not secure."

"Why is he sending Hussein and not Jamil?"

"Hussein is more of a logistics guy while Jamil is all about intelligence," Khalid replied.

"Yes, I noticed that," I said. "Jamil is certainly not your average Ray."

"The best ones aren't," Khalid said. "That's why average is hardly ever good enough. Won't get the job done."

"I thought average means the job gets done as often as not," I replied. I was too tired to stop myself from being argumentative and also irritated that Khalid couldn't keep his pedantic instincts in check.

Khalid laughed. "I see it differently. Average is almost always good enough for the easy stuff and usually good enough for the ordinary tasks. But for real challenges, and I believe we can both agree that finding Paul Blocher constitutes a real challenge, average is rarely good enough."

He was right, as usual. Another reminder never to play the player.

"Be that as it may," Khalid continued, "with Jamil you get the best of both worlds—the toughness on the battlefield, and the sensitivity and emotional intelligence away from it. Jamil has been through a lot in his young life and has been able to find the inner strength to channel his own hardship so that the resentment does not consume him. The Sheikh already saw that in him when Jamil was a little boy. There is not a single person he trusts more than Jamil. It is Jamil who draws the most sensitive assignments, from managing the Iranians to the covert discussions with the Israelis."

For an instant I thought I detected a pang of regret in Khalid's voice for revealing too much information about Jamil's clandestine life.

"Well then," I said, feeling suddenly more upbeat, "in that case, I suppose we can see some light at the end of the tunnel."

"Not so fast, *habibi*," Khalid deadpanned. "That light you see might be a train barreling toward us."

Khalid sure knew how to put a damper on my temporary euphoria. "So what do we do now?" I asked.

"We eat dinner."

"I mean, what's our next move?"

"We wait."

FIVE

I LEFT ISTANBUL the next morning on the first flight to New York.
Khalid had been in a jovial mood over dinner, and we parted on a warm
note. He promised to get in touch as soon as he heard from Jamil. The
departure lounge—the same one in which I had met Jamil just thirty
hours earlier—was humming with travelers, and I felt a childlike satisfaction that none of them knew the secret of my last visit before the flight to
Beirut. As I walked down the steps to the bottom floor, I almost expected
to be met by Jamil's piercing green eyes.

I was sipping a coffee when I noticed a discussion playing on a television screen mounted on the wall behind me. The program was a
commemoration of the horrific sarin gas attacks in the Ghouta region
on the outskirts of Damascus one year earlier, in which, by conservative
estimates, more than fourteen hundred people, including four hundred
children, had been killed. A group of panelists was debating the histor-
ical and political significance of these repeated large-scale deployments
of chemical weapons by the Assad regime.

One panelist mused in a detached, clinical tone whether these casu-
alties really constituted a "genocide" or whether they were merely part
of an ordinary "civil war." Another wondered whether jargon such as
"mass murder" or "massacre" was really applicable to a conflict that he
believed was nothing other than criminal gangs settling scores. This discussion was yet another distressing reminder of how out of touch the
rest of the world had become with the depravities repeated every single

moment in Syria. The mere fact that these experts felt the need to parse their words so carefully to draw theoretical lines between a genocide, a mass murder, or just your average civil war evidenced a complete loss of empathy. All their chatter about whether this wasn't just that same old story of primitive, uncivilized tribal societies killing one another barely concealed their disdain for the refugees trying to escape the killing fields or their fleeting discomfort of having to look at the picture of a dead Syrian toddler swept facedown onto a Mediterranean shore.

I was about to get up and look for a spot where I would not have to hear the blaring television when I overheard two men seated near me discuss the TV program in loud German. The first man, a portly German in a sweat-stained shirt, proclaimed that this was just the way wars were—millions would still have to die in Syria, and the war would end only when there was no one left to die. The other person, a slim man in his thirties sporting green horn-rimmed glasses and a tight pink polo shirt that clashed with his bright carrot-red hair, was quick to agree, explaining matter of factly in a thick Swiss-German accent that the universal laws of nature would determine how many more people would still have to die in Syria. He called the war an act of natural selection and population control and stated that there was simply no more room for all those refugees in Europe. The German fellow nodded and mumbled, "*Es reicht schon mit diesen Scheissarabern*"—enough already with these shitty Arabs—to which the Swiss man added, "*Ja wirklich, das Boot ist voll*"—yes indeed, the boat is full. As I walked away, I heard them both snicker. Apparently not much had changed in Europe over the past seventy years.

I fell into a deep sleep on the flight home and dreamed of the green house in Beirut and of sweet Aliya and her brother, Sami. In the dream, I was playing a game with them when I suddenly noticed Paul Blocher sitting all by himself in the corner of the room. I tried to invite him to join us in our game, but each time I approached him, he vanished into another corner of the room. Eventually, I gave up and focused on Aliya and Sami. When I looked for Paul a little later, he was gone.

On my way home from the airport, I had to laugh at the terrible state of the roads in New York; the potholes were the size of craters, and it felt like driving in a war zone. In fact, the roads in Beirut, a city that had experienced civil war, occupation, and countless bombings, were in better shape than the ones in New York, the world's financial center. Once home, I sent Huby a text message with a request to call me at his convenience. My phone rang two seconds later.

"How are you? Do you have any news?" Huby asked, sounding very apprehensive.

"Yes, I do have some information," I said. "I'd prefer to meet in person rather than talk on the phone. Any chance you can come to New York in the next few days?"

"I am in DC at the moment. I can be there tonight," Huby replied eagerly.

"Tonight won't work, I just got back. I'd like to spend the evening at home with Laura and the kids. How about tomorrow morning?"

"Yes, of course. But can you tell me anything? Good news or bad news?" he asked.

"Neither," I said, remembering Khalid's brutal putdown of my light-at-the-end-of-the-tunnel optimism. "But we have a trail."

"So that's good news," Huby said. "Good enough to let me fall asleep tonight and hope to live another day. Or is it live to hope another day? It doesn't matter. A trail is good news for me. I'll take it."

We agreed to meet at nine in the morning in the thirty-fifth-floor lounge of the Mandarin Oriental hotel. I knew that Huby had a residence there with an incredible skyline view of the city.

HUBY WAS WAITING for me the next morning when I stepped out of the elevator.

"You're late," he said impatiently.

"Seriously? It's eight fifty-eight!"

"I know. But you're not early enough. I've been waiting for twenty minutes."

Huby could tell from my look that he needed to calm down. "Forgive me," he said. "I've been a wreck. I'm terribly anxious to hear what you have to tell me."

We found a seat by the window with panoramic views of Central Park and midtown Manhattan and ordered coffee. I gave Huby a run-down of what I had learned in Beirut, without revealing any names or the meeting with the Sheikh. When I mentioned the Anas connection to Captagon and other drugs, Huby pricked up his ears and asked me to repeat what I had just said. He had an expression of shock on his face, as if he had just seen a ghost.

"What's wrong?" I asked.

"The drug trade," he started before his voice trailed off. "What was the name of the drug you just mentioned?"

"Captagon."

"Captagon. Hmm. I have heard that name before," Huby said.

Huby looked me in the eyes. "How about we get out of here and continue our conversation over a walk in Central Park?"

"Why not, it's a beautiful morning," I said, a little surprised at his abrupt suggestion. "Is everything okay?"

"Not sure," Huby replied. "Let's talk during our walk. We'll have more privacy."

Huby paid for our coffee, and we made our way to the elevators. We did not speak until we had left the building and crossed Broadway toward the entrance to Central Park. The park was pleasantly empty at this time of day, just the occasional jogger and bicyclist.

"That drug you mentioned, Captagon," Huby said as we strolled across Heckscher Fields toward the expansive Sheep Meadow. The

immediate contrast to Manhattan's congested streets was a big part of
Central Park's magic, and the high-rise buildings framing the park now
seemed like a faraway movie set. "I knew I had heard that word before,
but it took me a moment to connect the dots. Then the penny dropped.
A friend of mine, a former French intelligence officer whom I have
known for decades since our days in the Foreign Legion, once mentioned to me that someone Paul knew—a friend or an acquaintance,
I'm not sure—was suspected of being involved in the Captagon trade.
Apparently this acquaintance and his father used to be close to Rifaat
al-Assad, President Assad's uncle. My secret service friend used to track
Rifaat and the Assad family for years, as far back as the late seventies,
and for a period of three years he was one of their main handlers in
the region.

"So when Rifaat recently moved from London to Paris, the French
intelligence service roped my friend back in from retirement because of
his familiarity with this particular cast of characters. From what he tells
me, Rifaat is not much of a caballero, as our friend Jacques would put
it, allegedly involved in all kinds of nasty things, from the Hama massacre to the Hariri assassination to drugs and embezzlement.* But Rifaat
al-Assad also has some powerful friends, which I can attest to from my
time in Saudi Arabia."

Huby was speaking at a rapid pace. "I don't understand," I interrupted
him as I pulled out my notepad to write down the details. "What does
Rifaat al-Assad have to do with Paul Blocher? And was this Captagon-
dealing friend the reason Paul went to Syria?"

Before Huby could reply, he had to duck to avoid being hit in the

---

* In June 2020, a French court sentenced Rifaat al-Assad to four years in prison after convicting
him of money laundering and the misappropriation (looting) of Syrian public funds. The court also
ordered the confiscation of his assets and properties in France and Britain. Following this court
ruling, the nongovernmental organization Sherpa called on French president Emmanuel Macron
to strip Rifaat al-Assad of his Légion d'honneur that was awarded to him by President François
Mitterrand in 1986, four years after the Hama massacre.

head by a Frisbee. It crashed into a tree behind us. I picked it up and
threw it back to the boy who had hurled it.

"It does seem bizarre," Huby said. "Like yet another unlikely case of
two or three degrees of separation. But apparently, from what my friend
told me, the father of Paul's acquaintance did something to disrupt the
drug trade of Rifaat al-Assad's associates in Syria, and both father and
son paid for it with their lives. The reason I am bringing this up now
is that the particular drug in this affair was Captagon—the very same
drug you just referred to. I remember it distinctly because I had never
heard of this before my friend mentioned it, and I had to educate myself
about it."

I was even more confused. "I still don't understand. Why did your
Foreign Legion buddy—thanks, by the way for dropping that piece of
information, I did not know that you had been a mercenary—why did
this French intelligence officer mention Paul to begin with? Just like
that, out of the blue?"

"*Ex*–intelligence officer," Huby corrected me.

We turned into the beautiful tree-lined Mall toward Bethesda Terrace,
stopping beside a fountain with a bronze female winged angel statue.

"This angel has healing powers," Huby said. "It's the angel from the
Gospel of John, blessing the pool of Bethesda. Would be nice if Paul had
such an angel, wouldn't it?"

I nodded, and we continued to walk toward the edge of the terrace,
from where we had a frontal view of the Central Park Lake.

I resumed our conversation after a few minutes. "So, again, why
did this ex–intelligence officer even bring up Paul in the first place?"
My thoughts were buzzing all over the place. Had Huby withheld critical information from me until this point, and was it possible that Paul
Blocher himself was a Captagon dealer? I worried that I might have to
call Khalid immediately to let him know that we had been working with
incomplete information and was already dreading Khalid's calm but

pointed scolding. I urged Huby to fill me in, without leaving out any details. Even though I continued to take notes, I also took the phone out of my pocket and started recording to make sure that no detail would get lost. Huby noticed and nodded.

Huby seemed to be weighing his words carefully. "You asked me whether I believe Paul had gone to Syria to look for this missing friend or acquaintance. Here's what happened: About three months ago, I had asked my intelligence contact to run some discreet background checks on Paul's acquaintance. This was just under four weeks before Paul went to Syria. Paul had called me late one evening sounding very upset, almost panicked. We didn't really speak that often, so I was surprised to hear from him. The same way you are confused now, it also took me a while to understand what he was talking about. He told me about some friend who had gone missing in Syria. Paul was distressed, very emotional as he spoke. He kept mentioning how this friend had told him that he and his father planned to get out of the drug business after this one last, big deal. After this strange call from Paul, I asked my Foreign Legion pal to look into the matter. I didn't care about Paul's friend. It was Paul I worried about. His concern for this friend troubled me."

"Do you think Paul was in any way involved in this drug trade?" I asked.

Huby shook his head. "I don't think so. Paul was a naturalist, a vegetarian, even a vegan, I think. He didn't smoke, didn't drink. I cannot imagine any drugs in his life. He was so connected to nature. Sorry, he *is* so connected to nature."

"So are drugs," I said, then quickly added, "though I suppose the synthetic, counterfeit Captagon they manufacture in those Syrian labs has very little to do with nature."

"My secret service friend told me that they are troubled by how easily Syrian-made Captagon is making its way into France and being used as an amphetamine by some of the disaffected youths in the banlieues—the cesspool of homemade Jihadists. Apparently the amount of Captagon in circulation is staggering, and when customs officials manage to make a bust, they sometimes catch hundreds of thousands of pills. So just imagine how many more pills actually find their way into the country! One of the insidious things the dealers in France do is package the pills in blister packs of ten, which gives users the false sense that they are taking medication rather than a dangerous and highly addictive drug. But compared to how this drug has spread in the Middle East and the Gulf, the problems in France are small fry. If it's a health problem in France and some other countries in Europe, then it's a full-blown pandemic in Saudi Arabia. And from what my friend tells me, it has also become everyone's favorite drug in the Syrian war."

"Because it is used as an amphetamine by fighters?" I asked, remembering my conversation about Captagon with Bassel and Jamil two days earlier in Beirut. Everything Huby was telling me jibed with the information I had about this pernicious drug.

"Yes, and also because it is a big part of the war economy," Huby explained. "So many ways to make money off it—manufacturing and trading, or taxing and policing the manufacturing and trading. It has the same value chain as a mafia operation, and it's the most effective way to fight unemployment in Syria. Thousands are involved directly and indirectly in the Captagon business, and it's much too profitable to be curtailed, let alone shut down."*

---

* The profitability of the Captagon business also extends to the safekeeping of its enormous cash profits in special warehouses in the Middle East and Southeast Asia through military-grade operations, and the reinsertion of this cash into the interbank market with the help of disreputable individuals within some of the most reputable global banks. Huby confirmed what Khalid had insinuated independently—that the same tight-knit group involved in laundering these Captagon profits in the banking system had also been providing these services to autocrats and their families for decades, starting with Muammar Gaddafi in Libya in the 1980s, Sani Abacha in Nigeria, Hosni Mubarak in Egypt, Saddam Hussein in Iraq in the 1990s, and José Eduardo dos Santos in Angola from the late 1980s through the 2000s. One name that keeps popping up in this context is Bashir Saleh Bashir, a former aide to Muammar Gaddafi and head of the Libyan African Portfolio, a sovereign wealth fund that invested Libya's oil wealth internationally. He has been referred to as "Gaddafi's moneyman."

We turned right and found a bench near the boathouse, where we sat down. A group of children nearby were playing hide-and-seek, and their joyful shrieks and giggles belied the heaviness of our moods.

"I really hope the Captagon connection with this Anas fellow is purely coincidental," Huby said. "Though the older I get, the less I believe in coincidences."

I smiled. "As Jacques once put it, a coincidence is just the Creator's way of leaving you with the illusion that he is not involved."

"Bravo!" Huby exclaimed. "The Creator and Jacques both have a sense of humor."

A couple sat down on the bench next to ours. I got the distinct impression that the woman was trying to eavesdrop on our conversation. Huby also seemed to pick up on that, because he got up and suggested we keep walking.

"So what's next?" he asked after we were at a safe distance from the couple.

"I'm waiting to hear back from a contact who is trying to locate this Anas. It's our only semi-hot trail. The Kurdish fellow in their party, Alan, has not been heard from since the same time Paul disappeared."

"A contact?" Huby asked in a mocking tone. "Does your contact have a name?"

"Sure he does," I said.

"Care to share?" Huby asked.

"Not really," I replied. "Remember, up until half an hour ago I didn't even know that you had served in the Foreign Legion. You've chosen not to tell me your intelligence pal's name, and now you are expecting me to reveal my contact's identity?"

"Okay, okay, Captain Secrecy!"

"I'm just learning from the best," I said. "In any event, as soon as I hear from him, I'll go back to the region to find this Anas person."

"Thank you, Daniel. I am really grateful for this. I would feel much better if you allowed me to compensate you for your efforts. At least let me pay for your flights."

Once again, I explained to Huby why I couldn't accept any payment from him or Paul Blocher's family. I assured him that I would never fail to follow up on a lead because of the expense involved and promised to let him know if financial constraints did become an impediment to helping him, which I did not foresee. Besides, as I told him again, I had to travel to the Middle East anyway for my work. When Huby looked at me skeptically, I reminded him of the rude manner in which that official had threatened him with prosecution if any money ever changed hands as part of a ransom payment. Only then did Huby finally relent and drop the issue. I promised to get in touch as soon as I had new information, and we shook hands.

Huby set out for the Metropolitan Museum in order to distract himself, and I headed in the opposite direction to Manhattan's West Side. The conversation with Huby left me with a lot to chew on, and Paul's seemingly random connection to drug traders in Syria was troubling. I sent Khalid a text message, asking him for a Skype call when he had a moment. He replied an hour later, suggesting we talk the next morning.

KHALID WAS NOT his usual jovial self when he picked up. Immediately, I envisioned some bad news regarding Paul, and my heart sank. This roller coaster of emotions every time I got involved in the search for a missing person in Syria was draining—from the hopeful high whenever I received encouraging information to the pit in my stomach each time those hopes were dashed.

"Is everything okay?" I asked. "You sound discouraged."

"I *am* discouraged," Khalid replied. "But it has nothing to do with Paul Blocher."

"Glad to hear that," I said, instantly abashed at my sense of relief. "Sorry, that came out the wrong way. I'm sorry you are having a rough day."

"It's all right, Daniel," Khalid said in a slightly acerbic tone. "What can I do for you?"

I told Khalid about my conversation with Huby and about the strange connection to Captagon and Rifaat al-Assad. Khalid listened intently without saying a word.

"Are you still there?" I asked.

"Yes."

"Well, any thoughts?"

"If nothing else, it shows that there might be more to the Anas connection than meets the eye," Khalid said.

"Have you spoken to Jamil?" I asked.

"Yes, but not on our matter."

I hesitated to push Khalid. His answers were monosyllabic, which was his way of asking me to tread lightly. "Is there any chance you could urge him to speed this up?" I asked, stupidly ignoring my gut feeling that it might be better to keep my mouth shut. "A life is on the line."

"I am aware of that, Daniel," Khalid shot back. "Many lives are on the line, and most of them don't have any voice. They are helpless, too. This war is not just about Paul Blocher."

Again, I was ashamed, this time for having pressed Khalid. He had done so much already, as always, without asking for anything in return. I deserved this dressing down.

"You're right, I'm really sorry," I said. "Forgive me, I was being selfish."

Khalid was gracious. "It's okay, don't worry. You're just trying to help another person, as am I. But don't forget: Jamil is a Ray, and Rays are not like us. They may look like us, but they belong to a different species. Compassion is not what drives them, so it is something else we have to appeal to."

"I understand. But if not out of compassion, why does Jamil help us?"

"Leverage, *habibi*, leverage. Collecting chips, to be cashed in at the right time," Khalid said. "I will owe him a favor or two for this. Got it?"

I remembered how tender and affectionate Jamil had been with Aliya and Sami in the green house and wondered whether perhaps my friend pegged him wrong. But my behavior on this call had already been so abysmal that I decided against challenging Khalid on this point. Still, his words raised a different question, one I'd been wanting to ask him for a long time.

"Then why are *you* doing this?"

Khalid laughed. "That's a conversation for another day. Besides, what makes you so sure it's not all about leverage for me, too?"

"I'm no longer sure about anything," I said, not certain whether he meant leverage against me or Huby or someone else.

"Relax," Khalid said, as if he had read my thoughts. "Jamil is clever enough to collect chips and still frame the whole thing to his advantage. Collecting chips at both ends, or cashing a chip while collecting it, to be more precise. He is a virtuoso illusionist when it comes to using up a favor while giving the impression that he is the one doing the favor. Anyway, I'm sure I'll have some news on our matter in the coming days. Jamil mentioned that he was going to Damascus tomorrow night. I'll be in touch."*

---

* I remembered that Khalid had told me in Istanbul after my return from Beirut that the Sheikh had sent Hussein to Damascus rather than Jamil. Based on how Khalid had described it at the time, I was under the impression that this was the way the tasks between Hussein and Jamil were generally divided and that Jamil was too valuable to the Sheikh to be sent off to Syria. Even though this contradicted Khalid's statement on our call, I decided not to probe.

SIX

TWO DAYS AFTER our Skype conversation, Khalid text-messaged me, asking that I phone him as soon as possible. I was about to get on a previously scheduled call and asked how soon he needed to talk. I received a short reply: "ASAP was not urgent enough?" I canceled the other call and dialed Khalid's number. He got straight to the point.

"I just received a call from Jamil. Apparently Bassel's friend in Damascus was able to track down Anas in Amman. Can you be in Jordan tomorrow?"

I was thrilled and distraught at the same time—on the one hand, Anas had been located, but on the other hand I could not fly to Amman immediately. I had an appointment at the Justice Department in Washington, DC, the next day, one that I had already postponed twice, even though it was a meeting I had requested concerning one of our foundation's initiatives in Mongolia. I had given my word that I would not bail again on this meeting, and I worried that if I took another rain check, my contact would refuse to meet another time.

"That's wonderful news, thank you," I said. "The only problem is that I cannot be in Amman tomorrow. I have a commitment tomorrow in DC that I can simply not miss. "The earliest I can be in Jordan would be late afternoon the day after tomorrow."

The line fell silent.

"Khalid, are you still there?" I asked.

"Yes, I am here," Khalid said in an ice-cold voice. "Maybe, in light of your other priorities, you should refrain next time from reminding me that a life is on the line."

That stung. I felt terrible, but there was nothing I could do. "I'm really sorry, Khalid. I have no choice."

"We always have a choice," he shot back, still in that frosty voice.

"Well then, this is the choice I need to make."

"No, Daniel. This is the choice you are *deciding* to make, the choice you *want* to make. If you *needed* to make it, it would not be a choice."

"I don't want to argue with you, Khalid," I said, irritated that he was being so persnickety. "I am fully aware of how important it is that I catch Anas. I will fly out tomorrow evening. Hopefully it won't be too late."

"I hope so, too," Khalid said, his tone now slightly thawed. "Apparently he stays at the Four Seasons when in Amman, where he meets with his partners. I don't know how long he will be there, but from what Bassel's friend could gather, Anas is continuing on to Dubai soon."

"I was planning to fly to Dubai anyway, so a stopover in Amman works out well," I said, instantly regretting my words. It sounded like I was placing my convenience above the requisite sense of urgency.

Khalid didn't miss a beat. "Glad we could fit this into your schedule, Sheikh," he said sardonically.

"Please stop beating me up, Khalid," I pleaded. "I am extremely thankful that they were able to track down Anas, and you know full well how grateful I am to you."

"I know," Khalid said. "Sorry for being so harsh. These past few days have been a little difficult."

"I'm sorry to hear that. Is there anything I can do?"

"Not at the moment, thanks, though I might at some point in the future ask you to reach out to your friend Mr. Hubertus so that we can find out more about this former French intelligence agent friend of his."

There it was, the universal principle—*quid pro quo; do ut des.* The Romans must have been world champions at back scratching, given how many of these phrases they coined.

"What is your interest in this intelligence officer, if I may ask?"

"It's not *my* interest," Khalid replied. "It's Jamil's. I recounted our last conversation to him, and he was very keen on learning more about this French guy. I'm sure you can put it together."

I understood. By his approximate age as a retired agent, Huby's friend could have been serving in Syria around the same time as Jamil's biological father. Perhaps it even was one and the same person, as freakish as that coincidence would be.

"Do you really think it could—" I asked.

"I don't know," Khalid stopped me. "Stranger things have happened—after all, my own life has unfolded somewhere in between happenstance and providence, hasn't it? We shouldn't need any proof that God is pulling the strings in this world. Look at the Middle East— only the Almighty, with all his superpowers, could mess up a region so thoroughly. Coincidence and fate alone will not get that done."

I smiled. Khalid really did express himself unlike anyone I knew— though his views on God were very similar to the way Jacques felt about the Creator. "Just say when, and I'll check with Huby about his friend."

"Not yet," Khalid said. "Now is not the time. I'll wait for Jamil to ask me again. The more important it is to him, the more chips in my basket. By now, you should have a pretty good sense of how this works."

It seemed that the leverage game never stopped for people like Khalid and Jamil. I swore to myself never to forget that.

"Anyway, I will send you a few pictures of Anas, which we got from Damascus. There are also pictures of his partners, which I will add to the email. And don't worry about the hotel room; I'll take care of it. Please try to get to Amman as soon as you can and let me know once you've arrived there."

"I will." I would have preferred to handle my own hotel arrangements but didn't want to hurt Khalid's feelings by turning down his offer.
I believed he was still on friendly terms with one of the shareholders
of the Four Seasons in Amman, Sheikh Hamad bin Jassim Al Thani,
the former prime minister of Qatar, and as a result Khalid always had a
room there at his disposal.

Khalid hung up before I could thank him. Ten minutes later, I
received an email with some pictures of Anas and his partners. The men
in the photographs looked like a nasty mix of bouncers in a grungy bar
and pimps in a seedy red-light district behind the train station. Not
exactly an uplifting sight.

SEVEN

I ARRIVED IN Amman two days later around midnight on a late flight via Frankfurt. At the top of the escalator leading down to passport control, a tall man in his midthirties walked up to me.

"Excuse me, sir, are you Mr. Daniel?"

"Yes. Who are you, please?"

"I am Fuad. I work in airport security. Please follow me."

"May I ask what this is about?" I had not given anyone in Amman advance notice of my visit and didn't expect to be met by any person, and certainly not by airport security. In a flash, I imagined that Anas and his friends had somehow gotten wind of my arrival and alerted a contact at security to intercept me. But I dismissed this thought since no one other than Khalid knew about this trip. Still, a certain trepidation did linger.

"Do not worry, sir," Fuad said in a no-nonsense tone. "I'm here to take care of you."

"That's very kind of you, Mr. Fuad," I said, "but how did you know I was arriving in Amman, and why are you taking care of me?"

"It seems that you have an important friend," Fuad replied. "My boss told me that Sheikh Khalid had called and asked us to take excellent care of you during your stay in Amman."

Good old Khalid! His reach was truly impressive.

"Pardon my question, Mr. Fuad, but I don't think I shared my flight details with Khalid. I mean Sheikh Khalid. So how did you find me?"

"Sheikh Khalid told us that you would be arriving today and sent us a picture of you. Blue eyes, no hair, Semitic nose. You were hard to miss."

I laughed. "That pretty much sums me up. But tell me, how long have you been waiting here?"

"Since eight in the morning."

"That's over sixteen hours! I am so sorry!"

"It's no problem, sir," Fuad said amicably. "It is our pleasure to do anything for Sheikh Khalid. It is as if His Majesty the King asked us for something. Now, may I please have your passport?"

"Don't I need to purchase a visa?"

Fuad shook his head and stretched his arm out in my direction. "Please."

I handed him my passport, and he cut to the front of the line straight to the immigration officer who immediately barked at the family standing before him to scoot to the side in order to accommodate us. The family had the appearance of ultraconservative Muslim Salafists—the man's beard was long and wild, dyed with reddish-brown henna, and his upper lip was clean shaven in homage to how the prophet Muhammad is purported to have worn his beard fourteen hundred years ago. His wife was dressed in an all-black abaya cloak with a niqab veiling her entire face other than a narrow slit for her eyes. She was rocking a sleeping infant in her arms while trying to comfort another child crying in a stroller. The man was holding the hands of their two sons. He muttered something under his breath as he backed up to let me pass. I followed Fuad guiltily, avoiding the resentful stares of this man and the other travelers in line. The immigration officer stamped my passport without looking and handed it back to Fuad. We walked toward the exit and out of the terminal. A car was waiting for us, and we both got in.

"Sheikh Khalid informed us that you would be staying in the Four Seasons," Fuad said. "Is that correct?"

"It is."

"Good. This should not take too long at this time of the night. No traffic." He told the driver to get going, then handed me his phone. "This is a secure phone. Sheikh Khalid asked that you call him when we're in the car."

I dialed Khalid's number. "*Masaa al-khair, habibi*, good evening." He answered in a jovial mood, as if this conversation on some Jordanian security officer's phone was the most natural thing in the world.

"*Masaa al-noor*, Khalid, good evening to you. Why didn't you tell me that you would arrange to have me picked up?"

"Well, you did not share your flight plans with me, so I did not share your arrival plans with you. Let's call it a draw."

I laughed. "Your logic is impeccable as usual. Anyway, thanks for looking out for me."

"You're welcome. There's some information I wanted to share before you try to find those guys in the morning. First, there is a chance that Anas left Amman this evening. Bassel's contact is not sure. His mobile phone signal still originates in Amman, but he sent an email from a Dubai IP address late last night. In any event, one of his partners, who goes by the name Mike, seems to be at the Four Seasons every morning at ten for breakfast. He is the ugly fellow next to the skinny guy in the picture I sent you after we last spoke."

"Yes, I received the picture, thanks," I said. "Where is this Mike from? Is he also Syrian?"

"No, Mike is from Dearborn, Michigan, but originally his family is Palestinian. His real name is Malik, but he has Americanized it to Mike. Apparently he's not the sharpest tool in the shed and not very pleasant either."

"I look forward to meeting him."

"I'm sure you do," Khalid said. "Thugs can be so entertaining, after all—especially those called Malik, as we found out in our last go-around."

"I really hope I didn't miss Anas," I said, ignoring his reference to a nasty and dangerous experience Khalid and I had endured a few months earlier with a Lebanese wannabe gangster called Malik in Istanbul. It had been a case of mistaken identities and intentions: Khalid and I were trying to acquire a key piece of information on a member of the Assad family, while this Lebanese fellow thought we were trying to purchase drugs. Khalid and I ended up spending most of the night driving through Istanbul in separate cars in order to confuse and shake this Malik off our tail. Only at six in the morning, as the sun was rising, did he give up and drive to the airport to catch a flight out of town. Khalid and I returned to the Kempinski hotel for a sumptuous breakfast. We still laughed about this crazy adventure, which had a slapstick feel despite its perilous nature.

"I also hope you did not miss Anas," Khalid said. "But just in case you did, Jamil expects to get the contact information for Anas's ex-wife who lives in Dubai. Apparently she's no longer all that fond of Anas, so she might be willing to help you find him just out of spite."

"Let's hope that won't be necessary."

"One more thing, Daniel," Khalid said. "I know you are a fully grown man who can take care of himself. Still, some of these fellows are a little rough around the edges. And the nice ones are usually disingenuous. So don't trust anyone. At the same time, don't allow your outrage to trip you up."

"What do you mean?" I asked a little defensively.

"These people are sharks. Remember what I told you in Doha many years ago. When a shark does something aggressive, when a shark attacks people, it makes the shark neither good nor bad. It's not about morality. It's stupid and nonsensical to get mad at a shark because he tries to eat you—it's what a shark does! So now that you know that these guys are sharks, brace yourself and stay cool and calm rather than angry and incensed. Try to get what you need out of each person you'll meet.

Above all, always remember that you are either controlling the narrative or you are allowing it to happen."

"I understand."

"Good luck. And please don't treat your stay in Amman like your clandestine flight. Keep me posted on what's going on, so that I don't have to keep troubling my friends in security."

"I will. Good night, and thanks again for your help." I handed the phone back to Fuad.

WE ARRIVED AT the hotel a few minutes later. As we approached the driveway leading up to the entrance, we had to meander around large cement barriers and multiple security checkpoints, which had been set up after the deadly simultaneous bombings in 2005 of three Amman hotels that killed and wounded many people, including a large group attending a wedding. Despite the calm and orderliness of the Jordanian capital's commercial center, these massive cement impediments were a grim reminder of the region's violent reality.

I stepped out of the car and was greeted by a loud sound of chirping crickets. The evening was surprisingly chilly, and I shivered in my thin shirt. Floodlights illuminated the entire parking lot and hotel entrance, leaving me with that same eerie sensation that I had felt after landing in Beirut a week earlier. Two armed guards were standing at the main door, pointing with an impassive motion toward the metal detector and the conveyor belt at the entrance. Before I walked inside, Fuad gave me his phone number and asked me to call him if there was any problem or if I needed anything. He promised to stop by the next afternoon to check on me.

As I lay in bed, Khalid's words kept spinning in my head—either I would be the one controlling the narrative or someone else would do it for me. There seemed to be so many factors beyond my control, so many unpredictable plot twists. I lay awake for hours contemplating all possible scenarios should I succeed in meeting Anas, as well as backup possibilities in the unfortunate event I had missed him. The more scenarios I could think of, the more anxious I became. I finally fell asleep at seven in the morning.

When my alarm clock went off at nine, it took me a long time to figure out where I was. During my travels, I try to keep my eyes closed when I wake up in some hotel bed until I become fully aware of the place I am in—my small pre-exercise exercise routine on the road. This morning, I just could not figure it out. I was completely disoriented. I struggled to open my eyes; they felt like they had been pasted shut. I had a massive headache and felt groggy. It took me three cups of coffee and some Advil before I finally regained my bearings.

I stepped into the breakfast area a few minutes past ten and immediately spotted two of Anas's partners from the picture Khalid had sent me—the one he had identified as Mike as well as the other, rather thin person—sitting at a corner table with two men I did not recognize. Mike looked as unappealing in person as he did in the photograph. The two unfamiliar men were wearing black suits, white shirts, and black ties, pulp fiction–style, trending toward Middle East–inspired Blues Brothers, while Mike and the other man from the picture were sporting fashionably torn jeans and tight polo shirts with raised collars. To my great disappointment, none of the men was Anas.

There was something unkempt and repulsive about Mike. He was chubby with thinning, greasy curls, and he had a permanent grin with a dull, unintelligent expression under an uneven stubble. As I approached their table, Mike grabbed the apron strap of a waitress as she passed by him and held on to it until the bow opened and the apron fell to the ground. As the waitress bent over to pick up the apron, Mike lifted her skirt and let out a loud belch-like grunt. The waitress mumbled something under her breath and dashed off.

Anas's other partner from Khalid's picture seemed to be the polar

opposite of Mike. He was short and wiry, clean shaven with dark, penetrating eyes that exuded an intense energy. I took a seat at the adjoining
table, ordered some coffee, and placed my phone against the plate at an
angle that allowed me to take a surreptitious picture of Mike, his partner, and the two pulp fiction mannequins. I then turned the phone to
flight mode and started recording. One of the dark-suited fellows was
checking me out, then mumbled something to Mike, who looked at me.
I nodded casually and got up to help myself at the buffet. I spotted a
beautiful classic Patek Philippe watch on Mike's wrist, which seemed
a little out of character, given his boorish appearance. By pure chance,
it was the very same watch my friend Riad had bought in Zurich last
time we met, and I had to smile as I remembered Riad's proud exuber-
ance when he showed me his trophy acquisition. I decided to use Mike's
watch as an icebreaker when I returned to my table.

"Pardon the interruption. I couldn't help but notice your gorgeous
watch," I said. "One of the nicest ones Patek has ever made. In my opinion, the most exquisite specimen of its Grand Complications." Silently,
I thanked Riad for his extensive horological explanations, which might
have been a little tedious at the time but sure came in handy now.

Mike's eyes lit up. "Why don't you join us?" he asked as he motioned
for the two dark suits to scamper. Even though Khalid had told me that
Mike was from Michigan, I was still surprised by his broad midwestern
accent and the high pitch of his voice, which did not match his large
frame.

"Thank you, that's very kind," I said, and claimed one of the seats
that had just been vacated by what I concluded were his bodyguards. We
shook hands, I introduced myself, and Mike introduced the other man
as his friend Imad.

Mike reeked of cologne. The sweet smell was nauseating, especially
since I was still nursing the remnants of that nasty headache. A waiter
came and moved my coffee to their table.

Mike was chatty, especially once he heard that I lived in New York. He was obsessed with American sports, and he followed the Detroit teams with childlike enthusiasm.

"Man, the Lions suck something fierce," he exclaimed. "God damn it, do they fucking suck! I mean, those guys blow some serious chunks. Seriously, dude, ever since Barry Sanders retired, I have nothing to look forward to other than draft picks at the end of the season. I have the NFL package downloaded on my iPad, and nobody is allowed to talk to me on Sundays and Mondays during the season—not that the fucking Lions ever play on Monday night football! You will not believe the places I end up watching the games on my iPad!"

"Really? Like where?" Mike's sports talk was hard to bear.

"Man, you have no idea!" Mike said, his voice raised in excitement. "In the most desolate areas near the Iraqi border, in no-man's-land driving through Oman, in some stinking shithole in Egypt, or when I'm crossing from Turkey into Syria."

As he spoke the last words, I saw Imad glare at him. Mike winced and stopped talking for a moment but quickly recovered.

"It's not just the Lions," he continued, without giving me a chance to zero in on his mention of Syria. "Don't even get me started on the Detroit Pistons." Enunciating the basketball team as the "Deee-troyt Peees-tens," he sounded like a sports announcer stirring up the crowd. "Man, I miss the Bad Boys days. I was in middle school at the time. And the Fab Five at Michigan—I'm still trying to recover from C-Webb's time-out brain freeze! Good times, man, good times!"

Mike stopped talking for a moment. This was my opening. I tried to come up with the most inconspicuous way to ask Mike what had brought him to such a dangerous place as Syria. Even though I had run through this kind of scenario countless times in my head just a few hours earlier during my sleepless night in the hotel room, an adrenaline rush blocked the words in my throat. Before I had a chance to regain my composure,

Imad turned to me. "What brings you to Amman, Daniel?" he asked as he looked straight in my eyes. Imad's features had an unusual, powerful intensity, and when he spoke, his expression exuded spartan efficiency and calculation. His jaw and cheekbones suddenly had hard, angular edges. Not a single gesture was redundant.

"I was hoping to meet someone," I answered warily.

Imad looked at me suspiciously. "What do you mean, 'hoping to meet someone'? You flew all the way over here without a confirmed meeting?"

Clearly, Imad's senses were a lot more attuned than Mike's. His English was perfect, with a slight French accent.

"It's a complicated story," I said, choosing my words cautiously. "I don't want to bore you with it."

Mike was grateful for the opportunity to turn the conversation back to sports. "Tell me, Daniel, which New York team do you root for?" he jumped back in. "Giants? Please don't say the Jets! God damn it, they fucking suck!"

Before I could reply, Imad looked at Mike with that same harsh glare. "Hold on, Mike," he said sharply, "I'd love to hear Daniel out. Besides, I've had it up to here with your American sports!"

"But—" Mike tried to object.

"*Halass!*" Imad hissed. "Enough already, Mike!" Turning to me, he asked, "So, Daniel, what's the story?"

"Well, to keep it short, a friend of mine asked me to help him find a young man, the son of a friend of his, who seems to have disappeared in Syria."

Now both Imad and Mike were listening intently.

"What do you mean, 'disappeared'?" Mike asked.

"Vanished, without a trace," I said. "Or, rather, almost without a trace."

"Where did he vanish?" Imad asked.

"Apparently somewhere in northern Syria, after crossing the Turkish border," I said.

"When?" Imad wanted to know.

"About two and a half months ago," I answered.

"Where was he heading?" Imad continued to grill me in a tone that sounded more like a demand.

"To Aleppo, I believe," I said, "though he never made it there."

"You said that he vanished almost without a trace. What do you mean, 'almost'?" Imad seemed completely focused, and I vowed to myself never to underestimate this man. His alertness reminded me of Jamil in Beirut.

"Well, they were a party of three," I started carefully. "Two of the three vanished, but it seems that one is still around. This third person is the little I have of a trace."

Mike was about to say something, but Imad stopped him immediately by putting his index finger in front of his lips.

"So, this third person, is that the one you were hoping to meet here?" Imad asked.

Before I could answer, Mike blurted out: "This has to be Anas!" As my heart beat in excitement, Imad stared at Mike with a look of abject contempt. Mike winced, realizing that he had just made a very dumb mistake. I resisted the urge to check that my phone was still recording.

"Why don't we move to a quiet spot in the lounge?" Imad suggested. "Mike, settle the bill and join us in a few minutes."

Mike sulked but did as told. He tried to get the attention of the waitress whose skirt he had just lifted, but she turned her head away in disgust. As another waiter rushed over to Mike, Imad and I walked to the lounge and found a discreet sitting area.

"Well, was that the person you were trying to meet?" Imad asked as soon as we sat down.

"Yes, that is the name of the person," I replied. "Do you know him?"

"That depends."

"On what?"

"That also depends," Imad said.

"I don't understand. It depends to the second power?" I asked.

"Something like that." Imad smiled. "First, it depends on whether this is the same Anas. And second, assuming—just as a hypothetical, of course—that it is the same Anas, it depends on who is asking, why this person is asking, and how much it's worth to the person who is asking."

"Wow, that's almost to the fourth power."

Imad laughed. "You're right. So, if we stick to pure hypotheticals, if it happened to be the same Anas, and if we work on the assumption that you are the one asking, let's move straight to the third power, to use your line of thought: Why are you asking?"

I hesitated for a moment. Imad was clearly suspicious. His mind worked quickly and precisely. A mistake now, even a slight miscue, and Imad would probably walk away, causing this door to be shut for good. I needed to give Imad enough information with a satisfactory answer of why I was asking about Anas, so that I could clear this threshold and move to the last stage—the fourth power—and allow Imad to name his price. In my thoughts, the tactical steps seemed straightforward, but there were minefields all over the place. I decided, for now, less would be more.

"It's exactly as I said earlier," I began, "no hidden agenda. A friend asked me for help in locating this young man, because I have some decent relationships in the region."

"If I didn't know better, I'd say you're stalling, Daniel. Besides, in this region your decent relationships are not going to do you much good. It's the *indecent* ones you will need if you want to get something done in this godforsaken part of the world."

As if on cue, Mike joined us at the table. Imad motioned for him to take a seat and keep quiet.

"I figured as much," I said after Mike sat down. "Which is perhaps why I am trying to connect with this Anas gentleman."

"Tell me, Daniel," Imad said, ignoring my subtle jab at Anas, "was this missing person a government employee?"

"No."

"A journalist?"

"No."

"A doctor or an aid worker?"

"No, not to my knowledge."

"Then tell me, my friend, why the hell was he traveling to Syria? It's not exactly high on the list of most sane people's travel destinations." Imad's tone was harsh. "Did he have any relationship with a person or group in Syria, or was he going there for any specific purpose?"

"Not that I am aware of," I said. "As far as I know, this was more of a self-discovery adventure than anything else." There was a piercing quality to Imad's questions, like a drill that penetrated deeper and deeper in tight, circular motions. I had hoped to wrest from Imad valuable information about Anas, but instead Imad was interrogating me.

"For most people, a trip to Syria ends up being a one-way journey," Imad said. "That's one hell of a self-discovery! It had better be worth it."

"I am just doing this as a favor to someone who wants to help one of his closest friends. That's all there is to it," I said, trying to transition to level four of Imad's challenge.

"You are doing this for free?" Mike jumped in. Again, Imad stared him down, but this time Mike refused to be silenced—too preposterous was the idea that I would do this without a financial incentive. "Seriously, dude, for free?" he repeated, and shook his head with a look of revulsion when I nodded. "God damn it, what a sucker!"

"Thank you for your invaluable insights, Mike," Imad said, then turned back to me. "Now that Mike has done all he can to help you lower the price for our fourth power level, let's talk about it."

"Huh?" Mike grunted.

"It's okay, Mike, just try to follow," Imad said patronizingly. "It's a little easier if you only listen and don't talk. We'll make an effort to speak slowly."

Mike looked completely lost. "I don't get it. What do you mean?"

"I mean shut the fuck up!" Imad replied in a raised voice.

I hesitated to say anything for fear of getting caught in the middle of their spat. Mike's face had a vapid expression. Finally, he sighed loudly and shrugged his shoulders. This did not seem to be the first time Imad had spoken to him this way.

"So, Daniel, now that we've cleared the first three levels—in other words, it's the same Anas, you're the one asking, and you're doing this out of the kindness of your heart," Imad said sarcastically, "let's talk about what this is worth to you."

This was the tricky moment I had been dreading. "It's important to me," I said, "so by that measure I suppose it's worth a lot."

"Dude, seriously," Mike jumped in again. "We're not in the favor business. Imad means how much money! Cash!"

"Thank you, Mike," Imad said, then turned to me. "So beyond the emotional or even spiritual importance of this quest to you, are you ready to discuss a price?"

Imad's directness made it hard to avoid this topic, and stalling would have been an insult to his obvious intelligence, so I decided to be equally direct. "I'm afraid there is no payment on the table for this information, Imad. And even if there were—which is not the case—I could not name a value without knowing what I am getting. I'm not really big on sight-unseen deals."

"That's clever, especially in this part of the world," Mike interjected.

"Once again, Mike, thank you," Imad said. "You've been an inspiration to us all. The patron saint of all negotiators."

Mike got up in a huff. "I've got to take a piss," he said as he stormed away.

"Please forgive Mike," Imad said. "He doesn't know that he's an idiot. Then again, if he knew, he would not be one."

I tried in vain to suppress a smile.

"Now that we've got that dull instrument out of the way," Imad continued, "I'd say our foreplay has lasted long enough. Two words: How much?"

His bluntness stung. "Look, Imad, I appreciate your direct style," I tried to hedge. "As I said, money is not on the table. It cannot be—not for any information on the missing person, just like I cannot be compensated for my efforts."

"Actually, Daniel, you've got this all wrong. This is the one stage of this process where money *can* be on the table. If we agree on the terms, and you get the information you need, you might end up being able to locate the young man you are looking for. At that stage, you will want to free him, right?"

I nodded, though I had frozen the moment Imad mentioned "the young man." I had never divulged Paul Blocher's age. Was this a slip of the tongue and an implicit admission that he knew about Paul, or was it just a generic description of a person that held no special meaning? Or was it a subtle way for Imad to insinuate that he had the goods while preserving full plausible deniability if pressed on this point? My bet was on the latter.

"Daniel, stay with me, please. Focus!" Imad said tersely, noticing my distracted state. "You want me to give you the information on Anas and then presumably for Anas to give you the information on how to find this young man, right? Assuming, of course, you are not looking for Anas so that you can spend an evening philosophizing on the horrors of war and the dark side of human nature. It's this young man you are trying to find, right?"

Again, "this young man," twice more. I nodded.

"Well then," Imad continued, "up until that point, there is nothing that would keep you from offering money for information. It's not illegal, not illegitimate, not even unethical, assuming you even give a shit about that. Am I missing something?"

I shook my head, weary of doing or saying anything that could be construed as consent. I was also aware of my phone recording this potentially compromising conversation about money changing hands, even just for information, and even if everything was carefully constructed to avoid the appearance that the payments had been made for this purpose. I had to chuckle at my own predicament.

"Good." Imad chuckled back. "Now, it's once you have all the information that your problems really kick in."

"What do you mean?"

"Let's assume I connect you to Anas. And let's assume you meet Anas and he directs you to the place where this young man is. Hypothetically, of course," Imad added with another smile.

"Of course," I said. "Maybe that's why it's called an assumption."

Imad's smile vanished. "Well then, since you're so quick on the uptake," he said, "you will also readily appreciate how illegal it is to pay any kind of ransom to release someone in captivity in Syria. Unless, of course, you can get the Qataris to pay the ransom for you, the way they do for most of the kidnapped Americans, Brits, and Frenchies—you know, wink-wink, with all those fake denials! But if you can't finagle that, then paying a ransom puts you knee-deep in illegal shit. Are you following?"

I understood. I remembered Huby's repeated attempts to pay me for my efforts as well as our walk in Paris, when he told me about the government official who had warned him that he would be prosecuted if he offered to pay any ransom for Paul's release. And this warning was not an isolated instance, as I knew from personal experience. Imad's words brought back painful memories. Nine months earlier, during a search for another person who had gone missing in Syria, a Lebanese

American middleman demanded an extravagant fee for arranging a ransom payment, without offering any proof of life, let alone any evidence that he was in communication with the missing person's captors or that he had the ability to get him released in return for the ransom payment. I refused and severed my ties to this shady go-between, thinking that this would be the end of it. A week later, I found out that he had tried to sell these same ransom services to an American intelligence official in Beirut and was warned in no uncertain terms that he would be arrested and prosecuted if he tried to do this again. The middleman vanished, as did any trace of the missing person. I had never stopped thinking about that experience and kept obsessing over the conundrum of giving in to ransom demands. As much as it pained me to admit it, I realized that Imad was right—the only time it was not illegal to make a payment was now, when all I was seeking was information.

Imad seemed to read my thoughts. "I can see that you might need a moment to think this over, maybe even call your friend," he continued in a softer tone. "If it helps you wrap your mind around it, think of it as a foray into Islamic finance."

"Islamic finance?"

"Sure. Let me walk you through this," Imad said, clearly pleased by the prospect of schooling me. "We might as well have a little fun and learn something new while we get to know each other. As you probably realize, Sharia law places strict prohibitions on interest payments, right?"

I nodded, even though I had no idea where he was going with his lecture.

"Good. So some clever person has come up with these ingenious structures to get around the prohibitions, you know, *sukuk* bonds and all that, which place some asset or property in the investment so that the payments can be called 'rent' instead of 'interest.' And when the *sukuk* expires, these rent payments miraculously expire with it."

I nodded again, even though I still did not know why he was telling me all this. Imad's entire discourse on Sharia-compliant bonds seemed utterly out of context. I was very confused.

"My point is that an interest payment still needs to be made, but one has to find a legal way, or rather a way that is not strictly illegal, to make it. Satisfy the letter of the law, and ignore its spirit, if you follow me."

I was beginning to understand.

"I can see that you are starting to see the light," Imad said. By now, I had convinced myself that this shrewd man was able to read my mind. I wondered whether I could perhaps trick him with a fake thought, like a red herring. It was the same kind of absurd tactical trick I would use as a child when trying to hide a bad thought from God. It failed then as thoroughly as it would fail now with Imad. "It's the same concept here," he continued. "You can make a payment to be connected to Anas and then from Anas to the young man. A slightly inflated payment, perhaps, because the inflation will also have to cover a possible consideration for those who might be holding this young man. Without calling it a ransom payment, of course. The principles of Islamic finance—but made in order to be circumvented, like all religious laws."

I got it. Again, I remembered the delicate fact that my phone was recording our potentially incriminating exchange. This guy was quite brilliant but also the type of person who would never respect someone who surrendered too easily. "That assumes, of course, that you and Anas would pass on the inflation value, or that this is not just a ploy to increase the price and there is no further step after Anas," I said. "What if the young man is no longer alive? A dead end, in every respect."

"Well, my friend, that's a risk you're just going to have to take, isn't it?" Imad said callously. "Remember, you've approached us empty handed. A beggar at least has a cup, yet you come with nothing. We have the information, which, in war as in peace, is everything. Information is gold, so to speak."

"Okay," I said carefully.

"And I assume you know the golden rule, don't you?"

"I'm not sure what you mean," I answered. "Which golden rule?"

"He who has the gold rules. Or, if you prefer, he who has the gold makes the rules—*that* golden rule!" Imad replied triumphantly. "As I said, the information you are seeking is as precious as gold. Give it some thought, then let me know. I'll be back in the hotel this evening. If you want to talk, you can find me at the bar. If you don't show up, I'll have my answer, and you'll never see me again."

Without another word, Imad got up, turned his back to me, and walked away. No handshake, no niceties. Gone was all the playful fourth-power and Islamic finance banter of a few moments earlier. As he moved toward the hotel entrance, he spotted Mike and signaled for him to follow. Once they were out of earshot, I pulled out my phone and stopped the recording.

I tried to retrace the past minutes in my mind. I had been unable to slow down the conversation with Imad to a point where I would have enough time to consider the repercussions of my words. It was evident that Imad and Mike knew Anas and were in a position to connect me to him. They presented it as a business negotiation—information for cash. There seemed to be little room to move this into something softer—information for information, information for a favor, or information for the vague assurance of a relationship—the smallest carrot I could dangle before them. While Mike seemed slow on the uptake, Imad was clearly sharp as a tack and utterly unsentimental. There was no way he would give me something for nothing, and he was hardly the type to be easily fooled into doing so unwittingly.

BACK IN THE room I paced back and forth. I feared that a failed negotiation with these fellows would prompt them to warn Anas not to meet with me in the event that I might be able to track him down by some

other means. This trail would go cold immediately. It was the only one I
had, and I had to find a way to take advantage of it. I needed to clear my
mind. The hotel had a lovely pool, and I decided to go for a swim.

To my relief, there was not a soul in the pool, and the water felt
soothing as I sunk in. The conversation with Imad was playing in my
head as I swam lap after lap. It occurred to me that Imad might actually
possess the same information I was hoping to get from Anas, but since
he had not offered that in our last conversation, he was unlikely to do
so in our next one—even if for no other reason than that the addition
of the Anas layer would also mean another opportunity to demand a
higher price. There would be no stalling Imad. By the evening, we would
either come to terms, or this door would close for good. Even though I
kept telling myself that I had done everything in my power to find this
Anas, I struggled to come to terms with my failure, which was looking
more and more likely with each lap.

Twenty minutes into my swim, as I was about to turn for another lap,
I saw two men in suits near the edge of the pool. As they approached
me, I recognized them. They were the pulp fiction characters from the
breakfast area, the same two whom Mike had forced to vacate their seats
to make room for me. I stopped swimming.

"Can I help you?" I asked.

"Our boss wants to talk to you," the smaller one answered.

"Now?"

"Now."

"Here?"

"Here."

"Would you mind if I swim a few more laps? I'm almost finished, just
five more minutes."

"Now," he repeated, leaving little room for debate.

I got out of the pool, dried off quickly, and wrapped myself in the hotel
bathrobe. Only then did I spot Mike sitting at the other corner of the

pool deck. I walked over to him, escorted by my two new black-suited friends.

"So sorry to interrupt your swim," Mike said with a conceited smirk.

"It's all right, Mike, what can I do for you?"

"I feel like we never had a chance to finish our conversation and really become friends this morning," Mike said. "Imad was quite rude, actually, and I wanted to have a chance to get to know you better. It's only right, given that we're in business together."

"We are?"

"Yep, that's the plan. Anyway, you were looking good in the pool. Did you swim in college?" Clearly, Mike could not stay away from his beloved sports for very long.

"Afraid not," I said. "Both because I never went to college in the US, and also because I am not such a good swimmer."

Mike gave me a pitying look. "That's too bad. Michigan has an amazing swim team. One of the best, like most sports programs at U of M."

"Good to know," I said, a little annoyed that I had to end my pool session early for this idle chitchat. "So, Mike, what is it you wish to talk about?"

"Straight to the point, I like that," Mike said. "Well, I felt like we parted on a bit of a sour note this morning. As I said, Imad can be rude, a little rough around the edges, and I wanted to make sure that his abrupt style did not leave a sour taste in your mouth."

"No worries," I said. "I'm glad he didn't beat around the bush. At least I know where I stand."

"So, where do you stand?" Mike asked.

"Now?" I asked. "You want an answer now?"

"Why not?" Mike said. "There's no time like the present."

"I thought I would have until this evening. At least that's what Imad said."

"God damn it, I'm not Imad." Mike raised his voice. "Fuck him. You're dealing with me now." All of a sudden, there was a dark threat in Mike's tone. Unlike my earlier conversation with Imad in the hotel lounge, where my main worry had been that I might make a mistake that could end my chances of ever finding Anas, the interaction with Mike suddenly carried the possibility of a violent confrontation. The two suits moved closer to us, as if they might need to interfere. Mike waved them away.

"I'll try to be as clear as Imad, since that's the way you like it," Mike continued. "Either we come to terms now, or we never come to terms. The price I will give you here and now will be far below what Imad would have asked for this evening, so if we cannot shake hands now, there will be no need for you to have a drink with Imad this evening."

While Mike lacked Imad's quick wit and finesse, he had no difficulties getting his point across. I concluded that my best hope was to extract some information from him without giving him a firm commitment of a deal—something I would never be able to pull off with Imad.

"I hear you, Mike, I really do," I said. "But before we discuss price, how do I know that you have the goods? I have no evidence that you know the Anas I am looking for."

"You're right, you have no evidence," Mike said. "But I get to dictate the terms here."

"Why's that?" I asked.

"For the same reason dogs lick their balls," Mike said gleefully. "Because I can."

I laughed, hoping Mike would be pleased that his joke had been so well received.

"Anyhow, don't you trust me?" Mike asked, still very satisfied with himself.

"Sure I trust you, Mike, of course I do. After all, we're old friends," I said. "But from one sports enthusiast to another, how pathetic would it be if I just surrendered and agreed to a price without any proof that you have what I'm trying to buy. I'd be negotiating with myself. Very unsportsmanlike."

He took the bait. "You're right, Daniel, we sports fans have to stick together. Anyone who can appreciate the greatness of Barry Sanders and my beloved Wolverines is my brother."

As ridiculous as Mike's sports obsession was, it provided me with a fortuitous opening to bond with this bizarre person. I happened to know just a little bit about the Detroit teams because Laura was a proud Detroiter and a former colleague of mine used to be a rabid Lions fan. When Barry Sanders, the team's star running back, retired in 1999 at the peak of his career, my colleague was stunned and depressed, as many in the American football-loving world were. This was my opportunity to show off the little sports knowledge I did possess. I went for it.

"Yeah, Sanders was great." I laid it on thick. "The day he retired was one of the saddest days of my life. It still hurts."

Mike's eyes lit up. "You're the man!" he shouted. "Give me a hug, brother!" He stood up and gave me a bear hug. My bathrobe flew open, and I was standing there bare-chested, enveloped by this large man.

"Man, I cannot tell you how good it feels to talk to someone who knows Barry Sanders, let alone recognizes greatness when he sees it," Mike said. "Barry was a beast! If he had been able to run behind a decent offensive line, it would have been game over in the greatest-ever debate. I mean, God damn it, just think about it, if he'd had the Cowboys' offensive line . . . can you even imagine that! Emmitt fuckin' Smith, my ass! Barry would have shattered all the records. The dude ran for a hundred and fifty yards in his sleep! Man, I am so damn happy to be able to share this stuff with someone who can appreciate it. I almost want to cry. It's like being banished to the desert out here—nobody has a clue about the NFL. All they care about here is soccer, man. Soccer!"

"Hard to believe, isn't it," I said.

"No kidding," Mike sneered, completely missing my sarcasm. "Anyway, back at the ranch, where were we? Oh yeah, how do you know that my Anas is the one you are looking for? Maybe this will help," he said as he pulled out his iPhone. Which reminded me that I had forgotten to record this conversation. Instinctively, I put my hand in the right pocket of my bathrobe and considered taking out my phone, but there was no way for me to start recording now in a safe, inconspicuous way. Mike scrolled though some pictures, then held up the screen for me to see. "Does this dude look familiar?"

The man in the picture was Anas. The same one as the very large person in the photograph Khalid had sent me. There was no doubt. I tried to hide my excitement as Mike kept scrolling on his phone. "You want to see more? Here, this is me and Anas, somewhere in Idlib. Man, that was crazy, bombs everywhere. And here's one with both of us and Imad in Raqqah. Talk about nasty! But boy, did we make a lot of money there! Just raked it in, man. Fucking raked it in! And here's an old one of Imad and Anas from the wedding."

"Whose wedding?" I asked, amazed that Mike was sharing these pictures.

"Anas and Loubna's wedding in Damascus, many years ago," Mike said. "They're divorced now—it got ugly. What a dumb shit, our boy Anas! Loubna is one smoking-hot chick! Smoking, I tell you! Who leaves someone like that?"

Mike seemed to have forgotten the reason for our meeting and was showing me pictures as if we were old friends sharing family photos, including pictures of his brother and sister and some other friends. He was in a zone, and I decided to press my luck.

"So this Loubna, where does she live today?" I asked in as flat a tone as I could muster.

"In Dubai of course," Mike said, as if I were a complete fool for asking such a preposterous question. "She used to be involved in our operations there, you know, the girls and all that, but then she and Anas had some huge motherfucking fight, and she kicked him out of the house."

"What happened?" I asked, hoping Mike would say more, perhaps also about "the girls" he had just mentioned.

"She caught him several times banging other women," Mike said. "But the final straw was when she walked in on him humping her own sister in their bed."

"Lovely," I said.

"I know, right?" Mike said, laughing. "I mean, who does that? You don't screw your wife's sister in your own house. You do it at the sister's place. Duh!"

I kept quiet as Mike continued to scroll through the pictures on this phone. "Here's one more: Anas and I near Kobane."

"Who's the third guy?" I asked, pointing to the other man in the picture.

"Some Kurdish dude called Alan," Mike replied.

I held my breath. Alan—the same name Huby had mentioned in Paris, the one confirmed by the Sheikh in Beirut. Alan was from a village near Kobane. It *had* to be the same person.

"Anyway, enough of these pics," Mike continued as he put his phone back in his pocket. "I assume you're convinced by now that I have the goods."

"Yes, thank you." I said. "By the way, is Anas in Amman?"

"You missed him by a day," Mike answered. "He left for Dubai late last night. Tough luck, brother. Bad for you, good for me. So, let's get down to business, shall we?"

Just then, my phone vibrated. It was Khalid. I pressed the volume control button to stop the vibration. I thought about turning on the recorder now but reconsidered. If Mike noticed, it would certainly jeopardize his astonishing eagerness to share information and pictures of Anas.

"So, here's my price," Mike continued without waiting for my answer. "One million for me to connect you to Anas."

"One million what, Syrian pounds?" I asked, hoping to insert some levity into the situation and also trying to buy myself some time to come up with a strategy for the inevitable money conversation I was facing.

"Yeah, right, that's like five thousand bucks!" Mike said, clearly not amused. "No dude, one million dollars. US dollars. One million bucks. Bones. Greens. However you prefer it, so long as it's cash. And I don't take IOUs or credit cards."

"That's quite a bit of money for an introduction," I said.

"Not just any introduction," Mike said. "*My* introduction. And remember, it'll be a lot more if you wait till this evening to speak to Imad. You'll get a sense of inflation, Syrian-style."

"Still, a million dollars just to connect me to Anas," I said, trying to squeeze some more information out of Mike. "Surely, for this price you can throw in a little more."

"There's nothing more to throw in," Mike barked.

"Then let's discuss the price, if you don't mind," I said.

"God damn it, dude, do I look like I'm negotiating? I don't think you get it, there's nothing to discuss," Mike scoffed. "It's a take it or leave it kind of thing. And every hour, the price goes up by ten percent. Think of it as a war premium."

"A war premium?"

"Yeah. The guy you are looking for got lost in Syria. Syria is at war. War is a business. And business is good!" Mike stretched the "good" like a used car salesman would in a cheesy TV jingle.

Before I could answer, a hotel guest entered the pool area. Mike shouted across the pool: "Sorry, closed for a private event."

The guest seemed unimpressed. He ignored Mike and took off his bathrobe.

"Sir, the pool is not available at the moment!" Mike shouted a little louder.

"Excuse me, but who the fuck are you?" the guest shouted back.

Mike looked at his two goons. "Go explain to this cocksucker who the fuck I am."

They walked over to the hotel guest, and one of them handed him his bathrobe while the other blocked the access to the pool. The guest looked at the two men, shook his head, and muttered something under his breath. Without a word, they escorted him out of the area. "Try the gym," Mike shouted after the guest. "I hear it's real nice."

Mike turned back to me. "Asshole. Okay, where was I before we were so rudely interrupted? Oh yes, the price. It's not negotiable."

There was no way for me to stall any further. I would probably not get any more free information out of Mike, and a payment of this magnitude was not in the cards. I had managed to find out that Anas was in Dubai and had received confirmation of Paul Blocher's Kurdish handler, Alan, as well as Anas's wife, Loubna, who lived in Dubai. It was a lot more than I could have hoped for and one hundred percent more than I could have expected to receive for free. "Then I'm afraid I'm going to have to pass," I said.

"That would be a mistake," Mike said. "This might be your only chance of finding that lost dude."

"That's a risk I'm just going to have to live with," I said. "But I do appreciate the offer."

For a brief moment, I considered jumping back into the pool to finish my swim but decided that it might send the wrong signal, especially after the scene I had just witnessed with the other hotel guest. I stood up and shook Mike's hand. "Thanks again for your offer, Mike. Go Blue!" It was the battle cry of the University of Michigan sports teams. Mike did not react. As I turned to leave, Mike's two goons returned and retook their position behind him. "See you around," I said.

I had taken a few steps when one of the goons came up to me. "Our boss would like to talk to you."

"Again?"

"Again."

I turned around and walked back to Mike. "What's up?" I asked.

"Have a seat," Mike said.

"Here's the deal," he continued as I sat down again. "Rumor has it that you've been paid ten million bucks to find this missing dude."

"Come on Mike, that's nonsense."

"Oh yeah, ten million!" Mike said with a hearty laugh. "In fact, rumor has it that you asked for twenty but only received ten. And now you're too cheap to spend one of those ten to find the guy and maybe save his life. You'd rather pocket it all and fuck that lost dude."

"Seriously, Mike, what's this about? We both know this isn't true."

"Yeah, I know it's not true, and you know it's not true," Mike said with a wink. "But it's what I'm going to tell the world. This is how rumors get started, my brother."

"So you're going to spread lies about me just because I didn't accept your offer?"

"Yep, that pretty much sums it up," Mike replied with a huge smile, visibly pleased with himself.

"Why?" I asked. "So we didn't come to terms on the price. So what? No harm done. We just part ways, perhaps to meet another day. Why would you do this?"

"Because this way, everyone else will know better than to reject my offers. Nobody messes with Mike, right guys?" Mike looked at his two companions, who both nodded robotically. "Think of it as the Keyser Söze rule. You know, from *The Usual Suspects*—my favorite movie, by the way. Destroy the first one, even if he's family, and word will spread."

"So you're telling me that you will make this stuff up just to send a message to anyone else you might possibly negotiate with one day?"

"That's *exactly* what I am telling you. Clever, right?"

I was completely cornered. My only option was a convincing bluff. "Well then, I suppose it's a good thing that I recorded this conversation on my phone," I said as calmly as I could.

"You what?" Mike blurted out incredulously.

"I recorded our conversation, just in case," I said as I pulled my phone out of the pocket of my bathrobe. "Looks like 'just in case' just happened."

Mike suddenly turned pale. His jaw dropped, and little specs of saliva appeared in the corners of his mouth.

"I started recording our conversation when I pulled out my phone a few minutes ago, remember?" I continued, thinking of Khalid's call that I had silenced. "It's the beauty of these modern smartphones: you can start recording with two quick taps on the screen. Very practical."

"No w-way! I d-don't b-believe you," Mike stuttered in a weirdly high pitch. All his bravado seemed to have vanished. He had the look of someone who had just been abandoned by his date at the high school prom.

"Well, this one's a risk *you're* going to have to live with," I said as I stood up. I decided to leave before Mike had a chance to recover from this setback or before he could get his goons to grab me or my phone. "Pleasure meeting you," I said as I walked away without turning around. I heard no voices or footsteps behind me.

As soon as I reached my room, I locked and bolted the door and sat on the edge of the bed. The adrenaline rush of my bluff with Mike, fueled by the fear of getting called on it by this thug and his two bouncers, started to drain from my body. My shoulders slumped, and I slowly slid from the bed to the floor. I closed my eyes and tried to regulate my breathing until I regained my composure. I needed to get my act together quickly and contemplate my next steps, so I sent Khalid a text message, asking him to let me know when he was available to Skype. Five minutes later, Khalid replied that he was ready. He picked up in a good mood. I told him about the events of the day, from the breakfast encounter and morning conversation with Imad to the pool meeting with Mike a few minutes ago, and why I had not been able to answer his last call. When I finished, Khalid laughed.

"All in all, I'd say it has been a fairly productive day," he said. "You've received a fair amount of free information, though now your reputation is in tatters. We'll have to find a way to fix that. Ten million dollars! You could have at least offered to share some of that plunder with me."

"Very funny, Khalid," I said, not quite as amused as he seemed to be.

"Oh, take it with a sense of humor," he said. "This Mike guy sounds too dumb to see through your recording bluff. I would have been more worried if this had happened with the other fellow, Imad. But, then again, he sounds too smart to threaten you with that silly rumor to begin with."

Khalid's words were balm for my soul. "So what do we do now?" I asked. "After the pool scene, I'm starting to feel a little paranoid."

"Remember, it's not paranoia if they're really after you," he said with a chuckle.

"Thanks, Khalid. You're in rare form today."

"Relax. It seems that you have accomplished everything there is to accomplish in Amman," Khalid said. "Time to skip town, the sooner the better. Try to move up your flight to Dubai. I'm sure there's one every few hours."

I was relieved that Khalid was too much of a gentleman to bring up the fact that I had missed Anas because I hadn't traveled to Amman quickly enough. He reminded me to call Fuad before I left so that he could take me to the airport and through security. I promised Khalid to keep him posted.

I called the airline and rebooked my scheduled flight to Dubai to one that would leave in just over two hours. Cutting it close, perhaps, but feasible with Fuad's help. I rang the front desk to inform them that I was checking out early. Then I called Fuad, who told me that Khalid had just texted him. He would be at the hotel entrance in ten minutes. I hopped in the shower, barely dried off, packed my bag, and left the room. On the way to the elevator, I received a text message from Khalid letting me know that Fuad was already downstairs and also informing me that he had another passenger in his car—someone whose appearance might shock me and that I should brace myself. I was in too much of a hurry to pay much attention to his strange forewarning.

As I stepped out of the elevators, I spotted Fuad walking toward the reception desk.

"You're all set with the checkout," he said. "Let's get going. One more thing—there is someone in the car, whom I had not intended for you to meet. But I had no time to drop him off at home when you called ten minutes ago, so he'll have to come with us to the airport. I apologize for that."

"Of course. Not a problem," I said, confused by Fuad's apology on the heels of Khalid's ominous alert a few moments earlier.

As we left the hotel, I saw a black SUV with tinted windows speed up to the entrance and screech to a halt. Just in time, I managed to step behind a column next to the main door in order to avoid being seen. Out the driver's side of the SUV emerged Mike, who demonstratively threw the keys to the valet. Out the other door came Imad, who was berating Mike with some choice words. It was evident that the two were in the midst of a heated argument. Two pigeons were madly bobbing their heads, trying to get out of Mike's way as he approached the main entrance. One pigeon managed to escape, but Mike's kick caught the other one with all his might. The unfortunate pigeon smashed with a thump against a glass door, with feathers flying everywhere. "Fucking rats with wings!" Mike cursed loudly as he entered the hotel. I made sure I remained concealed by the column as I turned around and hurried toward Fuad's car.

"They did not see you," Fuad said, reading my thoughts. "But let's get out of here. I'd rather not push our luck by dillydallying, as much as it would be fun to watch these two lovebirds fight."

I got the sense that Fuad was fully aware of my interactions with Imad and Mike, either from Khalid, or because he had found another way to witness them.

Right away, Fuad confirmed my intuition. "The good news is that Mike's either too stupid to realize that he gave you all that free information earlier today or too embarrassed to admit it to Imad, who would skin him alive if he found out."

Fuad motioned for me to get into the backseat on the passenger's side. In front of me was a young man, probably a teenager, wearing a baseball cap. The skin on the back of his neck was completely discolored and bore huge scars. Still, I was not prepared for what I saw when he turned around to mouth a soundless hello as Fuad started the car. I was looking at the face of a completely disfigured young man who had suffered massive burns. One eye shut or missing, I could not tell. He was also missing most of his nose and the left side of his mouth. His expression and body language signaled the most severe pain and exhaustion. He was hard to look at, and impossible not to. I was instantly struck by an overwhelming fleshy smell emanating from this young man, like raw meat that was about to go bad. It was the smell of immeasurable sadness. For a few seconds, I choked up, unable to say a word. Finally, I mumbled that I was pleased to meet him, and he turned around again.

"This is Saif," Fuad said as we drove off.

"My goodness, what happened to him?" I whispered. I was instantly ashamed of my reaction and hoped that Saif had not heard me.

"You don't have to speak so softly," Fuad said as he looked at me through the rearview mirror. "Saif is deaf in one ear and almost deaf in the other. He got caught in one of the chemical attacks in Syria, then in a cluster-bomb explosion as they tried to evacuate the victims. His entire family was wiped out. All of them. Mother. Father. Three older brothers and his young sister. How he survived is beyond me. It seems that God still has plans for Saif, as cruel as that may be. In his young life, he has suffered more than any human would be able to endure."

I sat in frozen silence. "Why is he with you?" was all I could muster after a minute.

"My wife wanted to adopt a Syrian refugee," Fuad replied as he calmly navigated the last remnants of Amman's rush hour. "We don't have any children of our own, which has been very hard on her—and on me, too. So one day we drove to Zaatari."

"Zaatari?"

"Yes. Zaatari is the refugee camp in the north, close to the Syrian border. Since the war began, it has grown into a full-size city. Actually, it's a hellhole, not a city. It's like a city that had an abortion that lived."

Fuad spoke these words with palpable emotion. As we drove, I could not stop myself from thinking about Paul Blocher and what might have happened to him in Syria. Had he been injured like Saif; was he maimed or disfigured? Saif seemed to embody the war's atrocities and horrendous suffering—a human reminder of all that had gone wrong with humanity. Even though I told myself that I was just reacting to Saif's frightful appearance and that there was no particular reason to assume the worst for Paul, I could not shake the sinking feeling that he had suffered a similar fate. Fuad pulled me out of my thoughts with a heavy sigh as he observed me through the rearview mirror.

"I'm sorry, Daniel," he continued with a mournful voice. "There is such loss and destruction, entire generations that will never come back, children who will never, ever have a normal life. Look at Saif. Imagine the sadness. Even a heart of stone will break."

I just shook my head and looked to my right out of the car window. I was worried I would tear up if my eyes met Fuad's in the mirror.

Fuad continued. "So my wife spotted Saif sitting by himself. 'I want *him,'* she said as she nodded in his direction. I asked her whether she was sure. She gave me the death stare and declared, 'We are not leaving without him.' This is how Saif came to live with us. That day, I became an old man. Saif has been with us for one year. And my wife has never been happier."

Saif looked at Fuad and uttered something. It sounded like a low-pitched groan, and I could not make out the words. Fuad nodded and put his right hand on Saif's shoulder.

"What did he say?" I asked.

"He wanted to know if you are my friend," Fuad said. "Saif is terribly fearful every time he meets a stranger. He thinks he will be taken away from us. Every night he wakes up screaming. These cries are unlike anything I have ever heard. Deep, guttural sounds from a dark, dark place. Like an animal being slaughtered. It takes us hours to calm him down and get him to fall asleep again."

"How old is Saif?" I asked.

"Fifteen," Fuad replied.

"You and your wife are doing something incredible," I said. "I admire you. It must be so hard."

We had arrived at the airport. "Actually, it's the exact opposite," Fuad said as he pulled up next to a police car parked on the side of the terminal. "Saif saved us, saved our marriage. My wife is unable to have children because of a condition in her uterus. She had been in a deep depression ever since she found out only a few months after our wedding. I even worried that she was suicidal. One of her sisters has seven children, the other one has five, which her parents are kind enough to mention whenever they have a chance. But since Saif has entered our life, my wife has found a purpose, and so have I. Saif has been our blessing, our salvation."

Fuad got out of the car and waved to a man a few feet away. I could not hear what Fuad told him, but the man got in the car and sat in Fuad's place next to Saif.

"Is it okay for me to say goodbye to Saif?" I asked as I got out of the car.

"Of course," Fuad said. "And my colleague here will stay with him until I get back. Saif knows him, so he won't be scared."

I went to Saif's door and waved. Fuad opened the door. "Don't be shy," he said with a smile.

I stretched my right hand toward Saif, who gave me his left hand. Only then did I realize that he was missing his right hand. His left hand had only two fingers remaining, which were curled, giving the impression that he was pointing at something to the right of his body. Saif's wrist was mangled and twisted sideways. I held his hand with my left hand as gently as I could and shook it. I tried to detect some sign of emotion in Saif's expression as I wished him all the best, but the muscles in his face were completely rigid.

"Thank you for shaking his hand," Fuad said as we walked into the terminal. "Most people are too frightened to look at Saif, let alone touch him. And those curved fingers scare everybody away."

Fuad asked for my passport, and we walked to the check-in counter. As soon as we received the boarding pass, Fuad took me to a colleague at security who waved us past the queue.

"Your flight is boarding, let's hurry up," Fuad said as we speed-walked toward the gate. "I apologize for surprising you with Saif."

"You have nothing to apologize for," I said. "I am sorry to be such an imposition. You have been so kind to take such good care of me here. Besides, I am honored to have met Saif."

Fuad beamed. "No person who has the courage to touch Saif remains untouched. An angel."

We arrived at the gate. Almost all passengers had already boarded. I gave Fuad a hug and thanked him once again.

"Good luck, Daniel," he said. "I hope you find the person you are looking for."

On the plane, I closed my eyes and tried to sleep, but the impressions of the day kept me awake—from Mike and Imad, for whom the war was nothing but a lucrative business, to Saif and all the unspeakable suffering he had endured. I ended up staring out of the window for most of the three hours we were in the air. Finally, the pilot announced our approach to Dubai, and I could see the city's bright skyline and the mammoth Burj Khalifa skyscraper with its sparkling lights.

EIGHT

I WALKED OFF the plane feeling forlorn yet relieved that this time, unlike in Beirut and Amman, I would not be accompanied or picked up by anyone. It felt oddly comforting to stand in line at passport control, like thousands of other ordinary travelers, and have no security officer or anyone else waiting for me.

Traffic was light as we left the airport and zipped toward the hotel. The roundabout on Sheikh Zayed Road near the old Trade Center was covered with huge billboard images of Sheikh Mohammed bin Rashid, the ruler of Dubai, Sheikh Khalifa bin Zayed, the ruler of Abu Dhabi, and the late Sheikh Zayed himself, the revered unifier and first president of the United Arab Emirates who had died ten years earlier. These giant adulatory placards were all over the city—ubiquitous vanity monuments plastered on buildings, hanging from lampposts and construction cranes, even on tinted car windows. I wondered what Sheikh Zayed, whose early years before the explosion of oil wealth had been simple and humble, would have thought, had he seen his likeness splashed every-where on this Dubai thoroughfare that bore his name.

It was past midnight when I walked into the lobby. I checked in and stepped into the elevator. As the door was closing, two men squeezed in, followed by two women. The men were in their sixties, one short and heavy, the other tall and skinny. They were talking in Arabic with a Lebanese accent, debating which one would get which woman. The women were tall and beautiful, one with short platinum-blonde hair, black lips, and tattooed eyebrows and the other with long jet-black hair and bright red lips. The women whispered in Russian to each other and kept rolling their eyes at the men, who were immersed in their animated negotiation. "*Eto pizdets*," the blonde woman kept repeating. This is really screwed up.

The elevator stopped on the floor before mine while the two men were still in the midst of their heated argument—they both wanted the blonde woman. During this entire negotiation, they stood in the elevator door, preventing it from closing and holding me hostage to this bizarre scene. Finally, the tall, skinny man sighed in resignation, and all four stepped out. The short, heavyset man, with a victorious grin on his face, grabbed the blonde woman by the hand; the tall man pointed to the black-haired woman with the look of someone who had to settle for a consolation price. The last thing I heard before the elevator door closed was the black-haired woman snarl, "*Idi na khui.*" Fuck off.

I finally arrived in my room and dropped the bag on the floor. I opened the drapes and saw the familiar nightly show of Dubai's bright skyscrapers. I had a close-up view of the landmark Emirates Towers, among the most recognizable structures in this remarkable city, each with the obligatory needle on top to create the illusion of even more height. Prior to the Burj Khalifa, I had considered these two towers to be the modern-day Tower of Babel. But once the Burj Khalifa was completed and staked its claim as the world's tallest building, it became impossible not to see it as the incarnation of that Babylonian attempt to reach the heavens. Despite the silliness of all these vanity projects, there was something magical about this nightly display of light.

I was drained from the past twenty-four hours but knew that I had no time to waste. I missed Anas in Amman because it had taken me too long to get there, and I desperately wanted to avoid making the same mistake again. The foundation matter, my initial purpose for being in Dubai, would have to wait for now. It was far more important to catch up with Anas—assuming he really had traveled from Amman to Dubai, as Khalid had told me. I text-messaged Khalid to let him know that I had arrived.

An hour later, I was woken by the ping of my phone. It took me a moment to find my bearings. I had fallen into a deep sleep on the couch, seated and fully dressed. It was a message from Khalid, suggesting we speak on Skype.

"So sorry to keep you up so late, *habibi*," Khalid said in a pleasant voice. "I could not break away the very moment I received your message. I hope you had a pleasant trip. Please forgive me for not arranging a special pickup at the airport."

"Actually, I was grateful," I said. "Though I am starting to worry that you are losing your touch."

Khalid laughed. "Be careful what you wish for."

I was too tired for our playful banter. "I just wanted to let you know that I am in Dubai. Ready to roll."

"Good," Khalid said. "I just got off the phone with Jamil. He was able to track down the wife of this Anas. Actually, it is Jamil's friend Bassel, the person you met at the kiosk in Beirut, who managed to find her. I think he located her through the contact list in Anas's phone and then proceeded to hack her phone, too. Not sure why. Though, with Bassel's skills, why not, I suppose."

"Remind me to stay on Bassel's good side," I said.

"No kidding." Khalid laughed. "Anyway, here's what he found out. As you already know from this Mike fellow in Amman, Anas was married to a woman called Loubna."

"Yes, that's what he said."

"Well, it seems that this Loubna is quite the businesswoman in her own right," Khalid went on. "She has an office in Jumeirah but actually spends most of her time meeting people in a place called The Address at Dubai Mall. Do you know it?"

"I do. It's very fancy."

"Indeed. Apparently Madame Loubna has developed a fine taste for expensive things. In any event, from what Jamil told me, this woman is as beautiful as she is cunning."

"I'll be careful."

"You cannot be careful enough. This is a Syrian woman! Believe me, that's an entirely different species—something my father found out the hard way when he fell for his own Syrian beauty many years ago."

"So how should I make contact with this Loubna?" I asked. "From what you say, she's too smart to believe me if we just happen to bump into each other at The Address, and I just happen to ask her about Anas."

"That's exactly right," Khalid said. "I know someone in Damascus who used to be a friend of Loubna's father before he died. I will ask him to arrange the meeting. He will introduce you as someone who might be good for Loubna to know. He will also mention that there is something important you need to ask her, so that it won't look like some less-than-credible coincidence when you inquire about Anas. Instead, you are a reasonably well-connected foreigner who could be helpful to her. He might have to spice you up a little bit and oversell your importance, but that's all the bait you'll need."

It was a classic Gulf maneuver, where everyone is described in hyperbolic terms and everything is embellished beyond recognition. A man cannot just be financially secure or even wealthy, he has to be the billionaire of billionaires; he cannot just be intelligent, he has be a generational genius who predicted every financial or political event years before it took place; a woman cannot be merely attractive, she has to be the most gorgeous, desirable Victoria's Secret model in the world who turned down marriage proposals by multiple sheikhs. An employee morphs into a supervisor, a supervisor into a boss, and a boss into a chairman. The region has without a doubt the highest VIP per capita density. These frenetic exaggerations extend to all things: a car cannot just be fast, it has to be the fastest in the world; a shack turns into a house, a house becomes a villa, and a villa becomes a palace. It was a constant inflation of words to the point where they lost all value and meaning.

"Okay, that sounds good. Can you send me her contact information?" Immediately I heard two pings on my phone. The first one was Loubna's mobile phone number, followed by her profile picture.

"Thanks, that was fast," I said.

"My pleasure," Khalid said. "And if you want more photos of her, have a look at her Instagram page. She's a prolific poster of her own pictures and has over a hundred thousand followers, so she's quite the celebrity in Dubai. Remember, the amount of Instagram followers and Facebook likes has become the preeminent popularity contest in the Gulf, though from what Abu Fadl tells me, at least one-third, maybe even one-half, of these Instagram followers are fake. And Abu Fadl would know—he's the Ray in charge of monitoring social media."

"Who?" I asked. The name sounded vaguely familiar, but I couldn't quite place it.

"Abu Fadl," Khalid repeated with a trace of exasperation. "You know, my Saudi intelligence friend, whom you met in Istanbul the evening before your Beirut trip to meet the Sheikh."

"Oh yes, sorry. I had forgotten his name."

"You might want to memorize the names of the people you meet for the remainder of this journey," Khalid chided me gently. "Starting with Loubna."

"I'll do my best." Khalid's dressing down over something so minor irritated me, but I knew he was right. It didn't help that I had a poor memory for names.

"Don't be offended, *habibi*," Khalid said. "No mistakes allowed on this mission. Every detail matters. I see you taking notes when we meet, and you told me that you sometimes record your conversations with the phone. All I'm saying is that this is not the time to stop being your usual diligent self."

"You're right, sorry." I had to smile—I had been taking careful notes throughout this call with Khalid. Nothing got past this man.

"In any event," Khalid continued, "back to Loubna's Instagram followers: don't be surprised if complete strangers walk up to this woman and greet her like an intimate friend or ask to take a selfie with her. Social media popularity is probably the closest this region might ever get to a democratic election. Aside from all that, she is seductively beautiful, so please try not to fall for her. You wouldn't be the first, from what I hear."

"Don't worry," I said. "I'm all set in that department."

Khalid laughed. "That's what they all say. The most innocent ones fall the hardest."

"I never said I was innocent," I said with a chuckle, "just that I'm all set when it comes to romance. But I'll keep your words of caution in mind."

"Two more things," Khalid continued. "First, it might be useful to know that Loubna's mother was an Alawi woman from Qardaha, the town near Latakia where Hafez al-Assad was born.* Her family was dirt poor, like many Alawis in those days. Out of desperation, her parents—Loubna's grandparents—sold her to a Sunni family in Damascus. As disgraceful as that was, they saw it as their only way of survival. It is something Loubna's mother never forgave her parents for. She ended up marrying the son of the Sunni family into which she had been sold—Loubna's father. But this sense of betrayal, especially by the men in her life, made her bitter and cynical—traits she passed on to her daughter Loubna."

---

* Hafez al-Assad was the president of Syria from 1971 to 2000. In the 1980s, he had favored his brother Rifaat al-Assad as his successor, then, after some nasty internecine infighting, changed this choice to his oldest son, Bassel al-Assad. When Bassel al-Assad died in a car accident in 1994, Hafez al-Assad started to groom his second-oldest son, Bashar al-Assad, who had trained to be an ophthalmologist and had never displayed any particular leadership aptitude, as his successor. Upon the death of Hafez al-Assad in 2000, Bashar al-Assad became president of Syria.

"All *that* Bassel was able to find out by hacking a few phones?" I asked incredulously.

"Not just phones," Khalid replied. "This Bassel seems to read everything he can get his hands on, including the files kept by the Syrian intelligence services, the Mukhabarat. Apparently not everyone appreciates his passion for reading, which is how he found himself cooking breakfast at a kiosk in Beirut."

"And the second point? You mentioned two things." My notes were coming in handy.

"Yes, you're right," Khalid said. "The second point is related to the first one. From what Jamil tells me, Loubna hates her ex-husband Anas ferociously. I don't know what happened between those two, but it has got to be something rather unpleasant. Maybe it's what this Mike fellow told you in Amman—that she caught Anas sleeping with her sister. But I have the sense it's something else. Women in this part of the world are used to cheating husbands, though doing it with the sister-in-law does demonstrate a special touch. The wives almost expect it. In Loubna's case, however, this seems to go deeper. You might want to keep that in mind."

"I will, thank you."

"One last thing," Khalid added before I could say good night. "Please be careful and alert at all times. And, above all, be prepared. You may end up talking to Anas sooner than you think, and you'll have to have your tactics and your strategy all worked out. You don't want to be the dog that catches the car."

"What do you mean?"

"You know, dogs always bark at cars and chase them down the street, but they never catch them. If the dogs did catch a car, what would they do with it? Attack the fender? Bite a tire? What's the plan?"

I laughed. "They'd probably just keep on barking. But I get your point. I'll be ready for the moment I catch up with Anas."

"Good," Khalid said. "Don't fall into the trap of assuming that a single one of these people is stupid. Evil, perhaps, but not stupid."

I promised to keep him posted after I made contact with Loubna, and we hung up. I got undressed, crawled into bed, and fell into a deep, dreamless sleep.

I WOKE UP in the morning with a pounding headache. When three cups of coffee did not help, I decided to take a hot shower. Eventually, the tension of the past days started to ease away, and the headache dissipated. I got dressed and took the elevator to the lounge on the thirty-third floor to have some breakfast.

The staff in the lounge had barely changed in the twelve years I had been staying in this hotel. Charles and Dalia from Kenya, Kevin from the Philippines, and Dev, the cook from India. I was particularly fond of Dev. He looked like he was well into his seventies, always with a sweet smile and a few kind words. Everyone loved Dev, from the guests to the staff. Kevin greeted me warmly and showed me to the table by the window, overlooking Sheikh Zayed Road and downtown Dubai. Charles poured me a cup of coffee, my fourth this morning, and Dalia brought me my usual orange-carrot juice mix. The lounge was empty except for one table at the other end, where two gentlemen were having breakfast. Upon closer look, I realized that they were the two men from last night's elevator ride. Their two female companions were nowhere in sight.

I walked over to the buffet. Dev was behind the counter, ready to make eggs or pancakes or anything else the heart desired. I was just about to ask him for some scrambled eggs when the shorter and heavier of the two men cut in front of me and barked at Dev to make him three fried eggs over easy. Dev looked at me with an expression that asked whether it was okay to serve this guest first, since I had been so rudely pushed aside. I nodded. The last thing I felt like was an argument over a queue. Dev took an egg and cracked it over the frying pan. Before he could crack the second egg, a scream pierced the air in the room.

"How dare you!" the guest yelled at poor Dev. "This is just completely unhygienic! To crack eggs with your bare hands! I am disgusted!"

"I'm so sorry, sir," Dev said with a whisper.

"Sorry?!" the man shrieked at the top of his lungs. "*Sorry?!* I'll give you sorry! I don't want your naked, grubby, dirty Paki fingers on my eggs!"

"I'm Indian, sir," Dev objected quietly.

"Shut your mouth! Don't you even dare talk to me!" the man screeched, his voice cracking. "Indian, Pakistani, Bengali—who gives a damn! You're filthy, all of you! You will wear some damn gloves when you cook for me! Do you understand?"

"I'm very sorry, sir," Dev repeated, pulling vinyl gloves out of a drawer and hurrying to put them on his hands. "I apologize, sir."

"It's too late for that!" the man shouted. "I will see to it that you never work another day in this hotel. I'm going to complain to management and have you fired immediately!"

Dev just stood there, paralyzed in fear in front of this red-faced man full of indignant rage.

I had seen enough. "Excuse me, but considering where your body parts were last night, this cook's bare hands on your precious egg shells are the least of your hygiene problems."

The man looked at me with an expression of sheer disbelief, and for a few seconds there was not a sound in the entire lounge. Suddenly he started to shake violently and turned deep purple. I thought he was having a seizure.

"I . . . I . . . I will have you fired, too!" he finally stammered nonsensically. He dropped his plate to the floor, where it shattered into many pieces. "You will regret this!" he shouted as he left the lounge. His tall, thin friend hurried after him to the hallway, where I heard loud cursing until the elevator arrived.

Dev was crestfallen. "This is very bad, sir," he said to me. "I appreciate your help, but now they will fire me and send me back to India. I cannot stay in Dubai without a job."

"Don't worry, Dev," I said. "I will speak to the management. You did nothing wrong. I'll make sure you suffer no repercussions." Dev nodded, but the broken look in his eyes was that of a doomed man awaiting his imminent execution.

Ten minutes later, the hotel manager walked into the lounge and made a beeline for Dev's area. I got up from my table and walked over.

"Dev, please come with me," the manager said.

"I'm sorry to interrupt," I said to the manager, "but I would like to have a word with you, if you don't mind."

"What?" the manager snapped at me.

"Come again?" I said sharply.

The manager realized that he had just made a mistake by being rude to a hotel guest. "I have to deal with an internal discipline issue here. Please excuse me."

"No, I don't think I will," I said. "You are neither in a position nor in a condition to talk to me that way."

"I'm sorry, sir," he said in a contrite tone. "A guest just complained bitterly about the cook, and I have to address the matter."

"Yes, I am aware of that. This is what I would like to talk to you about. I witnessed the whole thing." I described the entire scene to the manager and assured him that Dev had done nothing wrong and in fact had conducted himself impeccably. The manager listened intently.

"Sir, I appreciate your description of the whole thing, I really do," he said when I finished. "But this guest was really irate, and he will not relent until we fire the cook. He demands his pound of flesh!"

"About that pound of flesh," I said. "Doesn't your hotel have a strict no-prostitution policy?"

The hotel manager gave me a befuddled look. "Yes, prostitution is illegal in the United Arab Emirates, and in this hotel we pride ourselves on adhering to the strictest of standards," he said pompously, his assertiveness increasing as he spoke. "Not a single prostitute gets past our guards, with or without a hotel guest."

"That's interesting," I said, "because last night I rode the elevator with the very same guest who just complained about the cook, together with his friend, who happens to be another hotel guest. They were in the company of two prostitutes. In fact, I got stuck in the elevator with these two fine gentlemen and was forced to listen to a lengthy and rather distasteful negotiation about who would get which prostitute."

I watched the color and the confidence drain from the hotel manager's face. "Are you sure?" he asked meekly.

"Absolutely sure," I said. "Coincidentally, I am on friendly terms with one of the government prosecutors in Dubai, who will be very interested to hear what I have to tell him."

At this point, the hotel manager's face was white as a sheet. "Please sir, I'm begging you sir, please don't say anything," he pleaded. "If this comes out, I will lose my job, and they will send me back to Romania."

Apparently the irony of his statement was lost on him. "Which is exactly what you are trying to do to the cook, who has done nothing wrong," I said coldly.

"Please, sir, please," the hotel manager implored me, almost sobbing, "I'm begging you! Please don't say anything to your prosecutor friend or to anyone else. Please!"

I stared at him for a moment. His rapid switch from rudeness to groveling brought out the inner asshole in me. "Here's what I'd like you to do," I said. "You will not fire the cook. From this moment on, you will be his personal protector. You will write an official letter to the hotel management company commending the cook for his exemplary behavior toward hotel guests in general and toward this one cantankerous, disgusting hotel guest in particular. You can mention me as a witness, and I'd appreciate a copy of this letter. If I have this letter before I finish my breakfast, the prostitution matter will not come up when I meet my prosecutor friend. If I don't have this letter, or if anything happens to Dev, you can go ahead and book your flight to Bucharest. Do we understand each other?"

The hotel manager nodded and grabbed my hand. "Thank you, sir, thank you, sir! I'll have this letter to you immediately, thank you, thank you." He made a mad dash for the elevators.

I returned to my table. Charles came over with a wide grin and poured a fresh cup of coffee, and Dev brought me a steaming plate of eggs and baked beans. "Three fried eggs over easy, with some extra spice in memory of that bad man," he said, smiling. "Thank you for helping me."

I was still eating the eggs when the hotel manager came running back into the room. For a moment, he did not see me. "He left already, oh my God, he left already," he wailed to no one in particular. "This is a disaster, what will I do?"

Dalia tapped him on the shoulder and pointed in my direction. Her twinkling eyes revealed how thoroughly she was enjoying herself.

"Thank God, you are still here," he exhaled as he hurried over to me. "Here it is." He placed the letter on my table. "Please read it and tell me if it has everything you need. I wrote it myself. Please, sir, read it right away."

I read through the letter. It was incredibly effusive. He praised Dev in the highest terms and colorfully denounced the nasty guest, culminating in his emphatic recommendation to ban that person in perpetuity from this hotel and all the hotels owned by the same chain.

"Yes, this will do," I said. "Thank you."

"Oh, thank *you*, sir," he said. "I am so very grateful to you."

"Don't mention it," I said. "I look forward to seeing our friend Dev during my next stay in this hotel, and during all my stays after that."

The hotel manager nodded incessantly. "Yes, sir, yes, sir."

"If you don't mind, I'd like to finish my breakfast now," I finally said when he made no effort to leave. "The eggs are delicious."

"Of course, sir," he said, walking away backward as he continued to face me.

After a few minutes, I got up to leave. As I waited for the elevators, I received a text message from Khalid, informing me that his friend in Damascus had reached Loubna and that she was expecting my call. I called her as soon as I was back in my room. She did not pick up. Five minutes later, I got a call from an Omani number.

"Who is this?" a woman asked in a throaty voice when I picked up.

"Is this Loubna?" I asked back.

"It is not nice to reply to a question with a question," the woman said tersely. The accent of her English was an unusual blend of Arabic and French.

"Perhaps, but it is also not nice to ask the person you call who he is." We were certainly starting off on a snippy note.

"I received a call from your number. I'm trying to find out who called me." Her tone was acid.

I decided to surrender. "This is Daniel. I was told that you were expecting my call."

"Ah, Daniel," she said in a sweet voice. The instant transformation was remarkable. "Why didn't you say so?"

"So you are Loubna?"

"Of course, who else would I be?" Loubna said. "Where are you staying? I would like to meet you." Loubna told me that she hadn't answered my call because my phone number was *too ordinary*: unless at least five of the seven digits were identical, the caller would in all likelihood not be someone worth talking to. A VIP filter, Dubai-style. But then her curiosity got the better of her; fear of missing out had trumped the dread of wasting her time on an unimportant person.

We agreed to meet one hour later in the lounge of The Address. I sent Khalid a message to let him know that I had made contact with Loubna. Khalid sent a peculiar reply, advising me not to be disappointed if that first meeting with Loubna ended up being unproductive. Apparently his contact in Damascus had told him that Loubna liked to get an initial impression of a person before deciding whether to pursue the relationship any further. I thanked Khalid for his counsel, even though the notion that this first meeting would be some kind of audition struck me as a tad melodramatic. But it did remind me of my initial encounter with Jamil at the airport lounge in Istanbul.

I ARRIVED AT The Address a few minutes early. A strange scene was playing out in the lounge. The place was full of attractive women, dressed to kill, who were meeting with men, many of whom, judging by their loosely cut, traditional white kanduras, were local Emiratis. The guests all seemed engaged in intense conversations, but at the same time each person who entered the space was checked out closely by everyone present. I found a spot at the edge of the lounge, where I had a good view of all the tables. I quickly spotted Loubna at the other end of the room: she stood out like a queen bee. She was gorgeous, dressed in elegant business attire, though with a lot of cleavage for a professional setting. She was immersed in a close tête-à-tête with an Emirati man. I decided to wait and give her time to finish her meeting. A moment later, she saw me and waved me to her table. As I walked over, I pulled out my phone and turned on the recorder.

Loubna had the brightest green eyes I had ever seen. "Mr. Daniel, please meet Mr. Ali," she said before I could introduce myself.

"Madame Loubna has told me wonderful things about you," Ali said as we shook hands. "It's a pleasure to meet you. I've got to leave now, but please let me know if you come to Abu Dhabi. It would be my honor and privilege to host you. Madame Loubna has all my contact details."

As Ali walked toward the entrance, I looked at Loubna. "You told him wonderful things about me?"

Loubna laughed. "This is Dubai, Daniel. None of these words mean anything here. It's all hype and hot air."

"So does he now expect me to contact him?" I asked.

"Of course not. Just because words around here are inflated does not mean everyone's an idiot. Ali's very clever. He's a Bedouin. He knows that I know that he knows that I know that we're all just playing this game of illusions."

My phone rang, and I hit the volume control to turn off the sound. Chagrined, I realized that the recording had stopped, too, because I had forgotten again to switch the phone into flight mode. I returned it casually into my pocket, annoyed at my own carelessness.

I suddenly noticed that the entire lounge was staring at us. Actually, the women were staring resentfully at Loubna, while the men were looking at me in bemused disbelief, wondering what I had done to deserve a date with such a beautiful woman.

Loubna must have read my thoughts. "Don't pay attention to the others. Focus on me, please."

"Gladly," I said, "though I am sensing a thousand daggers in my back."

"The men here can't control their eyes," Loubna said with a smile. "They're like boys who just got their hands on their first *Playboy* magazine. Show them a little cleavage, and the blood no longer flows to their teeny brains."

I laughed, though there was something bitter, even angry, in the way Loubna seemed to be talking about *all* men. "Eventually, that must get a little tedious," I said, failing to come up with something more witty.

"It does, once the thrill of wrapping someone around your little finger wears off. Listen," Loubna said abruptly, "I'm terribly sorry, but I have to run to another appointment. If you don't mind, I will call you this afternoon."

Before I could say anything, Loubna stood up and left. I remembered Khalid's warning about Loubna's habit of vetting people she met for the first time. Given how brusquely she had just ended this meeting, I was sure that I had failed to clear the bar. As soon as I saw her get into a car, I walked out and hailed a taxi. On the drive back to my hotel, I tried to understand what I might have done or said to offend Loubna but couldn't think of anything. I was in a dejected mood, made worse by the realization that I would now have to come up with another plan to find Anas.

I had just arrived at the hotel and was chatting with one of the doormen when my phone rang. A local number I did not recognize.

"I hope I am not bothering you," Loubna said in a pleasant voice.

My heart jumped. "Not at all, Loubna."

"I apologize for ending our meeting at The Address so harshly."

"It's quite okay," I said.

"No it's not. It was rude, and I'm really sorry. Unfortunately, that place was not only packed with hungry eyes but also with thirsty ears, some of which are attached to the heads of Syrians I would rather avoid."

"I understand."

"In any event, Daniel, I would very much like to see you again." Her tone was flirtatious and businesslike at the same time.

"That would be great. What do you have in mind?"

"Do you know the restaurant Flooka?" Loubna asked.

"I think so," I said. "It's in Jumeirah, at the Beach Resort, right?"

"That's right," Loubna said. "Let's talk over dinner. It will be a nice evening, not too hot, so we can sit outside on the balcony, where I can smoke. I'll make a reservation for nine p.m. if that's fine with you."

"Yes, that works, thank you. See you this evening."

Loubna's call significantly improved my mood. It seemed that I had managed to pass the first test after all. I called Khalid as soon as I got to my room.

"Hmm, interesting," Khalid mused after I finished the description of my interaction with Loubna. He then proceeded to break down Loubna's personality. He assessed her as someone of high intelligence and manipulation skills, who knew how to mesmerize others not because it felt gratifying to be admired or desired but because it allowed her to distract her targets and disguise her true interests and intentions. Khalid warned me again not to fall for her charms and never to lose sight of my real goal, which was to coax Loubna into guiding me in Anas's direction.

I told him that he was being a little dramatic and overly suspicious, that he was overthinking the entire situation and perhaps also romanticizing Loubna's Mata Hari charisma.

"Perhaps," Khalid said. "Just do me a favor. Pay attention to Loubna's appearance this evening. If she shows up in the same or a similar attire as the one she was wearing during your first meeting at The Address, I'm probably wrong and just seeing ghosts everywhere. But if she shows up with a completely different outfit, sending completely different signals, keep my words in mind. It means that she has reassessed you and made a deliberate decision to switch her facade in order to get what she wants."

I ARRIVED AT Flooka a few minutes before nine. A reservation for two had indeed been made in the name of Madame Loubna, and the waiter walked me to our table on the balcony. The evening was exquisite, a slight breeze was blowing from the beach, and the reflection of the moon was glistening in the sea. Despite the idyllic setting, or perhaps because of it, I felt out of place. The picturesque, romantic scenery stood in stark contrast to the reason behind my visit to Dubai. I kept thinking about Paul Blocher. Was he still alive? If so, how badly had he suffered? I could not stop my mind from racing to my own children and wondering whether I would always be able to keep them safe.

Loubna arrived at quarter to ten. Her appearance could not have been more different from earlier at The Address. Instead of the silky Armani business outfit with the plunging neckline, she was now wearing a plain, modest summer dress. Instead of the high stiletto heels, she had on ballet flats. Instead of the extravagant, wavy curls, her hair was tied in a simple ponytail. She looked like a completely different person, though no less stunning. Good old Khalid. I never should have doubted him.

Two waiters, like an honor guard, walked her through the restaurant to our table, and every single male patron turned around and followed her with his eyes. Only then did I realize that she was the only woman in the restaurant. It was as if a Hollywood star were visiting death row at a maximum security prison.

"So sorry I'm a little late," Loubna said with a sheepish smile as she sat down. She leaned over to air-kiss me on the cheek, and I smelled the unmistakable fragrance of Chanel No. 5. It was the only giveaway that her attire was not quite as nonchalant as the simple dress and flat shoes might suggest. Chanel No. 5 was never a random choice.

"No problem," I said. "I was enjoying the beautiful view of the sea. By the way, I don't see much of a difference between the hungry eyes at The Address and the way the men are looking at you here."

Loubna smiled. "You're right. But actually, it was the thirsty ears that had me worried at The Address, more than the hungry eyes. Just too many curious listeners in that place. You know who was at the table next to us at The Address? Mohammed Hamsho, a Syrian businessman who is very close to the regime. A real creep. In fact, he is related to the Assads by marriage. And yesterday I bumped into Rafiq Shehadeh there, you know, the Syrian general in military intelligence. Not exactly an enjoyable encounter. Very bad men, all of them."

I considered asking Loubna why she kept on going to The Address if so many evil men frequented that place, but I held my tongue.

"Anyhow, it has been a long day, time to relax," she continued as she lit a cigarette. Three waiters rushed to the table with ashtrays.

"Well, you certainly seem to have everyone's attention here," I said.

"Don't worry about them, they're just little boys," Loubna said as she exhaled the smoke. "I'm all yours tonight."

I had to think of Khalid's words. Loubna's flirtatious, slightly exaggerated intimacy showed me that the game had begun. It was time for me to find out what Loubna was trying to get out of this encounter. I was about to move the conversation in the direction of Anas when she suddenly rose. The abruptness reminded me of her precipitous exit earlier at The Address. Perhaps this time she really had changed her mind and concluded that a conversation with me was just not worth her time.

"I'm starving," she said. "All I've had today is coffee and cigarettes. Let's go pick the fish and order a few things, what do you say?"

I was relieved that she had decided to stay but dreaded the walk back through the restaurant to the fish tanks at the entrance, knowing that all the guests' eyes would follow Loubna's every step. Loubna seemed to notice my discomfort and took my hand.

"We might as well have some fun," she said mischievously. "If they think that I am with you, it will drive them even crazier. And they'll respect you."

She was right. The stares at Loubna were even greedier than upon her grand entrance, and I noticed some approving, even admiring nods in my direction. At the fish tank, she scanned the fish on display with an expert eye, then chose quickly and decisively.

"Tonight only the *halwayo* looks fresh," she said as we walked back to the balcony, all the eyes still following us. "It's a delicious fish, only eats algae, very clean, unlike these dogs here. Besides, it's mating season for some of those other Omani fish they have here, so they will not taste as tender as usual."

Once we were seated, we ordered a few appetizers and some wine, and Loubna lit another cigarette.

"I hope you don't mind if I smoke."

"Not at all, just like with your last cigarette," I said.

Loubna smiled and exhaled the smoke right in my face. Just then, her phone rang. She looked at the caller's name on the display, smiled, and switched off the phone. "As I said, I'm all yours tonight."

We spent the next hour enjoying the food and talking about the war in Syria and life in Dubai, a city Loubna seemed to loathe. "This place takes hypocrisy to new highs—or lows, depending on how you look at it. Here, it's not enough that people lie when they say they will call you tomorrow—no, they need to add God into the mix to make the lie complete. If you ever hear *bukra inshallah*, you can be one hundred percent sure that you will never hear back from that person. It's a promise *not* to do something. The kiss of death, delivered straight from God."

The waiters came to clear our table and refill our wineglasses. Loubna leaned back in her chair and lit another cigarette.

"You see, Daniel," she finally continued in a gloomy tone, "I know full well that people everywhere are false and dirty. It's just that the dirt here is a little closer to the surface than in other places. And there seems to be a little more of it." Suddenly her face brightened. "Let's talk about happier things."

"Such as?"

"Such as how you can help me get out of Dubai."

There it was, the angle that Khalid had expected. It was time to find out more specifically what Loubna wanted from me. "What do you have in mind?" I asked.

Loubna scrutinized every single person in the vicinity before responding. "Well, how should I put it, I am a Syrian woman in Dubai, here by the grace and at the mercy of some local sponsors.* Locals with voracious appetites, mind you. The higher up, the more voracious, all

---

* Foreigners seeking to establish and maintain a business in the United Arab Emirates are required to have local Emirati agents and nominee shareholders, referred to as sponsors. The fees for these sponsorship arrangements vary, and they can trigger resentment in excessive cases where they resemble a shakedown for protection money designed to benefit a few privileged locals rather than reasonably regulated registration requirements.

the way to the Sheikhs and their gatekeepers.* This can be good for business when channeled correctly, but that's not the business I want to be in, and besides, it's not exactly super helpful for my personal life. It is a lonely existence, ducking the ravenous eyes and eluding all those grimy hands and sticky fingers. It's time to plan my departure."

"So how can I help?"

"I was told by my friend in Damascus that you have good relationships with some governments," Loubna said in a sultry, seductive voice. "I would be so very grateful if you could put some of those relationships to good use and help me get a residence and a passport. Or two," she added with a coy smile. By the time she finished her sentence, her face was close to mine, and I was, once again, struck by her overpowering perfume.

How to reply? I had to keep Loubna motivated yet avoid raising expectations, all while trying to get information on Anas and at the same time not insulting her intelligence. There was no way to reconcile all these objectives, so I decided to play it straight.

"Look, Loubna," I started after a big sip of wine. "Let's get right to the point. After everything you've said about Dubai and the people here, I assume you don't mind a little frank talk. No games, no teasing. You tell me what you want, I tell you what I want. Deal?"

Loubna's expression changed dramatically. Gone was the playfulness; she was suddenly all business. She put out her cigarette, folded her arms, and again moved up close to my face. "Deal. I've told you what I want. I need your help to get out of here. I need to find a legal way to establish residence in Europe. Preferably in the UK or Germany. And none of that low-grade Malta stuff. Something respectable, please. I don't think I will

---

* Most sheikhs in the Gulf have one or several trusted people who are constantly in their company. These "gatekeepers" spend more time with the sheikhs than with their own families, and among their many functions is the total control of who may gain access to the sheikhs—the key to all success and well-being in the Gulf. They are often childhood friends from other prominent local families and remain with the same sheikh for the duration of their lives.

qualify for asylum, so let's look at investor visas. And from there, a path to citizenship. That's what I want. Frank enough for you?"

I was looking at cold eyes. My turn now to lay down my cards. "Yes, straight enough for me. So let me tell you what I want from you in return. I would like you to connect me to your ex-husband."

Loubna did not flinch. "What do you want from that scumbag?" she asked in a flat tone that did not reveal any emotion in spite of her harsh words. Her scent, on the other hand, did reveal her emotion. Gone was the Chanel No. 5. What I smelled now was very different. It was a rancid scent, like milk that had gone sour. I knew it well—it was a signal of deep-seated anger. The mere mention of her ex-husband Anas seemed to have triggered her rage.

"He seems to have some information I need," I answered.

"What kind of information?"

"Information about a person who has gone missing in Syria."

"A Westerner?" Loubna asked.

"Yes."

"Someone Anas knows?"

"I believe so," I said. "At some point, they were seen together. Now this other man has disappeared, and I would like to ask Anas for his help in locating him."

Loubna laughed. "Anas does not help people. 'Help' is not in his vocabulary. If you want to get anything from him, you'd better be ready to offer up something in return. A trade is your best option with that man."

"Just as between us, I suppose," I let slip.

Loubna smiled. "Sometimes honesty is overrated, Daniel. But yes, if you insist, just as between us."

I was disappointed in myself for not controlling my acerbic tongue. Loubna was right, sometimes honesty was overrated.

She seemed to read my thoughts. "It's okay, Daniel, I won't hold it against you. And it is a refreshing change from everything else in this place. I'll tell you where you can find Anas, but don't forget—he's a bad person who keeps really bad company. You'd better come prepared."

"I understand." After the Sheikh and Bassel in Beirut, Loubna now was the third person to warn that Anas was evil.

"He splits his time between Syria, Dubai, and Riyadh, with occasional stopovers in Beirut and Amman. I don't know where he is these days, but when he's in Dubai, he spends almost every evening in one of the restaurants at Le Méridien near the airport."

"Every evening at the same restaurant?" I asked. "He must like the food there."

"Actually, the food is not bad at Casa Mia, but that's not the reason he sits there."

"It's not?"

"No. He sits at a table outside the restaurant, because from there he has a perfect, unimpeded view of everyone entering and leaving the bar next door."

"What happens at the bar next door?" I asked.

Loubna did not answer immediately. She lit another cigarette and closed her eyes. Wrinkles appeared on a ridge at the center of her pristine forehead. "Jules Bar is where some ugly things happen," she said. "Some very ugly things."

Loubna slowly finished her cigarette, sipped her wine, lit another cigarette, and added, "That bar is *jahannam*. The first gate of hell. It is where the souls are snatched out of women."

I was about to ask Loubna a question about this Jules Bar, but she waved me off. Clearly, she did not want to discuss this any further. She remained steeped in her thoughts.

"Why don't we leave," I suggested, and asked the waiter to bring me the bill. "We can continue this conversation another time."

As soon as I had paid, Loubna stood up, walked to the entrance, and then down the stairs to the ground floor. Strangely, none of the guests who had been mesmerized by her earlier that evening were paying any attention to our exit. We had become invisible. We walked in silence through the foyer of the building. At the front steps, Loubna signaled for her driver to approach the curb. When he didn't start the car immediately, she snapped her fingers and loudly clapped her hands twice. Five seconds later, he was in front of us and jumped out of the car to open the doors.

"Come, Daniel, I'll give you a ride. My driver will drop me off at my home, which is just a few minutes away from here, and then take you to your hotel."

"Thank you, Loubna," I said, "but I am happy to take a taxi. No need to inconvenience yourself."

"There's no inconvenience to me, just to my driver. And I pay him to be inconvenienced." Loubna smiled. It was her first smile since before I had asked about Anas.

We got in her car and rode in silence. As we pulled up to a large house in Jumeirah, Loubna turned to me with a peculiar expression. "Why don't you join me for a drink in my home?" she asked.

"I don't think that's a very good idea," I answered. "It has been a long day and an enjoyable evening. Let's leave it at that."

Loubna gave me a long, hard look. "Every other man would have leapt as soon as I uttered the first three words of my invitation. You're different. I like that. Please sit with me in the garden, and I will tell you what you need to know about Anas. You don't even have to enter the house. My driver will wait here, and you are free to leave whenever you wish. How does that sound?"

NINE

LOUBNA PUNCHED IN the code to open the gate. Two housekeepers came running, but Loubna waved them off. She motioned for me to take a seat in one of the garden lounge chairs, and disappeared into the house. The garden was beautiful, full of flowers and fruit trees. The sweet smell of jasmine permeated the air. A few minutes later, Loubna came out barefoot, dressed in jeans and a tank top, holding a bottle of red wine and an ashtray.

"This garden is my refuge," she said as she poured the wine. "Damask roses and jasmine, to remind me of the Syria that once was. The scents and flavors of my childhood."

We sat for a few moments, appreciating the calm in the middle of the night. The bright lights of Dubai, the fancy sports cars speeding on Sheikh Zayed Road, the loud parties and the trendy nightclubs—they all seemed so far away.

"You have shown remarkable restraint this evening," Loubna finally began. "I respect that."

"Thank you." I was not sure whether she meant restraint as it related to her or to Anas.

Loubna lit a cigarette. "I promised to tell you about Anas, and I like to keep my promises," she said, slowly exhaling the smoke. "Anas is evil incarnate. Don't you ever forget that! There is not a single person who comes in contact with him—woman or man, child or adult, Arab or Westerner, Moslem, Christian, Jew, anyone—who stays clean. Anas is like a virus that infects every person around him."

Her phone rang. She answered and took a few steps away so that I could not hear the conversation. I pulled out my phone, switched it to flight mode, and tapped record. I placed the phone on the small coffee table by my side. Ten minutes later, Loubna returned.

"I'm so sorry, Daniel, it was my sister from Syria. There has been heavy fighting this evening in Daraya, and my sister and her family can hear the bombs from their apartment in Damascus. Her children crawl under their beds every time those booms start. They are completely traumatized. Usually they have some advance warning before the bombings, because, by some strange coincidence, the internet happens to go down. But this time, this did not happen, and the children woke up screaming when their house shook from the vibrations."

"Why doesn't your sister join you here in Dubai?" I asked.

"She was here with her husband and the three kids," Loubna said with a sigh. "They tried it for four months. But she hated life in Dubai. She could never get used to the people, to the weather, to the food. She kept saying that everything here is artificial, from the apples to the smiles. So they returned to Syria. Imagine how much a person must dislike a place in order to prefer life in that Syrian nightmare."

"Hard to fathom," I said.

"Anyway, where were we? Yes, Anas. I met him when I was fifteen years old. He was eighteen. It was an arranged marriage. I didn't have much say in the matter, and it didn't even occur to me to object—not that it would have made a difference. That's how these things were done those days, and that's how they're still done today. Our wedding night was pure agony. He was really violent and hurt me terribly. It was my first rape."

Loubna seemed to be fighting back tears. I didn't move, not even to pick up the glass of wine. A dog barked on the street, then another joined in. A car drove past the house, and the barking faded away. I thought of Khalid's barking dog metaphor—would I know what to do once I caught up with Anas, or would I be as clueless as the barking dog who catches the car?

Loubna looked at me and continued. "Our daughter was conceived that night. She turned fifteen a few months ago—the same age I was when I married Anas. Imagine that! My little girl. If nothing else, it proves that something wonderful can spring from something awful."

"What is your daughter's name?" I asked.

"You know, Anas was already wicked at birth," she said after a long pause, ignoring my question. "He was the first son after five girls, so his parents treated him like the arrival of the Mahdi, or the Second Coming, whichever you prefer."

"I don't really have a preference," I said quietly.

Again, Loubna paid no attention to my remark. "Anas was born in Hama, a couple of years before that famous slaughter, when Hafez al-Assad and his brother Rifaat butchered tens of thousands of innocent people."

"You mean the 1982 massacre?" I asked.

Loubna nodded. "Yes, that one, when the army hunted down the Brotherhood and killed everyone like dogs. Anas's family managed to flee just hours before the siege and the shelling of the city began. Apparently a cousin of his mother was serving in an artillery unit of the Syrian army and tipped them off. The family made their way to Damascus. But by then, at age two, Anas's character was already formed. He had been spoiled rotten by his parents from the moment he was born—actually already before that, after some magic healer told his mother that she would give birth to a boy. He was a bully as a little kid, and he has remained a bully ever since. He used to torture animals, light the tails of cats and dogs on fire, put firecrackers in the mouths of frogs and watch them explode—those kind of delightful things. Then, when he outgrew animals, he unleashed that same charm on women. He kept count of his scores—a virgin counted double, so he really pounced on the young girls. I'm telling you, Daniel, this person is pure evil."

Two men were suddenly talking in hushed voices in front of Loubna's gate. Her eyes widened alertly, and she put her finger to her mouth to keep me quiet. As I froze, Loubna grabbed the serrated fruit knife and tiptoed toward the gate. Immediately, the voices outside began to fade, and two car doors opened and closed. A moment later, an engine started and a car drove off. Loubna stood at the gate for another thirty seconds before returning to our lounge chairs. She lit a cigarette and refilled our wineglasses.

Once she had leaned back and exhaled the smoke, I asked, "When did you leave Anas?"

"The first time I left him was after our son was killed," she said.

I remembered that Jamil had referred to Anas as Abu Sayid—father of Sayid—when we were having breakfast at Bassel's kiosk in Beirut. Had Loubna not just mentioned their son, I would have probably forgotten this piece of information—something that might come in handy once I met Anas. "What happened?" I asked carefully.

Loubna had an anguished look on her face. "Our son was killed on his tenth birthday," she said, wiping the tears from her eyes. "He was playing in front of the house when a motorcycle drove by and sprayed him with bullets. I ran out immediately and saw the motorcycle speed away. Sayid died in my arms."

Loubna looked up at the moonlit sky for a long time. "I received a call that night from someone Anas used to work for. He told me that this is what happens to people who steal from him. It turns out that Anas used to be one of this mobster's main couriers."

"Courier of what?" I asked.

"Drugs. Different drugs, though mainly a drug called Captagon. You've probably never heard of it. It has become the drug of choice in Syria and also one of the country's main export items. Another one of Syria's invaluable contributions to humanity. Anas was such a successful courier that some people called him Captain Captagon, and others,

Captagon Anas. Anas being Anas, he was actually proud of these nick-
names. He developed a habit of referring to himself in the third person
as 'Mr. Big Time.' He started taking Captagon himself, sometimes as a
cocktail with steroids when he worked out. He became huge, all muscles.
The worst was the rage that these drugs would cause. Once, he broke my
nose; another time, my jaw. Another time, four ribs."

"I'm so sorry."

Loubna stared at me with steely eyes. It felt like she was looking right
through me. "It was either me or the children." The cigarette fell out of
her hand and landed on her other arm with a sizzle. Loubna picked it
up without flinching and put it out in the ashtray. "So one day Anas,
Mr. Big Time, decided to branch out on his own and start his personal
Captagon business. Turns out that Anas's ex-boss didn't appreciate this
independent, entrepreneurial spirit in his former protégé. Market share
is everything when it comes to the drug business, and these guys had
no intention of giving up market share to Anas, even if he was the great
Captain Captagon. So they sent a message in the form of bullets. But you
know what was the worst part?"

I shook my head.

"The worst part was what that man said at the end of the call. Before
he hung up, he told me not to be sad, that I had enjoyed my son for ten
good years. A good round number, so why be greedy and ask for more?
Then he laughed and hung up."

Loubna's eyes welled up again. "No mother should have to bury her
child. And yet this is all we Syrians do—bury our children."

I waited a moment to give Loubna time to compose herself. "So how
did Anas deal with this? After all, it was his son, too."

"Anas was not there when it happened," Loubna said icily. "He was in
the north, near the Turkish border. I called him immediately, of course.
He was quiet at first, then said something I will never forget, and I will
never forgive him for."

"What did he say?" I inquired when Loubna didn't continue.

"He told me that he was tied up with some urgent business and that I should not wait for him for the funeral." Loubna lit another cigarette. "Imagine that. A father who chooses business over his son's funeral. And not just any business. Drug business. That was the moment when Anas died for me and when I decided to leave him. I buried my son the next day, and the day after that my daughter and I were on a flight to Dubai."

"Why Dubai?" I asked.

"I had an uncle, the husband of my mother's sister, who lived here. He had moved to the UAE many years ago, after my aunt died. I called him, and he arranged for us to come here. He knew some muckety-muck in Abu Dhabi, who took care of all the formalities."

"So that was that, the end of your time with Anas?" I asked, remembering what Michigan Mike had told me in Amman, how Loubna had caught Anas with her sister.

"Unfortunately not," Loubna said. "Two weeks after I arrived here, Anas showed up. At first, he was all contrite, told me how much he missed us, and asked me to come back to Syria with him. When I told him that it was over between us, and that our—sorry, *my*—daughter and I would not return to Syria, his demeanor changed completely. He threatened to beat the shit out of me, as only he can put it, and then he said something that still sends chills down my spine." Loubna paused and took a deep breath. "He said that he had buried one child, so another wouldn't matter."

My expression must have reflected the shock I felt, because Loubna nodded. "Imagine that. A father threatening a mother with the death of their child. Animals don't do that. Even monsters don't do that."

"How did you react?" I asked.

"At first, I was angry. I told him that he did not scare me, and besides, his words were asinine, since he had not actually bothered to show up in order to bury our son. I told him what I thought of him. But deep inside,

I knew who I was dealing with. This person has no soul, no feelings, no love. I could not continue to live my life the way I was, in Dubai or in Syria, and expect him to leave me and my daughter alone. So I decided to play along until some moment would arrive when I could get away from him once and for all."

Loubna's phone rang again. She looked at the number and once more moved away so that she could speak out of earshot. Even though I could not make out her words, her pleading tone was unmistakable. She seemed to be repeating the same sentence in a loop, a high-pitch sound followed several times by a low growl. Ten minutes later, she returned with two tall glasses of water.

"Perhaps some water to dilute the wine? I'm starting to feel it," Loubna said as she sat down.

"Thank you," I said, gratefully gulping down the water. "So how was life with Anas after you resolved to play along?"

"At the time, Anas was expanding his trade routes in the region, and he decided to make Dubai his hub. He paid off some people at the airport—you know, police officers, customs officials, some of the guys in charge of cargo—and everything was running smoothly for him. I stayed in Dubai with my daughter while he spent about one week a month here. He had his routine—two weeks in Syria, one week in Dubai, one week in Riyadh. Every once in a while, he would carve a few days out of the Syria schedule to meet his homeboys in Amman or Beirut, but he never changed the Dubai and Riyadh pattern."

"Did you get involved in his business?" I asked cautiously.

Loubna gave me a long, cold stare. "What do you mean?" she finally asked in a frosty tone.

"I mean, the way you describe Anas, it would seem difficult to 'play along' without being part of what he does. You yourself said that he dirties every person who comes in contact with him, infects them like a virus."

Loubna cast her eyes down at her lap. "You're right," she said. "Yes, the same thing happened to me, I'm afraid. It's not something I'm proud of. But it is what it is. Anas really does ruin everyone he touches. Literally and figuratively." When Loubna looked up, the look in her eyes was softer. "I suppose you should have this information if you're going to meet Anas and try to extract from him the information you are looking for."

"I appreciate that," I said.

"As I told you, Anas runs a huge Captagon ring in Syria. He has far surpassed the group he deserted—you know, the people who killed our son. He controls most of the Syrian labs, and he orchestrates the main trade routes within the country and out of the country, to Turkey and Greece in one direction and all the way to Morocco in the other. He has the Mediterranean covered. In Syria, everyone is using Captagon, both for personal consumption and as a currency.

"Government militias use this drug, as do opposition groups, including Nusra and those ISIS freaks. They all see themselves as holy warriors, committing atrocities in the name of some god they know nothing about. These animals have managed to turn 'Allahu Akbar' into dirty words, into some perverse code for killing innocent people. Whatever. Anas once told me that throughout history fighters have used drugs to fuel their rage and boost their courage. He spoke in glowing terms of the Nazis and how they had their own amphetamines in World War II, their very own type of crystal meth. Even Hitler, Anas's personal role model."

I remembered my conversation with Huby in New York. The parallels between Loubna's description of Captagon, with its huge impact on the war in Syria, and the way Huby's French intelligence buddy had related it were uncanny. But while it was the job of an intelligence officer to know all the minutiae of the drug trade, I did not expect such a remarkable grasp of details from Loubna—unless, of course, she was more involved in the operations than she let on.

"You sure seem to know quite a bit about this." I sounded more sardonic than I had intended.

She grimaced. "When you are married to one of the region's biggest drug dealers, who has apparently also become one of the great drug historians, you tend to pick up a few tidbits. By osmosis, of course."

"Of course."

"Believe me, I had nothing to do with the drugs," Loubna said, evidently picking up on my suspicions. "It was the girls. The girls," she repeated with a sigh. "That's where Anas got me involved."

"The girls? I don't understand. What do you mean?"

She refilled our wineglasses and took a big sip. "Okay. Here's the deal. In addition to the drugs, Anas and his group have been placing young girls."

"Placing young girls?"

Loubna was clearly uncomfortable. "It all started with the drugs. One of Anas's ingenious innovations is to combine prostitution with drug distribution. Whenever and wherever he would ship the girls, first just within Syria and then increasingly to the Gulf, he would place the drugs with them, and sometimes in them."

"So the girls became unwitting drug couriers?"

"Exactly," Loubna said. "Remember, his specialty is young girls. They don't have a clue what is going on. All they know, if they know anything at all, is that Anas and his men promised the girls' parents to get them work as domestic help so that they can send money back home to their families. How ironic, considering that this is just like what happened to my own mother once upon a time. Anyway, the parents hand over their daughters in desperation, and those who refuse get some very persuasive encouragement from Anas's thugs. Most of the girls are shipped out of the country, though some are used in trades within Syria. Everything is bartered—drugs, girls, weapons, prisoners, anything. Even heating oil or diesel. And everyone trades with everyone. Suddenly, there are no enemies, only businessmen with one common goal: to make money. The government deals with Nusra and ISIS, just like these groups deal with the government. If they were as good at politics as they are at business, this war would have ended long ago and Syria would be the most prosperous and the happiest nation on earth. But you see, the war is the best thing that ever happened to people like Anas and the bigwigs on all sides of the war. It has made them immensely rich."

While I was eager to hear more, I also dreaded the information Loubna might give me. "You mentioned prisoners. They are also traded?" I tried to sound as casual as possible.

"Yes," Loubna replied. "Though their value is usually lower than that of a girl, especially a virgin. Unless we are dealing with a CIA agent or a Mossad spy or someone like that. Hunting trophies do come at a premium, after all. You see, the problem with prisoners, especially Westerners, is that you have to keep them alive. That costs money and also exposes their captors and wardens, especially when they have to move them from one place to another. And remember, most Western governments have abandoned those who got caught in Syria, have washed their hands off these poor souls. The doctors, the journalists— they have been forgotten by their governments. What was the person you are looking for doing in Syria?"

"I don't know. He was not a journalist, not a doctor, not an aid worker, as far as I know."

"A nobody, then," Loubna remarked matter of factly. "In that case, he has very little value to whoever has him, if he is still alive. That's too bad. Some of the others, especially the well-known journalists, had some value. And once their value as prisoners diminished, or if they became too much of a burden, there was always the shock value of their execution."

I was quiet. Her words did not inspire confidence that Paul Blocher might still be alive.

Loubna must have sensed my distress. "Don't torment yourself until you get some more facts. You never know in Syria. Everything there is completely unpredictable. Except that things usually don't end well," she added with a cruel sneer. "So I guess that makes it predictable after all, doesn't it? I suppose gruesome endings are the one thing we can safely predict in Syria."

"Thanks," I said. "I feel much better now."

"Look, Daniel," she said cuttingly, "I understand how you're feeling. We Syrians have cornered the market on despair. But nothing compares to what these poor girls go through. They are ripped away from their families, often no older than twelve, and either sold to fighters as sex slaves or exported to the Gulf as child prostitutes. Though prostitutes are usually paid, aren't they? These poor girls never see one dollar. It's nothing but slavery."

Loubna was very upset, and I waited a moment for her to collect herself. "So how do you fit in?" I asked.

She lit another cigarette and took a few drags. "As I told you, it's nothing I'm proud of. A few weeks after Anas had tracked us down here in Dubai, he started to send young Syrian girls my way. He told me in no uncertain terms that he expected me to take care of them for three days while he decided whether to deploy them in Dubai or ship them off to Riyadh, his other main market. I was responsible for them during this holding period. They were put up in an apartment near the airport, and I made sure they had enough food and water."

"Sounds like a prison," I said.

"Of course it was a prison." Loubna glared at me. "The first thing that would happen after their arrival was a thorough medical checkup, during which the girls would also be relieved of the drugs they had unknowingly smuggled to Dubai. Armed guards would come and haul away the drugs, sometimes in armored vehicles, sometimes in more creative vessels such as ambulances. After those three days, Anas's guys would show up and take the girls. That was the last time I would see them. But there were always new girls arriving—fresh meat, as Anas liked to say—to replenish the supply."

Neither of us spoke for a while. I struggled to process the horror that Loubna had just described to me. I thought of my own children, whose lives were so carefree and cheerful, and so very sheltered. Loubna's daughter had to be about as old as my own daughter. Her son would have been close to my son's age. I tried to come up with something to break this awkward, uncomfortable pause but was unable to utter a word.

"Is Anas still in your life?" I finally managed to ask.

"No, *alhamdulillah*."

"What happened?"

"It's a long story," Loubna said. "It's getting late, so I'll keep it short. We never formally divorced—Anas has refused to grant me a normal *talaq* divorce, so I'll go through a *qadi* and do the *khula* thing. Obviously, ever since I left him in Syria, I've not considered myself married to this monster for many years, so I never cared about his sleeping around, even with some of the girls he brought to Dubai. He no longer sleeps with the virgins—never ruin premium merchandise, as he puts it. But then, one day, he raped my younger sister here in my house."

I could tell that Loubna was fighting back her tears. She picked up the mobile phone that she had placed facedown on the table just minutes earlier. Suddenly that rancid scent returned, that same one I smelled earlier in the evening at Flooka, when I had asked her to connect me to Anas. And just like it had then, this odor obliterated all traces of her Chanel No. 5. This was not some slight annoyance at a bad memory. This was deep, visceral rage. I watched Loubna scroll through some photographs until she found what she was looking for. Without a word, she handed me her phone. I was paralyzed, horrified by the image of a young woman with a huge bloody bruise on her left cheek and the eye above it swollen shut. Her mouth was completely deformed, and most of the lower lip was covered in stitches that looked like oversized paper staples. Around her neck was an enormous hematoma with a deep purple-black hue. Judging by the depth and size of this bruise, Anas must have choked Loubna's sister half to death. I felt a wave of nausea come over me. The young woman's features were unrecognizable. All they screamed was pain and agony. Anas had beaten Loubna's sister to a pulp.

I put the phone facedown back on the table and saw that Loubna was observing me carefully. For a second, I thought I detected disdain in her expression—actually, more of a snarl—as she picked up the phone and scrolled through more photographs. A few moments later, she again handed me her phone. The picture showed her sister's wrists with deep red marks completely encircling them. They were the marks of Anas's hands. He must have applied incredible pressure, because each of his fingers had left a gaping imprint with defined contours. The marks reached from the woman's wrists all the way to her elbows. Anas's hands seemed to be gigantic.

I again placed Loubna's phone on the table, hoping that I would not have to look at any more pictures of Anas's sadistic assault. Loubna gave me an odd, almost condescending, look and, to my chagrin, again picked up her phone, scrolled to another photograph, and passed it to me. I was now looking at an image of two huge black hematomas but could not figure out to which part of her sister's body they belonged. I was sick to my stomach and couldn't bear to see any more pictures of this brutal, depraved rape.

Loubna watched me squirm uncomfortably as I laid the phone back on the table. She placed her hands on the inside of her thighs and moved them up toward her groin. It took me a moment to realize that she was signaling the location of those last hematomas on her sister's body—the location where Anas had beaten and abused her little sister as he raped her. My own body started to shiver, and I crossed my arms in a wrap as

I tried to stop these tremors. I shut my eyes and tried to unremember the awful images.

When I opened them, Loubna was staring right at me. "I wanted to go to the police," she explained, "but my sister begged me not to do it, because Anas had threatened to kill her if she said anything to anyone. Actually, he terrorized her as only he can. Do you want to know what he told her?"

I shook my head reflexively. I had seen and heard enough.

"Well, I'll tell you anyway." Loubna's face was hard, impassive. "You need to know these things about Anas. You must be prepared should you ever meet him. He actually told my sister that if she said anything to anyone, she would end up in a garbage dump bleeding to death because he would cut out her vagina and rent it to those clients who could not afford a whole girl. Actually, he used a different word for vagina, but I'll spare you. And then, when her vagina was all used up and no longer of any value to him, he would feed it to the first stray dog he saw on the street. That, Daniel, is the Anas you are trying to meet."

I sat there without moving. Despite sitting in Loubna's garden under the stars, I felt like my surroundings were closing in on me and that I was about to get crushed by the walls and the trees on all sides of the property. I realized that I was suffering an attack of claustrophobia—something I had never before experienced. I could hear Loubna call my name but was unable to respond. She finally pulled me out of my stupor by poking me sharply in the elbow. Only then did I notice that I had been holding my breath the entire time. I exhaled and slumped deeper into my chair. Loubna was nodding slowly in a rotating motion, like in some prayer trance, as if trying to expel the demons of these memories.

"I took my sister to the American Hospital and had to bribe the doctor so that she would not report the rape to the police. Then I changed the locks of the house, installed surveillance cameras, and hired armed guards."

"So that was when you broke off all ties to Anas?" I asked, trying to keep my composure and hide how much the pictures of her battered sister had shaken me up. If I fell apart in front of Loubna, she would lose all faith in my ability to get her and her daughter out of Dubai to start a new life in Europe.

Loubna grabbed the bottle of wine, saw it was empty, and placed it back on the table with a sigh. "Not quite. But it sure did harden my determination, and I started to hatch my escape plan. About one month earlier, I had met one of the sheikhs in Abu Dhabi and had figured out a way to let Anas believe that this sheikh was on my side and would not hesitate to destroy Anas if I asked him to. It was just the illusion of a threat."

"Did it work?"

"I never got to try it out, because Anas found a way to sink to new lows before I was able to put my plan into action."

"What happened?"

"Without my knowledge, he picked up our daughter at school and brought her to the apartment with the Syrian girls. His plan was for her to assist in comforting the girls. Most of those girls could not stop sobbing, while the others would just sit there in catatonic shock. He thought that another young girl like our daughter would do the trick to help these girls get over their misery. Thankfully, it never came to that. She texted me from his car, and I immediately figured out where they were heading. By some lucky coincidence, I was sitting with this Abu Dhabi sheikh and his gatekeeper, who happens to be my main Emirati sponsor, when my daughter texted, and I asked him if he could help me out in an emergency.

"I was wearing a similar outfit as the one you saw me in yesterday at The Address, and it seems that my cleavage put the sheikh in a giving mood. He agreed to drive me in his car to where I needed to be. We arrived just as Anas was pulling up in his Range Rover. He completely froze when he saw me step out of the sheikh's car. The sheikh and two of his bodyguards got out of the car, too, as did the gatekeeper who arrived just behind us in his car. I asked them all to stay back and walked up to Anas. Pointing at the sheikh, who gave me a thumbs-up, I told Anas that if he wanted to survive his stay in Dubai, he should never approach me, my daughter, my sister, or anyone in my family again. There would be no more warnings. The next time, I said, I would *end* him."

"That was it?"

Loubna nodded. "That was it. No one messes with this particular sheikh. Anas may be the worst person in this world, but he is not dumb. I took my daughter by the hand, and we got into the sheikh's car. One of his bodyguards moved to the gatekeeper's car to make room for my daughter, and we drove off. The sheikh behaved like a gentleman and never asked a single question, never mentioned the episode. This was the last time I ever heard from Anas."

Just then, I heard the muezzin's cackling call for the Fajr prayer at a nearby mosque. I looked at my watch—five in the morning. We had talked all night, and not once had I moved or checked my watch.

"I think it's time for me to leave now," I said as I stood up. "Thank you for everything you've told me. I will never forget this night."

"I kept my end of the bargain," Loubna said as she gave me an air-kiss on the cheek. "Now it's your turn. Remember to keep your end of it. Get me and my daughter out of this cursed, wretched place."

"I will," I said. "Though moving you and your daughter out of Dubai will require quite a bit of planning. Not exactly what I would call a bargain."

"Neither is leading you to Anas." Loubna unlatched the gate. The driver was still sitting in the car and ran out immediately to open the door for me.

"Good luck," Loubna said. She did not wave as we drove off and stood there motionless until we had turned around the corner into the main road.

TEN

LOUBNA'S DRIVER DROPPED me off at the back entrance of the hotel. Despite the hour, there were a good number of people lingering in the parking area near the door. Most were decked out in snazzy party attire, their night of fun and entertainment nearing its end. Just an ordinary Dubai scene. A guard asked me whether I was staying in the hotel, then abruptly turned his attention to a woman who was trying to enter next to me and blocked her way.

"Is this lady with you, sir?" he asked. I shook my head, and he motioned with both hands for the woman to scamper.

"Sorry, sir," he said as he turned his attention back to me. "I had to stop this person. No professional women allowed in this hotel. Management is cracking down on this. Please proceed."

I had to smile. I thanked the guard for his vigilance and walked toward the elevators. As the elevator door opened, two scantily dressed women waltzed out. One of the women, who with her stiletto heels was considerably taller than I, looked at me suggestively and turned the palms of her hands in a questioning motion. "No thank you," I said as I walked past them into the elevator. Before the door closed, I could hear them laugh. Apparently the hotel's crackdown was not exactly as advertised. The forces of supply and demand were just too powerful.

Back in my room, I took a shower and got into bed, but after only a few minutes I knew that I had zero chance of falling asleep. The conversation with Loubna, and especially the images of her sister's violent rape, kept playing in my head. I got up and sent Khalid a text message. Instead of a reply, he called immediately.

"Don't you ever sleep?" I asked.

"I could ask you the same thing," Khalid said. "Besides, I had to get up for prayers. What's your excuse?"

He was right; insomnia was becoming the norm for me. "I just got back to the hotel. I spent the night with Loubna," I said, then quickly added, "Sorry, that came out wrong!"

Khalid laughed. "I told you to beware of Syrian women."

I recounted the conversation with Loubna to Khalid, everything from dinner at Flooka to the long wine-infused hours at her home. Khalid listened without interrupting. When I finished, he took a deep breath.

"I hope you've not bitten off more than you can chew, *habibi*," he said.

"What do you mean?" I asked. "Loubna told me where I can find Anas. Once I make contact, I'll try to find out what he knows about Paul Blocher, and then I'm out of here."

"Hmm, just like that?" Khalid asked in a sarcastic tone. "That's an excellent plan, just march up to him and ask him for the information. Or, even better, appeal to his conscience and his humanity. He seems to suffer from an abundance of both."

I knew that Khalid was right. My adrenaline could cause me to overestimate myself and discount some of the dangers that lurked in an interaction with Anas. Still, I demurred. "Come on, Khalid, I never said it would be easy. I have no illusions about the person I am dealing with. But I've got to do this, it's what I came to Dubai for—to find a path to Anas and, through him, to Paul Blocher."

"Just remember, you have to be prepared. Plan your work, and then work your plan. And trust me, you need a plan for when you'll be face-to-face with this guy, this vile specimen. This rapist. He comes from a different world, a world that is poles apart from ours. You and I, we believe that humans are great when they are good. Anas believes that he is great when he is bad. We might understand that with our intellect, but we are never really prepared for it."

Khalid's words felt dark and heavy.

"And another thing," Khalid went on. "You need to be ready for the possibility of a physical altercation. What someone like Anas lacks in kindness, he makes up for in thuggery. I don't think you should go by yourself."

I considered Khalid's suggestion. My worry was that any of my friends in Dubai would want to know more about the reason for this trip to the Méridien compound and about the person I was hoping to meet. It was the same reason I had decided not to inform Fouad al-Zayat before my trip to Beirut to meet the Sheikh, even though it would have been reassuring to have a safety plan in case things went wrong. My friends were just a little too curious.

"I'll think about it," I lied.

"I know you better than that, Daniel," Khalid shot back. "But if you must go by yourself, make sure you always sit with your back to the wall."

"What do you mean?"

"At their core, people like Anas are cowards. They never fight straight up. Their specialty is beating up on the defenseless and stabbing in the back. If your back is protected by the wall, you can just focus on not being defenseless."

Khalid had a gift of reducing things to their bare essentials. I promised to keep his advice in mind. By now, it was seven-thirty in the morning and I was too wired to sleep, so I got dressed and went up to the lounge, where I was welcomed by Dalia with a high five. Charles poured the coffee, and Dev greeted me with a warm smile. Dalia brought the orange-carrot juice, and a few minutes later Kevin walked to my table holding a delicious-smelling plate of *akoori*, Indian scrambled eggs. "Compliments of the chef," he said with a grin. Dev waved shyly from behind the counter.

I looked out the window and saw the Méridien hotel complex in the Garhoud area in the distance, on the way to the airport. I thought about Khalid's admonition to go there with a plan. Traffic on Sheikh Zayed Road was light at this time of day, and I decided to head to the Méridien to scout it out. I finished my breakfast, took the elevator to the ground floor, and asked the doorman to hail a taxi. The air was surprisingly fresh, almost cool. Fifteen minutes later, I was there. I walked around the hotel and the outdoor restaurant area for a few minutes. Everything was closed, and the only people in sight were the cleaning crews in their overalls. At Casa Mia, I sat at one of the empty tables and tried to get a sense of the restaurants and bars in the immediate vicinity. Loubna was right—from that spot I had an excellent view of the entrance to Jules Bar next door. One table in particular provided the perfect angle to see and not be seen, and I made a mental note to look for Anas in that very spot. Just as I was about to leave, a Méridien employee came up to me and asked if everything was okay. I nodded and tried to walk past him.

"The action over there starts in the evening." He pointed at Jules Bar.

I played dumb. "What kind of action?"

"Oh, you know, sir, those loose girls," he said. "The ladies of the night."

"Thanks," I said as I left. I wondered whether anything about my demeanor had betrayed my interest in that bar or whether the hotel employee had simply assumed that any man in the area could only be there for one reason. Either way, I resolved to be more alert and surreptitious when I came back in the evening. Before I left, I walked one more time around the hotel and jotted down the various entrances and exits in my notebook. Next, I went inside and explored the lobby and reception areas in order to familiarize myself with possible corners where I could remain undetected in case things got ugly. Part of the exercise was also to memorize the spots that had good cell phone reception so that I wouldn't find myself unable to reach an emergency contact. Ten months earlier, at a different hotel in Dubai just a few miles from the Méridien, I had agreed to meet an unverified middleman who claimed to be in possession of valuable evidence on the whereabouts of a missing journalist. I regretted my decision the moment he showed up with two thugs and vowed never again to expose myself to such threatening situations without at least mapping out an escape route or hiding place.

Once I was satisfied with my reconnaissance expedition, I got into a taxi and returned to my hotel.

As soon as I opened the door to my room, I dropped into bed and fell asleep instantaneously. I dreamed that I was sitting on a swing that was going higher and higher. Just as I was about to reach the highest point, I jumped off. Instead of landing, I kept on flying, at first upward, then down, ever faster and faster. I woke up drenched in sweat. I had not had this dream in over forty years, since I was a little boy. I used to compete with other kids in the neighborhood by jumping off a swing and seeing who could fly the farthest. I often won and had the bloody knees and elbows to show for it, which had more to do with my recklessness than with any particular mastery of the laws of aerodynamics. In those days, I would frequently have this nightmare of jumping off a swing and never landing. At some point, I figured out that I had the nightmare only on the days that I played this game with my friends. Eventually, I stopped playing the game and the nightmares stopped, too.

I changed out of my soaked T-shirt and went back to sleep. I found myself in the same dream again, jumping off the swing, at first soaring high, and then plunging lower and lower into the abyss. As I fell, I saw my own face. But suddenly the face morphed into the face of Paul Blocher, his eyes wide open in horror. I woke up with a scream and a cramp in the calf of my left leg. I leaped out of bed and stepped with all my weight on my left foot until the cramp was gone. My left leg was stiff and the calf hard as a rock. I limped to the bathroom and splashed my face with cold water. It was time to end the sleep experiment for the day.

As soon as my calf recovered, I went for a swim in the hotel pool, and after thirty minutes I felt rejuvenated and clear minded. I got out of the water just as my phone vibrated. It was my prosecutor friend—the same one I had invoked to help out Dev in the hotel lounge—who asked me to let him know when I would next be in Dubai. Even though the timing of his call was eerily on point, I knew that it was a coincidence, as he usually called me every few days for a quick hello and, also, given his suspicious and slightly possessive nature, in order to make sure that I wouldn't even think of coming to Dubai without letting him know. Feeling busted, I sheepishly told him that I had just arrived. There was no way to wiggle out of seeing him, and we agreed to meet for a late lunch.

We met at Sammach in a Jumeirah mall, his regular lunch venue, which was usually pretty empty at this time of day. The only other patrons at the restaurant were a large Kuwaiti family. The father was dressed in a blue kandura that revealed his Kuwaiti identity: it was tight fitting, with a one-button band collar and cuff links, as opposed to the loose-fitting local Emirati kanduras with a long tassel and neither collar nor cuff links. He was seated at the head of a large table, with four children on each side. His wife was sitting next to the youngest child at the other end of the table. She was dressed in a beautiful black abaya with embroidered golden flowers and a matching headscarf; it was unusual for a Kuwaiti woman not to have her face veiled in public either by a niqab or an all-concealing burka, but sometimes a woman would take liberties in Dubai that she wouldn't take in another, more conservative place in the Gulf. The eldest son had just returned from a shopping expedition at the sports apparel store in the mall with two pairs of brand-new Nike Air Jordan sneakers. One of the shoes had apparently fallen out of his bag on the walk from the store to the restaurant, and the mother was berating the teenager for his carelessness. She ordered him to retrace his route and try to find the missing shoe. As the boy stood up, the father reached into his pocket, handed his son a one-thousand-dirham note, and told him to buy another pair of sneakers rather than waste his time looking for the missing shoe. The boy took off with a wide, triumphant grin, and his mother shook her head.

"Typical Kuwaitis," my prosecutor friend sneered. "Too much money. They are so wasteful, I can't even watch." He then proceeded to order an enormous amount of food—way more than he and I could possibly eat.

Over delicious meze dishes and fresh fish, I alluded, as inconspicuously as I could, to an interesting meeting that I was looking forward to that evening and mentioned that I might have to ask him for a favor if things got more than just interesting. He was gracious and offered his support, no matter what. I could tell that his senses were heightened and that he would in all likelihood come looking for me if he did not hear from me in the course of the night. I was grateful for his backing and relieved to have this contingency plan with such a reliable friend. After ending our meal as always with *dibs el-kharroob*, thick carob molasses with some added tahini—the world's tastiest and most effective digestif—we walked together to the mall exit. Outside, a young laborer ran up to us. My prosecutor friend searched his pockets, gave the man fifty dirhams, and thanked him for watching his car. Only then did I realize that he had left the engine and the air conditioner running throughout our meal so that the car would be nice and cool when he returned. I hailed a taxi, and we parted with a cordial embrace.

AROUND SEVEN, AFTER the sun had set, I got into another taxi and drove back to the Méridien compound. On the way, my anxiety started to build. What if I was too late and had missed Anas again, just as in Amman? Every day that passed, even every hour, could mean a tragic turn of events for Paul Blocher, assuming he was still alive. Time was not my friend, as Khalid had told me.

The outdoor scene at the Méridien was very different from the early-morning hours. The restaurants were bustling with people, and raucous music was blasting from many directions. I went straight to Casa Mia. I noticed that the table I had identified in the morning as Anas's ideal lookout was empty. None of the guests in the restaurant looked even remotely like Anas. I sat down at the table just next to the one where I had speculated I might find Anas and ordered a mineral water. When the waiter returned with the water, I asked him whether he knew a fellow called Anas. I could tell from his expression that he was genuinely drawing a blank, so I described Anas to him based on the pictures Mike had shown me as well as Loubna's account. Immediately, the waiter's face lit up. "Oh, you mean Mr. Big Time," he said with a wide grin. "No, I have not seen him in a few days. Why don't you have a look in the bar over there." He pointed to Jules Bar. "And if you see him, tell him we miss him here. He's our best tipper!"

I promised to pass on the message, paid for the water, and made my way to Jules Bar. I tried to avoid two men who were walking straight at me. One of them tumbled into my side just as I was passing them. He appeared drunk and cursed me out loudly in English with a strong Australian accent, flicking his cigarette at my chest. I was about to pick it up and flick it right back at him but stopped myself. I could hear their full-throated laughter and swearing as I continued toward Jules Bar. I was almost at the entrance when the door flung open, and another drunk man came tumbling out. He appeared to be in his fifties and was holding on to a woman who looked no older than eighteen. He bumped into me with a loud, alcohol-reeking burp and stumbled on with his young companion.

Inside, the techno beat was ear shattering, and on the stage a live band was getting ready to perform. The scene was mind blowing. I felt like I had landed on some crazy planet. For every man present, there were at least five women of all ethnicities. Within seconds, two young Chinese women came up to me. "One thousand dirham for the night," the first one said. Before I even had a chance to shake my head, the second one added, "Discount for two. Just for you." I walked past them without replying. I tried to find a good spot near the side wall, where I would be able to look for Anas without being accosted. But after a few steps, another woman grabbed my sleeve. "How about it? Why we don't disappear from here?" she asked in broken English with a heavy Hungarian accent. This place had the charm of a grungy meat market next to a slaughterhouse. Even if Anas happened to be here, it would be impossible to approach him and talk to him. Better to wait outside or at Casa Mia.

As I turned toward the exit, a man crossed my path. He was dragging a young woman, a girl really, by her hair, cursing at her and telling her to shut up. She was screaming in agony. He was holding a bottle of beer in the other hand and threatened to break it over her head if she did not stop bawling. But the girl's earsplitting screams continued; they had a low pitch, coming deep from her gut, then turning into groans that sounded like rolling thunder. Her childlike features were distorted by pain. As the man loosened his grip briefly, the girl's groans turned into quiet whimpers, but as soon as he yanked her again with full force, the anguished screams were back. Strangely, nobody seemed to pay attention, and everyone in the vicinity moved casually aside to clear his path.

I tapped the man on the shoulder. "Let go of her, please," I said.

He looked at me with a stare of total disbelief, which immediately mutated into glowering rage. "Get the hell out of my way, asshole, or I'll fuck you up!"

"Let go of her. Now!" I demanded. A circle of people had quickly formed around us, expecting a spectacle.

The man let go of the girl and squared up. "You're going down, asshole!" he shouted, then swung his beer bottle at my face. I stepped into his swing, placing my right leg behind him as I struck him in the nose with the palm of my hand. It was a move I had practiced thousands of times in all those years of martial arts training, but that awful, familiar sensation of torn skin and crunched bones still triggered a sense of nausea, suppressed only by the rush of adrenaline.

The man fell backward and hit his head on the floor. Remarkably, he managed to hold on to the bottle of beer and keep it from shattering, even though he was now bleeding profusely. One of his companions bent down and helped him to his feet. His nose looked like it was broken, and he was bleeding from the back of his head. He was wobbling badly but still had the presence of mind to take a swig from his bottle, which he was still clutching in his hand. The girl was nowhere to be seen.

"What the fuck's your problem, asshole!" His words were slurred. "What's that bitch to you?"

"She's my daughter," I said, pushing past him. It was the first thing that came to my mind, possibly because I hadn't been able to stop thinking of my own daughter since the evening with Loubna. I was haunted by those poor Syrian girls who were taken from their homes by Anas and his gang. As soon as I uttered those words, the crowd parted like the Red Sea, and I hurried toward the door. I was just about to open it when two security guards intercepted me.

"Could you please come with us, sir?" one of them demanded.

"What for?" I asked.

"You've caused a scene here," he said. "We have to escort you out of this establishment."

I was incredulous. "*I've* caused a scene? Are you serious? Some man is hauling a young girl, who happens to look no older than fourteen, by her hair, threatening to break a bottle of beer over her head, and *I'm* the one you need to escort out of this establishment?"

"Sir, we don't make the rules. We just enforce them. Please come with us."

I walked out of the bar, flanked by the two security guards. Outside, one of the two turned to me with an apologetic look. "I'm really sorry, sir. We don't enjoy this either. But in that establishment, the men can do whatever they want with the girls. The client is king, as they say. You are free to go now."

I stared at the two guards for a moment, then turned away, shaking my head in disbelief. I walked toward the taxi area, exhaling deeply in an attempt to keep my adrenaline rush in check. This was not the time to connect with Anas. I needed to go back to my hotel to decompress.

There were two people in front of me in the taxi queue waiting, when I heard a breathless voice behind me. "Excuse me, sir, excuse me, sir."

I turned around and saw a girl, who looked no older than sixteen or seventeen, running up to me. She was petite, with long dark hair and large brown eyes, and was wearing a short denim skirt with a white sleeveless blouse. I had never seen her before and was not sure she was talking to me, so I pointed at myself and looked at her with a questioning expression. She nodded. "Excuse me, sir," she repeated as she reached me. "May I please talk to you for a moment?" Her Arabic was not a local Emirati dialect; I couldn't quite place her accent.

I was not in the mood for any more talk, but there was something sweet and gentle about this person, so I stepped out of the queue, allowing the couple behind me to move up. "How can I help you?" I asked her.

"Please forgive me for chasing you down. I saw what you did in the bar," she said. "I hope you don't mind if I ask you, but why did you help that girl?"

"Like I said to that man, she's my daughter," I said tersely, in the hope of quickly ending the conversation.

"I'm sorry, sir, but I don't think she's your daughter."

"Why not?" I asked, taken aback at being challenged by this stranger.

"Because she's my sister. And I think I'd know if you were our father." She spoke without a trace of sarcasm.

I was speechless. I now recognized the strong resemblance to the girl at the bar, even though her sister's face had been distorted by pain. "I'm sorry," I said. "You are right. I'm not her father and not your father either."

She smiled. "Actually, I just wanted to thank you for coming to my sister's defense."

I felt a warm gush of pride and joy overcome me. "It's all right," I said, embarrassed that I was blushing.

"I hope you don't mind the question, but may I please ask you why you did that? Why did you intervene?" she asked.

"I don't know," I said. "Instinct, I suppose. I just didn't like what that guy was doing to your sister. I wasn't really thinking it through. I just reacted."

"I understand," she said. "Thank you. It was nice meeting you."

She started to walk away. I went to the back of the taxi queue and watched her. She had a bounce in her step, like a child skipping at a playground. Suddenly she stopped dead in her tracks, turned around, and came back toward me.

"Please don't take this the wrong way, but reacting without thinking can get you killed in a place like that," she said in a serious voice.

"I'll take that under advisement." Right away, I wished I could have retracted my flippant words.

"I'm sorry, sir," she said, looking at me with a disappointed expression. "It's just that there are some really bad people in Jules Bar. You don't look like someone who belongs there. It doesn't seem to be the proper kind of place for you."

"You're right," I said in a softer tone, trying to compensate for my earlier tartness.

"If I may ask," she said politely, "what were you doing there?"

"I was looking for someone."

"A friend?"

"Not really. It's not someone I've ever met before. I just know his name."

"What's his name?" she asked.

"Anas."

The girl stared at me in complete shock, as if she had seen a ghost. Gone was the warm, bright look in her eyes. They were suddenly filled with fear. "Anas?" she whispered. "What do you want from him? He is so evil that even the devil himself wants to have nothing to do with him. We call him Shaytan."

"You know this man?" I asked.

She glanced at the people around us. "Is it okay if we talk somewhere else?" Her voice was hushed. We walked to the side of the building where we found a bench.

"What is your name?" I asked her as we sat down.

"Reem."

For some reason, Reem instantly reminded me of little Aliya at the green house in Beirut. "Pleased to meet you, Reem. I am Daniel."

"Nice to meet you, Mr. Daniel," Reem said.

"Please, just call me Daniel."

"Okay, Mr. Daniel," she said, then corrected herself. "I mean Daniel."

"Tell me, Reem, if you don't mind the question, how old are you?"

"I am seventeen," she said. "And my sister Samar is almost fifteen."

Fifteen. The same age as my daughter.

"So, Reem, do you know this Anas?"

Reem looked down at her hands, which were folded in her lap. She did not answer immediately. "I do," she finally said in a whisper. "He owns me and my sister."

"What do you mean, he owns you?" I asked wearily.

"He brought us here from Syria. We are from Qatana, a city in the south of Syria. His men took us from our family and brought us to Dubai."

The expression on Reem's face was pure sadness, and I shuddered as I remembered Loubna's description of the Syrian girls she used to tend to after they were shipped to Dubai. Hearing Loubna talk about it had been awful, but nothing compared to the gut-wrenching experience of being face-to-face with someone who had suffered this fate herself.

"How does he own you?" I asked again. "Why did your parents let you and your sister leave with him? Did he threaten them?"

"This evil man does not threaten. He just kills," Reem said in a detached manner. "I don't know why my parents told us to go with his men. On the day they came for us, our mother was crying in the kitchen. Our uncle tried to calm her down, but she would not stop. Our father walked us to their car, and he also had tears in his eyes. He kept telling us to do everything these men asked us to do because they owned us now. When he kissed me goodbye, he told me to take care of Samar. The last thing he said was that we would meet again in heaven."

There was nothing I could say to relieve the despair of Reem's words. She pulled a tissue out of the front pocket of her skirt and blew her nose. "When we arrived in Dubai, Shaytan, I mean Anas, did something that I can never forgive him for. Samar had been holding on to her little doll since we were taken from our home in Qatana. It was her one and only toy, her pretend baby and her security blanket all in one. Our parents had given it to her for her fifth birthday, and she had never let go of it since. She slept with the doll, she took it to school, she ate with it—everything. The doll was dirty and tattered, but it was so real for Samar that the rest of us also considered it to be part of the family. My mother even knitted clothes for the doll—an outfit for summer and one for the cold winters.

"As soon as we got here, we were forced to line up in front of Anas. He immediately zeroed in on the doll in Samar's hand. He marched straight up to her and told her what a nice doll she had. Samar's eyes lit up. Anas asked her if he could play with it for a moment. Samar, who always shared her possessions with others, handed her doll to Anas. Anas took it from her and repeated how pretty this doll was. Then, without any warning, he ripped off the doll's head. He laughed in this really loud and disgusting way that I will never forget and threw the head of the doll far away. Then he handed the headless stump back to Samar. I cannot describe to you the look on Samar's face. And I don't even want to relive it by talking about it. There are no words. All life drained from my little sister. That was when she became faceless, like her doll and the rest of us."

"My goodness," I mumbled.

"Anas then told the other girls to listen up," Reem continued. "He said that what we had just seen would happen to any one of us who dared to disobey him or who tried to run away. 'This will happen to any bitch who tries to pimp the pimp'—those were his words. Then he said that he would kill us in this world, and after that he would follow us to hell and kill us again. He told us that from now on, we were his. His property. He said that we were no longer girls but prostitutes, nothing but bodies, fresh meat, which we would remain until our last day. I had no idea what he meant. Until my first time. Then I understood."

Reem blew her nose again and took a deep breath. "Shaytan sent me on to Riyadh. Samar stayed here. Separating from my sister was even worse than being taken from my parents. I will never forget the look in Samar's eyes when they told us that I was going to Riyadh. It was this look of horror, of betrayal, of abandonment. It was the look of death, and I died right there with her."

I felt tears welling up in my eyes. "I'm so sorry," I said in a barely audible whisper. It was hard to speak.

"It's okay," Reem said. "I'm back with my sister now. Though everything else is still the same. The same daily nightmare."

I suddenly was aware that Reem and I had been sitting on the bench for a while, and I worried that someone, perhaps Anas or one of his goons, would come looking for her. "Tell me, Reem, is it okay for you to be talking to me, to be gone this long?" I asked.

"Don't worry, they will think I'm with a client. When I get back to Jules, I will tell them that the client changed his mind and left without paying. This will cover the time we've been here—not more and not less."

"I see. So, if you don't mind talking about it, what happened in Riyadh?"

"Riyadh was a three-month rotation," Reem answered matter of factly. "It's different from what we have to do here in Dubai. In Dubai . . . well, I suppose you got a pretty good sense of our job here based on what you just saw in Jules. In Riyadh, it was a little different. There, they used us as a form of payment. We were treated more like money, like a currency."

"I don't understand. What do you mean, like a currency?"

A group of three men passed us. They looked at me, then at Reem, then again at me with dirty, knowing grins. She waited until they were out of earshot. "What I mean is that we were used as payment, as barter, for other services. For example, if a businessman stayed in a nice hotel, he would ask for two or three of us to go with him. When it was time to pay for the bill—the hotel bill, an expensive meal, or some other debt— we would be offered up instead of cash. We then had to go with the man who was owed the money. There were different prices for different packages."

"Different packages?"

"Yes. Let's say two girls are offered together. If they are not related, it's called the Basic Package. If they are sisters, it's called the Bonus Package."

"Sisters?" I asked incredulously.

"Yes," Reem replied. "It is not uncommon for sisters to be offered together. I don't know why they separated me from Samar and kept her in Dubai. Anas must have had his reasons."

"How awful!"

"Yes. So sisters are the Bonus Package. The next level up is virgins. If both girls are virgins, it's called the Jackpot. It's very expensive. Probably because it's only a one-time use. Though I think Anas and his guys lie about it—they seem to be recycling some of the Jackpot girls. And then you have the highest level, the most expensive package. That's when the girls are virgins *and* sisters. That package is called Jannah—heaven, or paradise. You know, the place where seventy-two virgins are offered to the martyrs. I guess this is good practice for the virgins," she added sardonically.

I just shook my head. It was beyond awful. Unfathomable.

"Anyway, Daniel, now that you know my story, and now that you know what Shaytan—what Anas—does for a living, why do you want to meet him?"

I decided to tell Reem about Paul Blocher and, in broad terms, about the path that had led me to Anas. She listened intently. "I'm afraid you missed him today. He was here yesterday, then flew to Riyadh. From what I was told, he is expected back tomorrow. Would you like me to let you know when he shows up?"

I nodded. I gave her my mobile phone number.

"He usually comes here around eight in the evening, so expect a message any time after that," Reem said as she got up. "If you don't mind, could you stay seated for a few moments while I walk back to Jules? It's better for us not to be seen together."

"Of course. Thank you for everything you've told me, and thank you for letting me know when Anas arrives. Are you sure it's safe for you to contact me?"

Reem nodded. "One more thing." She sat down again. "As you must realize by now, Shaytan is a very bad person. A monster. He will not just hand you the information about this missing person. You cannot appeal to his feelings, because he doesn't have any. Or at least not the kind of feelings that will make him help you. Before you meet him, you may want to think of something you can offer him, something he will want, or at least something that will make him curious. Or maybe even something that will make him scared, though that might not be easy. He's really evil and extremely cruel. But he's not stupid."

Reem's depiction of Anas matched what Loubna had told me, and her advice to think of something I could offer him for the information I was seeking was so similar to Khalid's counsel. Reem got up a second time. "Thank you again for helping my sister. It was the first nice thing anyone has done for us since we left Syria."

I remained seated on the bench for twenty minutes after she left. My mind went completely numb, unable to process the depravity that Reem had described. I pulled out my notebook and wrote down everything she had told me. When I stood up, my body felt like it weighed four hundred pounds. I shuffled over to the taxi queue. Five minutes later, I was in the back of a taxi, stuck in terrible gridlock.

"Sorry for the bad traffic. You like rock music, sir?" the friendly driver asked.

I nodded. The young driver fiddled with his phone. Suddenly a loud rock song filled the taxi, a song I had not listened to in many years: Frank Zappa's "Broken Hearts Are for Assholes!" As the driver sang along with gusto, I had to laugh at the absurdity of it all. "This is a great song, sir, great song!" he shouted over the blaring music. "And you know the best part, sir? The name of the album is *Sheik Yerbouti*! Get it? *Sheik Yerbouti*—shake your booty!" He laughed so hard that he accelerated inadvertently and had to brake violently in order to avoid crashing into the car in front of us. I had not buckled my seatbelt, and my head hit the back of the seat in front of me. But I was too drained to register any pain.

Back in the hotel, I sent a short text message to my prosecutor friend to let him know that the interesting meeting I had mentioned to him over lunch had been postponed, probably by a day, so that he would not worry and come looking for me. Then I sent Khalid a message on Skype, informing him of a possible meeting with Anas the next evening.

As I climbed into bed, I couldn't stop thinking about Reem and Samar. One day they are innocent children playing with their friends, and the next day they are tormented sex slaves, existing at the mercy of evil, rapacious men. I could not fathom how Reem found the courage and the strength to survive, let alone the ability to maintain her composure. How would she ever again interact with any man without feeling hatred and revulsion?

Eventually, I fell asleep. I dreamed of a train ride in Switzerland that kept making stops at increasingly remote alpine stations. At each station, I tried to find a chocolate bar I was suddenly craving but was told by a cascade of the main characters in my search for Paul Blocher— Huby, Khalid, Jamil, Imad, Mike, Loubna, Reem, and finally Anas—that it wasn't available. By the time I had reached Anas at the last station, I had shrunk to a tiny gnome-like figure standing before this giant who dismissed me with a caustic smirk.

I woke up on my back completely paralyzed with my mouth wide open, chin raised high, compressing the nape of my neck. I felt a searing pain in the back of my skull, as if the valves intended to allow the blood to leave my head were all blocked. Only after ten minutes of deep belly breathing was I slowly able to move my fingers, then my hands, arms, and gradually the rest of my body. As the pain subsided, I felt forlorn. Every detail of the dream remained unusually vivid, except that I was unable to recapture the sounds of the voices. I sat up and scribbled the dream on the nightstand notepad before it had a chance to evaporate. The dream made me think of "Spanish Train" by the Irish songwriter Chris de Burgh, a song I used to love as a teenager but had not heard in decades. It was about God and the devil playing poker for the souls of the dead. God has a good hand—a straight—and is confident he will win but doesn't notice how the devil slips another ace from beneath his cloak. Again and again, the devil keeps cheating and winning more souls, while God, well, "he's just doing his best."

I was suddenly overcome with a gloomy premonition that Paul Blocher was no longer alive. I tried to convince myself that the dream wasn't based on any facts and could only have been an expression of my own anxieties rather than some oracle about Paul's fate. It didn't work. I began questioning whether Paul was actually a good person, someone worth all this effort and sacrifice by people who didn't even know him. After all, the information Huby had received from his French intelligence friend could well mean that Paul himself might have been involved in the Captagon trade or some other unsavory dealings. But then I remembered the two pictures of Paul that Huby had shown me. In them, Paul's eyes had the look of an innocent, melancholy person. And I remembered the tender words Huby had used to describe Paul. I knew that I needed to continue my search and that the honor code of "leave no one behind," which had been instilled in me during my military service, applied just as much to unfortunate wanderers as it did to wounded warriors. But I could not escape the wretched grief I was feeling.

Thankfully, I had a meeting scheduled that morning with my close friend Salem from Abu Dhabi, which I hoped would distract me and calm me down. Salem was a retired official in the UAE government who had remained a confidant of several members of Abu Dhabi's ruling family and was still responsible for special projects. He was assisting the foundation in coordinating our efforts in Libya with the powers that be in the Gulf so that our wires would not get crossed in an unforeseen clash of interests and initiatives. Our Libyan initiative was similar to Project Bistar in Syria a few years earlier, and Salem's insights were extremely useful in identifying which Libyan candidates could play a role in the future rebuilding of the country.

Salem had proven to be invaluable in our past interactions because he had the ability to bypass the mighty gatekeepers of his country's rulers and connect us directly with the right decision makers, thus sparing us endless frustrations and inefficiencies that were so often part of the Gulf

experience. He had been the first person to predict—at a time when no
one else uttered this opinion—that Sheikh Mohammed bin Zayed, the
crown prince of the United Arab Emirates, would end up being the most
powerful and influential ruler in the Gulf, ahead of the Saudi king, the
emir of Qatar, and the crown prince's own half brother, Sheikh Khalifa
bin Zayed, the president and nominal head of the United Arab Emirates.*

We had agreed to meet at nine in the morning at my hotel, and at five
to nine, true to form, Salem called to let me know that he was five minutes away. I stepped out of the elevator just as he was walking into the
lobby. After a cordial embrace, we found a quiet corner. Salem updated
me on the particular individuals and militias that Abu Dhabi wished to
support and on the increasing efforts to prevent the rise of an Islamist
party in Libya. We parted after one hour and agreed to meet again the
following month in Abu Dhabi.

Back in my room, I spent the rest of the morning trying to think of
a plan that would draw Anas into a discussion and entice him to tell me
what had happened to Paul. All kinds of ideas were spinning through
my brain faster than I could process them. I needed to write down my
thoughts in order to unscramble the chaos in my head. I took six sheets
of the hotel's stationery and plastered them on the wall with some tape.

I thought of Reem's parting words and came up with three possible approaches. Plan A: Need. I had to think of something Anas would
desire, something valuable enough that he would be willing to exchange
Paul's information for this thing he needed. Plan B: Curiosity. What
could pique his interest to the point where he would volunteer Paul's

---

* Salem was also the only person who had predicted within a year of the death of the Saudi king
Abdullah bin Abdulaziz in 2015 that Sheikh Mohammed bin Zayed would play a major role in
the ascent of the ambitious Saudi crown prince Mohammed bin Salman by leveraging his deep
relationships in Washington, DC, both directly and through the ubiquitous, copiously networked
Emirati ambassador to the United States, Yousef Al Otaiba. Sheikh Mohammed bin Zayed's
prodding of President Trump, and even more effectively of his son-in-law, Jared Kushner, toward
an enthusiastic embrace of Prince Mohammed bin Salman proved to be decisive for the young Saudi
crown prince's rise to unchecked power.

information just to learn what I had to tell him? Plan C: Fear. How could I threaten Anas or insinuate the possibility of a threat to the point where he would agree to tell me what had happened to Paul?

I ordered a large pot of coffee and started to map out the three plans in all their tactical minutiae—two wall-mounted pages for each plan. Plan A was both the easiest and the hardest. The easiest, because it seemed clear what someone like Anas desired—money and power. The hardest, because I was unable to offer him money for Paul, and in any event I could not possibly put enough money on the table to entice someone like Anas, who was accustomed to astronomical profits. Moreover, the things that Anas was likely to covet would probably all be so repulsive that I would not be able to maintain the illusion of the end justifying the means. I tried to come up with other things Anas might want, but every single thing I could think of was either not enough of a tease or so hideous that I saw no tolerable way to offer it up.

Plan B was tricky. I tried to envisage some intriguing piece of information that would be valuable to Anas, something I knew only through confidential and privileged sources. Details of the recent crackdown of the Turkish authorities on drug dealers in the Kurdish areas, which would force Anas and his partners to find new distribution routes for his Captagon? New anti–money laundering rules that could complicate his cash-only business, even though the ingenuity of his cash couriers and their willing accomplices in many reputable banks turned this idea into a dud? Recent strikes by French intelligence against certain criminal Syrian rings around Rifaat al-Assad, which forced some of the principal players even further into the shadows? A conversation currently taking place between the leadership in Abu Dhabi and Riyadh about human trafficking and its potential for international embarrassment? The tracing of a prisoner-for-drugs swap between Syrian Alawi militias and an Islamist group? The problem was that all these pieces of information came with two significant handicaps: First, these nuggets were off the record. I had received them from Emirati and French government contacts during the search for two other missing persons and the nego-tiations over proof of life, and I would not be able to give Anas more than a superficial tease. Second, Anas was too shrewd to give me any-thing of value in exchange for just the tease of new information. Besides, even if I managed to obtain the approval to give him more than simply a hint of the valuable information, I knew that Anas was the last person on earth who deserved to know more about things that could be a threat to his evil empire. Again, as much as I tried, I could not convince myself that the end justified the means.

So I was down to Plan C. How does one put the fear of God into someone who does not believe in God? Or into someone who might believe in God but who does not fear him? Or, hardest of all, into some-one who thinks he *is* God? After meeting Loubna, I had been convinced that Anas was a very bad person, hard as nails, rotten to the core. But after listening to Reem, I now believed that he was evil incarnate. Shaytan. How do you intimidate the devil? Or, to borrow from Mike's favorite movie, *The Usual Suspects*, how do you convince the devil that he does not exist? It would take more than showing up with a prominent local, the way Loubna had done with her Abu Dhabi sheikh. I thought of my prosecutor friend, who was fearless, but concluded that he would not have the authority and the firepower to move the needle. I wondered whether I should call another good friend, a local poet who was close to one of the Emirati rulers, or perhaps involve Salem, who had unfettered access to the country's head of intelligence.* But in the back of my mind I kept remembering how Khalid had once described the voracious

---

* When I called Salem two weeks later to schedule our follow-up meeting in Abu Dhabi for the foundation's Libya project, he asked me whether I still might need his assistance in that unpleasant matter in Dubai. Noticing my confusion, he told me that I had mentioned something cryptic that morning when he had come to meet me in my hotel. I have no recollection of having mentioned anything to him about possibly requiring his help with Anas, but the fact that he brought it up means that I must have said or hinted at something.

appetite that some of the potentates in the region had for very young women, just like other powerful men all over the world, because it was, as Khalid put it, about power more than about sex. I had to consider the possibility that some of these mighty fellows could be Anas's clients—hardly an ideal starting point to exert pressure on him.

I thought of a Turkish intelligence officer I knew, who was in charge of tracking and intercepting unwanted incursions from Syria, but his focus was the prevention of terrorist attacks, not the disruption of drug and prostitution trade routes. He once told me that he couldn't care less about the drug dealers and the pimps, because they would never blow themselves up in a crowd—all around bad for business, as he put it. So I could not expect anything useful from him. I went through all my other contacts who could possibly pose a threat to Anas and his empire, but those who possessed the necessary capacity and perhaps even the willingness to help would only do so if I briefed them in full detail in person on what I was trying to accomplish—something I did not have the time to do. Anas would supposedly be returning to Dubai today, and my encounter with him could not be postponed. It was now or never. Plan C was no good either.

I was terribly discouraged. The six sheets of paper on the wall were covered with my scribbles, yet not one of my three plans appeared viable, and it seemed that I had turned into that car-chasing, barking dog Khalid had warned me about. Now that I was actually close to meeting Anas, I didn't have a blueprint for how to wring out information from him on Paul Blocher. I leaned back on the couch and closed my eyes.

Just moments after dozing off, I was awakened by my phone's ping. It was a text message from a local number I did not recognize: "A back in d, at cm this pm. R." Reem had kept her word and just let me know that Anas was back in Dubai and would be at Casa Mia this evening.

This was it! Finally! Reem's message was the jolt I needed. It immediately sharpened my mind. I suddenly understood that I had been thinking about this whole thing the wrong way. It was embarrassing how backassed my assumptions had been, how flawed my reasoning. Instead of starting with Anas's weaknesses and reverse-engineering my approach from there, I had stupidly been trying to map out three plans in a vacuum, without taking the traits of this particular adversary into account. Of course Anas would not be susceptible to my meager temptations, and of course he could not be intimidated into surrendering the information I was seeking. That was not who he was. He was the king in his kingdom, with all the means and the arsenal to preserve his power. I had missed the clues Loubna and Reem had given me. This was a person who referred to himself as Mr. Big Time, who exercised fanatically to build humungous muscles, which—as Loubna told me full of contempt—he constantly admired by flexing them in front of any mirror he could find, even in his reflection on the lenses of a stranger's sunglasses. This was not a person I could threaten. This was a person I had to flatter. A person whose ego could perhaps be stroked to the point of getting him to puff himself up and brag about his accomplishments. I thought of the Sheikh's despised "fist of flattery" that Jamil had explained to me when we were traveling from Istanbul to Beirut. *This* was the trap I needed to set.

I SPENT THE next hour refining my new approach, which became clearer with every passing minute. I had to allow for the possibility that Anas had been warned about me by Mike or, more likely, by Imad, and there was a remote chance that he might have been made aware of my interaction with Loubna by some of the curious Syrian ears she was trying to elude. There also was a chance that last night's waiter at Casa Mia had told Anas that some bald fellow had inquired about him or that Anas had heard about the brawl at Jules Bar. Most worryingly, he might know about my conversation with Reem.

There was nothing I could do at this point to mitigate those risks other than to be vigilant for early signs of hostility by Anas, which would have to trigger my immediate exit. Despite all the contingency planning, I knew that it was impossible to anticipate each and every situation, and it was plausible that the evening could turn unpleasant or even dangerous. For a moment, I thought about calling home to hear the voices of my wife and children. But I fretted that it would weaken my resolve and my concentration and that they would pick up on my anxiety and worry. Instead, I grabbed another piece of paper and wrote down all the different scenarios, with my action and reaction options under each bullet point. Once I felt comfortable with the full set of plots and their permutations, I went for a swim to clear my mind. For once, this dog would know what to do when he caught up with the car.

ELEVEN

AT SEVEN IN the evening, I made my way back to the Méridien complex. Traffic was fairly heavy, and it took the taxi over half an hour to get there. Casa Mia was still empty when I arrived, and thankfully a different waiter was working this evening's shift. I sat down at the table next to what I suspected would be Anas's table and ordered a coffee. I pulled out my phone, switched it to flight mode, and started recording. I had sent my prosecutor friend and Khalid text messages from my Swiss phone, asking them to contact me on that number if they needed to reach me in an emergency. Khalid responded by wishing me good luck.

About twenty minutes later, a group of three loud men came out of Jules Bar and walked toward the restaurant. I immediately spotted Anas in the middle. He was the largest and the loudest of the bunch, clearly the alpha male. There was something cartoonish about his appearance. He was enormous and broad shouldered and stood at about six foot five. His bulging muscles were even bigger than they appeared in Khalid's and Mike's pictures. He had a large moonlike face and a crew cut that revealed ugly waves of thick wrinkles on his skull, evoking a Shar Pei in a permanent state of fury. His face had a dark red, almost purple, hue, compounding the impression of a person with a really bad temper.

The waiter greeted Anas as if he were the Messiah and to my relief led him to the table next to mine. As he approached, I was hit by an overwhelming stench of aftershave—syrupy with an unpleasant tinge of sweat. Anas must have emptied an entire bottle on his face and body before leaving for this night out. He told his two companions to scamper. Apparently he was expecting some other friends to join him later and did not want these two around. When one of the men didn't leave instantly, Anas shouted at him to get lost, to take a long walk on a short pier. The few people in the vicinity laughed, except for the humiliated fellow who darted off.

Many times I had tried to visualize this moment in my head, and I had always assumed that my heart would be pounding when I finally came face-to-face with Anas. But to my own surprise, I was calm. It helped that I was mesmerized by Anas's gigantic, brutish appearance. He had the most powerful, titanic arms I had ever seen, and thick veins snaked around his biceps and forearm muscles like pythons around a massive tree trunk. His wrists seemed larger than my thighs, his neck wider than my shoulders. Even his fingers were huge and meaty, and I could not stop myself from imagining these hands around the neck and wrists of Loubna's sister as he raped her. There was something both repulsive and hypnotic about this enormous specimen of a man. He was wearing tight dirty-wash biker jeans and a black T-shirt with an incredibly bright spherical pattern in the center. I could not take my eyes off it, and Anas caught me staring.

"You like this T-shirt?" he asked in a loud, aggressive voice.

"Yes," I said. "I apologize for staring. I've never seen anything like it."

"You've got expensive taste," he laughed. "This T-shirt set me back a few hundred thousand dollars." His English seemed fluent, though with a scratchy, guttural intonation.

"You're kidding, right?"

"Not at all," he said proudly. "This is a Superlative Luxury shirt, very limited edition. Made entirely from renewable energy sources."

"How does that cost hundreds of thousands of dollars?" I was surprised that someone of Anas's ilk would be environmentally conscious enough to care about renewable energy.

"Aha!" Anas exclaimed triumphantly. "That's because I didn't mention the kicker. This bright pattern you've been staring at—any idea why it's so bright?"

I shook my head, trying hard to suppress my brooding ire at how Anas had been able to amass such ostentatious wealth.

"These are diamonds, man! Diamonds!" he said. "Sixteen beautiful white diamonds. That's why this T-shirt costs more than a Lamborghini!"

My jaw dropped, which seemed to egg Anas on. "See these jeans," he said as he stood up. "These are Balmain jeans. Two thousand bucks."

"They don't come with diamonds?" I asked.

Anas gave me a perplexed look, trying to figure out whether I was being facetious or serious. He broke into a wide grin when I smiled as innocuously as I could.

"That's a fantastic idea," he said with a laugh. "I'll suggest that to them. I'm sure they'll make a killing here in the Gulf with diamond-studded jeans. Do you want in on this?" He gestured magnanimously with both arms.

"It's all yours," I replied.

The jovial beginning to our conversation was reassuring. It meant either that Anas was not aware of my interactions with Mike, Imad, Loubna, and Reem or that he was aware of them but did not recognize me. Either way, I felt safe, for now.

"You're the shit, brother," Anas shouted, loud enough for everyone within a hundred feet to hear. "Come here, why don't you join me at my table?"

"Thanks, very kind of you," I said as I moved my coffee cup over to his table.

"What's that you're drinking?" Anas asked with a look of disgust. "Coffee after dark? What's up with that?" Turning to the waiter, he shouted, "What's a man got to do not to die of thirst in this joint? Kill someone?" The waiter raced over to our table. "Bring us a bottle of that wicked Barbaresco I had the other night. You know, that Nebbiolo

Costa Russi stuff. That was some good shit." Turning to me, Anas added, "You'll love that wine."

Before I could answer, his phone rang. He picked up and cursed at the person on the other end of the line in the vilest language imaginable, then slammed down the phone on the table. I half expected either the phone or the table to shatter. The waiter showed up with the bottle of wine and two large glasses. Anas smiled, as if nothing had happened. He tasted the wine and gave the waiter an approving thumbs up, which immediately mor- phed into an angry outburst when the waiter attempted to fill his glass.

"You fucking idiot!" Anas screamed. "Always pour the guest's glass first! Where are your manners?"

The waiter's face was ashen. His hands were shaking so violently that as he poured my glass, a drop spilled on my shirt. Anas looked at him with an expression of pure hatred. "Give me that!" he barked and grabbed the bottle. "Go back inside and cry your eyes out, you fucking pussy. And don't show your face until you've powdered your nose or done whatever else you fucking faggots do!"

The waiter stood there paralyzed after this volcanic eruption of anger. He moved only when Anas shouted "Go!" and stumbled into the adjoining table.

"Imbecile!" Anas said before turning to me with a wide grin. He filled his own glass before pouring mine. "So, where were we? Oh yeah, the jeans and the T-shirt. That was a great idea you had, stitching dia- monds on the jeans. We should name that line after you. So, what is your name?" he asked as he raised his glass.

I had been prepared for this question. "Dee," I answered, and raised my glass, too.

"Just Dee?" he asked.

"Dee Wolfson." We clinked our glasses. "What's yours?"

"Anas."

"Just Anas?"

"Just Anas," he said. "Though some people call me Anas BT."

"Beetee?"

"Yeah, BT. Short for Big Time." His grin showed impeccable, white teeth.

"Got it. Pleased to meet you, Anas."

We both took a sip of the wine. It was delicious, and I complimented him on his choice. He beamed in delight. "Some know how to pick 'em, some don't," he said. "I do." Anas leaned back in his chair and swirled the wine in his glass, then took another sip. "It's good to drink with someone who shares my appreciation for classy things." The diamonds on his T-shirt were sparkling as he spoke. "So, Dee, tell me, what brings you to Dubai?"

"I'm here for business and also to meet some friends."

"Friends? In Dubai?" He laughed. "There are no friends in Dubai. This is a place where everything is fake. The wealth, the success, the islands, the buildings, which are all empty. Everything. And of course the people. Even the beautiful women are fake."

"What do you mean?" I asked. "How are the women fake?"

"Dude, the hot chicks are all surgically enhanced. I mean, nothing about the good-looking ones is the way it was originally when they were rolled out of the factory, if you get my gist." Anas cracked himself up. "Look around you. See that girl walking by?" he asked pointing at a pretty woman passing near our table. "Some plastic surgeon got rich doing her up! Trust me, I know. I'm in the business. Besides, I used to be married to one of them."

"What do you mean?" I asked, hoping that he would volunteer some information on what it meant to be "in the business."

"My ex-wife," he said, missing my drift. "That bitch used to look completely different when I married her in Syria. But ever since she moved to Dubai, she's changed everything: new tits, new ass, new nose, new lips, tattooed eyebrows, slanted eyes, face-lift, forehead lift, tummy tuck, liposuction—Jesus, what has Loubna *not* done! Those green eyes all the men fall in love with—those are tinted contact lenses that hide very plain, brown eyes. Every body part of Loubna's is fake. That crazy bitch even removed a rib just to have a smaller waist. Given how much all this plastic surgery has cost me, I should own shares in those silicone plants and Botox labs! And now Loubna is banging some sheikh from Abu Dhabi. Good luck, is all I can say. To both of them. They deserve each other. Anyway, thank God I am better at my other business than I was at this investment."

"Sorry to hear about that."

"Don't be," Anas shot back. "Good riddance, is all I can say. He can have the bitch! She might be a hot piece of ass now—fake, but hot, I'll give her that—but some day, some time, this sheikh will also get tired of putting up with her shit. And that's when she'll be in for a rude mother-fucking awakening. You see, Dee, the dudes here get it right. When they are done with a woman, they throw her in the garbage and get a new model. And the good news is that the men can keep going forever. They are all hooked on Viagra. Nothing happens here without Viagra. Pfizer would have to close shop without the Gulf. This market never dries up. Not for Pfizer and not for me."

The waiter showed up carrying some plates with antipasto, carpaccio, and burrata. He placed them on the table without a word and left.

"See how easy this is?" Anas exclaimed triumphantly. "All you have to do is chew them out, and then they offer you all this food on the house. Guilt and fear are powerful motivators."

I didn't know what to say. How could I—without sounding sarcastic —compliment this man on his impressive ability to get free food while sporting a T-shirt worth hundreds of thousands of dollars? I ignored his triumph over the woeful waiter and tried instead to probe his strange Viagra comment. "What do you mean, the market never dries up for you?" I asked.

"Huh?"

"You said that the Viagra market never dries up. Not for Pfizer and not for you," I reminded him.

"Oh, that. You know, people will always try to procreate. It's what keeps the human race going."

"Sure, I get that," I said. "But how is that your market?"

Anas gave me a suspicious look. He seemed to be contemplating whether I was too nosy for my own good or just plain dense. Probably the latter, judging by the grin that followed his initial scowl. "Listen, brother," he said jovially. "I'm in the entertainment supply business. That means I supply the kind of entertainment the market asks for. Remember that seventies song, 'Sex & Drugs & Rock & Roll'?"

I nodded.

"Well, two out of three ain't too shabby, right?" Anas beamed triumphantly. "I'm not into the rock 'n roll part, but I've pretty much nailed the other two. And the good news is, the market on sex and drugs never seems to dry up. Demand always crushes supply, certainly in this part of the world. So all you've got to do is secure the supply, and you'll always be in a position to set your own price. All I need to do is control all forms of production, you know, the sources of production, and I'll have all the power."

"You and Karl Marx," I said.

"Who?" Anas asked.

"Forget it," I replied, regretting my snippy comment. "You were saying?"

"I was saying that I have what they crave." Anas did not miss a beat. "And they have what I crave—cash. A marriage made in heaven. What can I say—it's good to be me."

One of the two men who had accompanied Anas when he made his grand entry at Casa Mia came out of the restaurant, whispered something into Anas's ear, then looked at me. I froze. This was it, I was certain. I had just been busted, unmasked by Anas's aide. My worst fears had come true. My muscles tensed as I ran through the emergency escape route I had mapped out the previous day. I was going to move quickly toward the hotel and enter through a side door. Behind the front desk, there was a hidden space not visible from the lobby with good phone reception. I would make two calls—the first to my prosecutor friend and the second to my friend Michael, who lived in the apartment building right next to the Méridien. I had called Michael earlier to make sure he was home. I would ask him to swing by and pick me up with his car. If for any reason I could not reach him, I would wait for my prosecutor friend to come get me. And if even that failed, I would call the prosecutor's brother, who was a captain in the Dubai police force and was on duty that evening.

As I was about to stand up and make a dash for the bar in the open-air dining area, Anas motioned for me to remain seated. To my great surprise, his smile was warm and friendly, and I got the impression that he genuinely wanted me to stick around while he dealt with this irritating interruption. Despite the pit in my stomach, I stayed. Thankfully, Anas ignored me and instead kept shaking his head at his aide, who had started to sweat profusely. When he tried again to whisper something into Anas's ear, Anas grabbed the poor fellow by his shoulders and shook him violently. The man dropped his cell phone, and its screen cracked on the ground. Anas berated him even louder and pushed him into an empty chair. After showering the hapless aide with the ugliest invectives for five more minutes, Anas dismissed him and turned to me. His face was dark red with rage. I immediately picked up that familiar rancid scent I had smelled on Loubna at Flooka's and at her home when she recounted Anas's rape of her sister. After a few moments, it evaporated and his cloyingly sweet cologne was back. Gone also was the angry-red coloring of his face. Anas had calmed down.

I never found out what the aide had whispered into Anas's ear. I didn't care; all I felt was relief, as if I had been given a new lease on life. I was worried that I risked arousing Anas's suspicion if I went at him with more questions about his sex and drugs business, so I decided instead to cajole him into revealing more about himself. The challenge was how to accomplish this without Anas feeling interrogated—hopefully, plain old flattery would do the trick. I took a sip of wine for some liquid courage.

"Exquisite wine!" I said with an approving nod at the glass. "It does seem like it's good to be you. You look great! Do you live in the gym?"

Anas radiated pride. "Thanks," he said as he flexed his biceps. "Years of hard work, coupled with amazing genes. I suppose God rewards some of us more than others. Well deserved, I'd say, for the exemplary life I've led," he added with a dirty laugh.

My thoughts raced straight to Reem and Samar and Loubna's sister, and all the horrific things Loubna had told me.

"So, do you work out?" Anas asked, still basking in the glow of his own divine physique.

"I do, though it's hard to tell," I said. "I suppose I'm one of those God has skipped when handing out that muscle gene."

"Listen, Dee," Anas said, looking genuinely concerned. "If you eat properly and supplement your workouts with the proper vitamins, you, too, could look like me. Okay, maybe not like me"—he eyed me up and down—"but still pretty damn good and certainly better than your sad, scrawny self."

"Anas, your forearms are bigger than my thighs," I said. "I don't think there is any food or vitamin that can get me there, no matter how much I work out."

Anas laughed. "I never said it was easy. Listen, I eat six or seven meals a day, tons of protein—beef, chicken, salmon. In my gym in Damascus, I have someone serve me roast beef sandwiches on a tray while I work out, just like Ronnie Coleman in his Mr. Olympia years. I have to have those sandwiches, especially on chest and shoulder days. Those heavy presses are killers, and I need my red meat. No beef, no muscle."

"I don't eat meat," I confessed. "Maybe that explains it all."

Anas gave me a look of unadulterated disdain. "You don't eat meat? What are you, a vegetarian?" His tone dripped with contempt.

"Not quite," I replied in a meek attempt at salvaging my rapidly tanking reputation. "I do eat fish. A pescatarian, I suppose."

"More like a pussytarian!" Anas said, still disgusted by my unmanly food preferences. "Well, then, as I said, no beef, no muscle. But it's okay—there's room in this world for all kinds of people, even girlie men."

"So tell me, Anas," I said, trying to keep things moving, "aside from roast beef sandwiches, what else do you do to become this big? You mentioned vitamins. What kind of vitamins?"

"You know, vitamins," Anas replied. "Juice."

"Juice?"

"Seriously, man, what's wrong with you?" Anas sighed in exasperation. "Being a vegetarian has fried your brain. Juice—you know, PEDs, anabolic steroids. HGH. Stimulants. Amphetamines. Blood boosters. Testosterone. All that good stuff."

Loubna had told me about Anas's angry outbursts. Since sudden mood swings and uncontrolled, violent reactions—'roid rage—were well-known side effects of steroids, I resisted the temptation of asking him why such a manly man would need to increase his testosterone intake. I considered quizzing him about his impressive knowledge of performance-enhancing drugs—particularly amphetamines—in the hope that my flattery would lead him to brag about Captagon. But I still worried about seeming too inquisitive, especially on a topic that was hardly your typical dinner conversation material. I was about to say something mundane about the weather in Dubai when Anas started to wave his arms frantically at a person walking toward Jules Bar a few feet away.

"Abu Omar," Anas shouted in the direction of the man. "Abu Omar!"

The man turned around and saw Anas. His face lit up as he rushed to our table. "Abu Sayid, *kifak habibi*, how are you?"

Anas got up and greeted his friend effusively with a double kiss on the right cheek, followed by a kiss on the left cheek and another double kiss on the right side that came dangerously close to his friend's mouth. This overkissing blunder violated a subtle but firm code of conduct in the region, an odd faux pas that exposed Anas's eagerness to please and impress this person. In a flash, Abu Omar's mien revealed surprise, then revulsion, before reverting to the jovial expression of a moment earlier.

"Abu Omar, *habibi*, I missed you, it's been weeks!" Anas said. "How have you been, brother?"

Abu Omar was a tall, heavyset man in his late fifties with a thick goatee that was so dark, it appeared to be dyed with black ink. He seemed genuinely happy to see Anas. After a short exchange of pleasantries, he looked at me, then back at Anas. "Where are your manners, Abu Sayid? Aren't you going to introduce me to your friend?"

"Of course," Anas said in a cheerful mood, his disappointment concerning my deficient nutrition habits forgotten. "Abu Omar, this is Dee. Dee, this is my dear friend Abdullah."

Abdullah shook my hand vigorously as he placed his left hand on my right shoulder. "Pleased to meet you, Dee. What brings you to Dubai?"

Before I could answer, Anas motioned for the waiter and asked Abdullah, "Will you join us with a glass of this exquisite wine, or would you prefer something else?"

"No offense to your wine, but I'd prefer the usual," Abdullah said.

"Bring my friend here a tall, iced glass of Stoli. And another bottle of this Nebbiolo for us," Anas barked at the waiter. I realized that I had not even finished one glass of wine while Anas had devoured the rest of the bottle.

We all sat down. Anas and Abdullah spoke for a couple of minutes about people I did not know, completely ignoring me. The waiter showed up with Abdullah's vodka and our wine. As we raised our glasses, Anas proposed a toast. "To good friends! And to sex and drugs," he added with a laugh. "Let the losers keep the rock 'n roll."

As I took a sip of the wine, I saw Abdullah down half his glass of vodka with one gulp. He noticed my surprise and smiled.

"Growing up as a royal in Riyadh," he said, "I learned two things when it came to drinking—that is, if you don't want to get caught. First, drink something that looks like water. I hate tequila—it gives me a wicked hangover—so vodka became my beverage of choice. And second, whatever booze you are drinking—drink it fast! You never know when the *mutaween*, our special Saudi vice squad, will drop by for a friendly chat."

Anas and Abdullah both laughed loudly, and I joined in tepidly, still processing the fact that Abdullah had offhandedly dropped the tidbit of his royal pedigree. This blue-blooded Saudi had an easygoing demeanor. He raised his glass again and finished off what was left in it. Clearly, this was not a casual drinker. Anas beckoned the waiter over.

"I'll hold you personally responsible if my friend here dies of thirst," he threatened the waiter. "Bring him another glass of iced Stoli, and make it snappy, *ya manyak*!"

The waiter took off, again tripping over a table. Anas squealed in delight.

"So, Dee," Abdullah said as he turned to me, "are you married?"

I was not expecting this question. "I am. What about you?"

He laughed. "Four times over."

"Four wives?" I said, trying to inject some levity. "How do you do it? I cannot even live up to the expectations of my one lovely wife!"

Abdullah laughed. "You're looking at this from the wrong angle. Having four wives inserts some competition into the equation. It's like free-market economics applied to marriage. Each one of my wives knows that she needs to beat, to outperform, her competition if she wants to remain in the picture."

"Actually, it's more like survival in the wilderness," Anas jumped in. "Any wife of yours just has to make sure she's not the worst of the lot. It's no different than if you and your friend bump into a grizzly bear. You don't have to outrun the grizzly—you just have to outrun your friend!"

Both men laughed hysterically. The waiter arrived with Abdullah's vodka and joined in the laughter, even though he had not heard Anas's quip.

"Just put it down," Anas snapped. "Imbecile! Laughs for tips!"

"Keep the vodka coming," Abdullah told the waiter, who nodded and disappeared.

Abdullah took a big sip. "Ahhh, hits the spot. Anyway, Anas, as funny as your grizzly bear analogy is, it suffers from a fatal flaw."

"How so?" Anas asked with a frown, clearly peeved at being challenged, even in the mildest of forms and even by a good friend.

"Because no matter whether one wife outperforms another wife, I always have the option of replacing them both," Abdullah said earnestly. "Real competition does not mean that it is enough to be better than the worst performer. Real competition means that anything but the best will result in immediate termination and replacement with younger, better, and more eager models."

"Good point," Anas said, impressed by Abdullah's logic. "And I'm the one who can keep on supplying you with newer, better models. A win-win for everyone!"

Except for the wives, I thought.

"Talking about supply," Abdullah asked Anas, "have you been to Syria in the past days?"

"It's been a couple of weeks," Anas replied. "I just arrived from Riyadh, and before that I was in Amman with my homeboys."

"How *are* Imad and Mike?" Abdullah asked.

"Mike's still dumb as a fencepost," Anas answered. "One day, I think Imad might shoot him just for being stupid. Kind of like a mercy killing."

I looked for a sign in Anas's demeanor that he was aware of my interaction with Mike and Imad in Amman, but it seemed that Anas was just lamenting Mike's general lack of mental firepower rather than any specific event. Abdullah smiled knowingly and downed the rest of his vodka. As if on cue, the waiter showed up with a fresh ice-cold glass.

"So, what's it like in Syria?" I asked, trying to shift the conversation away from Imad and Mike.

"Syria has all the ingredients of a war that will never end," Anas said.

"Because both sides will never agree to share power?" I asked.

"Because *all* sides will never agree to share power," Anas corrected me. "If the war had just two sides, it could end when one side is defeated. But this war has so many sides. The West thinks this is just some tribal conflict—you know, Sunni versus Shia, Shia versus Sunni. But that's just the bullshit tribal narrative being fed to those clueless morons in the West. Sure, there are many Syrian groups that hate each other, but let's not forget that the foreign powers involved hate each other just as much, if not more. At this point, you have Iran and you have America, and you have the Saudis and the Qataris and the Emiratis, and you have the Turks. And since Bashar is not doing so well these days, he'll probably have to ask another country for help. Who knows? My bet is on Russia. Many of his intelligence officers studied in Moscow, and Maher* is very well connected over there. So my guess is that Putin will help Bashar, even if he doesn't like him."

"Why doesn't he like him?" I asked. I was impressed by how astutely Anas had made the case for a Russian intervention in Syria.

"Probably because Bashar is so much taller," he replied with a laugh. "Apparently Putin is not too fond of people who are much taller than he is. Maher is closer to Putin in height and is also a military man— two major assets in Putin's world. Helping the Syrian regime would give Putin a chance to mess with America and rub Obama's face in it."

---

* Maher al-Assad, the younger brother of Syrian president Bashar al-Assad, is the commander of the Syrian army's elite Fourth Division and the Republican Guard. Next to his brother Bashar, he is considered the most powerful and certainly the most feared and ruthless man in Syria, as well as the regime's enforcer and hardliner.

Anas's analysis seemed highly plausible.*

"You see, Dee," he continued, "these countries are all keeping this war going with weapons and money, but they're not the ones who are paying the price. So they don't really have an incentive to make peace happen. Do you really think this war would continue even for one week if Obama and Khamenei and all the others sat down and decided to stop the killing? If each of them brought their side to the table and said, 'Okay, boys, it's been a party, but let's wrap this one up'? If they wanted Assad to go, he'd be gone. And if they want him to stay, he'll stay. Nobody gives a shit about what the Syrian people want."

Anas seemed genuinely offended by foreign powers and their proxies having a stake in the Syrian war. "And don't forget," Abdullah jumped in, "with the exception of Turkey, you have nothing but weak or failed states surrounding Syria. Iraq—now a failed Shia state thanks to George Bush Jr.'s little adventure. Lebanon—please! The only real power there is Hezbollah, aside from Israel, of course. So two of Syria's neighbors, Iraq and Lebanon, are essentially Iranian satellites. And Jordan is weak, a few bullets away from the Muslim Brotherhood taking over and on the brink of collapsing under a tsunami of refugees. Besides, many of the ISIS fighters in Syria and Iraq are Jordanian, so that'll be fun when they return home!"

"What Abu Omar is saying is that no side can win this war, and no side can lose it either," Anas said, tag-teaming Abdullah. "This war can go on forever."

I was desperate to learn what had happened to Paul Blocher, but there was no inconspicuous way to probe more directly, and I couldn't ask flat-out. For now, I would have to stay engaged in their conversation. "At some point, the suffering might reach a point where the world can no longer look away," I ventured.

---

* Anas's prediction would prove true one year later, in September 2015, with the full-fledged Russian intervention in the war to support the Syrian regime.

"Really?" Abdullah stared at me. "Don't you think that point was reached long ago?"

I nodded. Abdullah was right; it was a silly comment.

"Look, Dee," Anas continued, "all sides to this war, inside and outside the country, they're all just looking out for their own interests, protecting their own power. Actually, the leaders of the different parties in this war, they all resemble each other far more than they resemble those they claim to represent. They all speak the same universal language—the language of power. That's why they get along and understand each other so perfectly. Come on now, just look at the Syrian players—the government, the opposition, ISIS—they're all just one and the same. They're all scum. It's like a filthy bowl of steaming hot shit staring at itself in the mirror!"

Abdullah high-fived Anas in approval of this delightful metaphor and finished his vodka. Immediately the waiter reappeared with yet another iced glass. I hadn't noticed him hovering near our table, and I wondered whether there was a hidden camera or a sensor in the glass itself alerting the bartender whenever the vodka in Abdullah's glass was approaching dangerously low levels.

"Attaboy!" Anas said approvingly to the waiter while handing him a hundred-dollar bill. "And this, my friends, is how you train a monkey. Carrots and sticks. Sticks and carrots."

"But there are some people in Syria who are trying to help, aren't there?" I asked, hoping to steer the conversation toward the aid organizations active in Aleppo and a little closer to Paul Blocher.

"Like who?" Anas sneered. "The UN?" He and Abdullah both erupted in hysterical laughter.

I sat there completely befuddled. "What's wrong with the UN in Syria?"

Abdullah hit Anas's thigh as they exploded in another roar. "What's . . . wrong . . . with . . . the . . . U . . . N . . . in . . . Syria!" Abdullah blurted between fits of delirious squeals, as if I had just said the funniest thing he had ever heard. "Tell him, Anas. Tell him."

"Where to begin, brother," Anas said to me. "The UN is so damn clueless in Syria. There are some things we wouldn't even be able to do without them."

"How so?" I had no idea what he was talking about.

"Man, the UN is great for business," Anas said. "Getting a piece of the aid money is the sweetest deal in the country. Nothing like those fat UN contracts!"

"Huh?" The expression on my face must have been bewilderment because both Anas and Abdullah started to laugh again as they took turns pointing at me.

Anas got hold of himself first. "Okay, let me explain," he said. "For starters, the UN can only operate in Syria with the government's approval. Nothing happens without that. So almost all the Syrian companies that get UN contracts are controlled by Bashar's buddies or his buddies' buddies. The best one of all is the blood supply to those poor war victims! All that money to support the Syrian national blood bank, and guess who controls that? The Defense Ministry! So it's the Syrian military that gets to decide who gets the UN-sponsored blood supplies. I mean, you can't make this shit up!"

"Hey, it just proves that the UN has a sense of humor," Abdullah piped in.

"No kidding," Anas continued. "The oldest brother of my man Imad is running this little enterprise in Damascus that distributes UN contracts and takes thirty cents on every dollar the UN spends. Man, he is raking it in! It's incredible! When the war started, he was a skinny man, maybe sixty-five kilos soaking wet. Now he has turned into a fat head honcho, a hundred-kilo pig in shit. And he's going to stay fat, I can promise you that! Because if this beautiful war ever ends, which I hope will never happen, then Imad's brother will be there to work with the Chinese who will invest billions to rebuild this damned country. He'll be more than happy to take their money, just as he did with the UN's.

It's actually kind of funny. Iran thinks that it will get a big piece of the pie when it comes to these future rebuilding contracts in Syria, but just because they saved Assad's ass doesn't mean that he won't screw them and give all those deals to the Chinese who can also finance the investments. After all, Iran is dead broke from all the sanctions, so there's not much they can offer Assad other than soldiers as cannon fodder. He'll just throw them a few scraps, maybe a sewage plant or some other stinking thing. Loyalty is way overrated. So you see, Dee, there are no good actors in Syria. Only bad ones, or dumb ones—you know, do-gooders."

"There's got to be some stuff the UN can do in Syria without the government, right?" I asked.

Anas gave me a pitying look. "Fuck man, you're some kind of stupid! You really think anyone can do anything in Syria without Damascus? What are you, retarded? When those UN staffers use their Syriatel cell phones, who do you think rakes it in? Rami rakes it in. Rami."

"Rami?" I asked.

"Rami Makhlouf—Bashar's cousin," Anas replied in an exasperated tone. "That's not all. When they need security protection, they go to another one of Rami's companies. And when they stay in the fancy Four Seasons in Damascus, who do you think owns a piece of that? The Syrian government. I could go on and on. Trust me, Dee, the UN doesn't as much as give a bottle of water to a homeless person in Syria without Bashar and his crew making money off it."*

"What about the food aid?" I asked. "Can't they distribute that directly without benefiting the regime?"

---

* In May 2020, an unusually public spat erupted between Rami Makhlouf and the Syrian regime's inner circle, when Rami Makhlouf accused his cousin Bashar al-Assad in a series of Facebook videos of confiscating his assets and mistreating his conglomerate's employees. Following the death of Anisa Makhlouf, Bashar al-Assad's mother, in 2016, the protection of the Makhlouf clan started to erode, but the primary reason for the fall in Rami Makhlouf's standing and the plundering of his assets was the regime's desperate need for money after a decade of civil war that had obliterated the country's economy, as well as other family members and insiders close to the president who had long coveted Rami Makhlouf's prime assets such as Syriatel, the country's largest mobile network provider.

Anas grinned and answered in an annoyingly slow cadence, as if he were talking to a child with special needs. "No, Dee. Not. Even. The. Food. Aid. Those distributions have to go through a Syrian charity. And you know who runs that one?"

I shook my head.

"Asma," Anas continued. "Innocent Asma, Bashar's trophy wife. She, too, makes a fuckload of money straight off those UN contracts. Good times, Dee. Good times."

Before I had a chance to ask Anas any questions about Asma al-Assad, he answered a call on his phone and screamed obscenities at the person on the other end of the line. It seemed to be the only way he knew how to use his phone. While Anas was on this call, Abdullah got up. "I'll be right back," he said as he headed toward Jules Bar.

I WAITED FOR Anas to finish his call, then resumed our conversation. "But surely not everything the UN and the aid agencies do is bad or stupid?"

"Only if you are someone who thinks that good intentions count," Anas said sarcastically. "I really hope I did not spend this past hour drinking with someone who believes that! Listen, it's not just the blood bank or Asma's charity. Those UN guys are so fucking clueless! Imagine this: we store a lot of our stuff in their camps, and we even use their vehicles to transport some of our hottest merchandise."

"What hottest merchandise?" I asked carefully.

"Seriously, dude?" Anas asked with a look of genuine pity. "You've still not figured it out? Drugs, uppers. Weapons. Even some chemical stuff. Contraband. Black money. Stolen car parts. Even prisoners."

I couldn't suppress my revulsion. "Wow!"

Judging by Anas's grin, he misread my reaction as an expression of admiration. "Listen," he continued, "just think of everything that you consider to be legal. And now think of the exact opposite. That!"

"Wow," I said again.

"I know—it's great, isn't it? One of my favorite stories is when we put some grenades and drugs in an SUV that the UN used to drive to the north of the country to deliver medical supplies. Our guys at the other end took out the grenades and traded them with Nusra for some other weapons and lots of cash. In Aleppo, our couriers made a stop to pick up some of the weapons that the rebels received from the Americans—high-quality stuff, sealed by your good old US of A, which we get at a huge discount in exchange for amphetamines—the perks of doing business with addicts! Actually, our trove included my favorite weapons—those kick-ass anti-tank missiles that the CIA gives the rebel groups it supports, who then turn around and sell them to me—at a sweet price, I might add. It's a beautiful thing. Turns out, ISIS and Nusra are horny as hell when it comes to these missiles—you know, kind of a missile-boner thing. So my profits are huge!"

I couldn't believe what I was hearing. There had been rumors of an active weapons trading market in Syria involving the CIA-supported rebels but nothing of the scale and brazenness Anas was describing. "Are you serious?" I asked.

"Oh yeah, baby!" Anas hollered enthusiastically. The wrinkles on the top of his head were becoming even more pronounced, evidencing a state of unbridled euphoria. "You'd better believe it! We're just cleaning up, man, shoveling in the dough. Last month, my guys even got their hands on some sarin and mustard gas—wearing gloves, of course. Get it? Chemical weapons, gloves, handle with care—get it?"

My eyes were wide open. I couldn't hide my shock and amazement.

"Relax, Dee," Anas continued proudly. "We really do handle the gases with care, so no one gets hurt."

"I'm pretty sure some people do get hurt," I blurted out before I could stop myself.

"Well, sometimes a few of my guys are careless and forget to wear masks and gloves. Good riddance, I say, natural selection." Anas had missed my reference to the actual victims of the horrific chemical weapons attacks. "Fuck 'em! Besides, we don't get near that VX stuff—that shit's nasty, and only the big boys deal with it."

"The big boys?" I asked.

"Yeah, you know, the big boys," Anas replied, for the first time shifting uncomfortably. "You know, the prez and his bro, you know, Bashar and Maher and their posse. Not gonna mess with those dudes. They'd get all medieval on my ass if I stepped on their toes. The VX is theirs. I was told that they get that shit straight from the North Koreans. And it's those fucking North Koreans, not the Iranians, who show them how to use the VX and how to store it. That's some really nasty shit! Really nasty." Anas shook his head in disgust.

"My goodness!" Anas had just casually confirmed the existence and use of chemical weapons in Syria one year after the international deal signed by the United States, Russia, and Syria, which followed Obama's infamous red line warning in August 2012. As to this VX trading, I had actually heard some rumors about the involvement of North Korean agents in Syria. The presence of North Korean military advisers in the region was nothing new. A former cash courier of Muammar Gaddafi* once told me how he used to deliver bags full of hundred-dollar bills from Libya to Egypt in the days of Hosni Mubarak in order to pay the North Koreans for their weapons and services. But their role in delivering VX to Syria and training Assad's men on how to handle and deploy it had not been more than an unsubstantiated rumor, bordering on a conspiracy theory—until Anas just confirmed it.

"Anyway, where was I before we got sidetracked with those chemical weapons?" Anas continued when I remained silent. "Oh yes, the stuff we transported in the UN's SUVs. We then sold the weapons plus some

---

* This cash courier reported directly to Bashir Saleh Bashir, the former head of the Libyan African Portfolio mentioned earlier in connection with the profitability of the Captagon business and the cash laundering in the financial system.

drugs from our labs in the north to ISIS for some more cash. A great deal all around. The fighters got drugs and weapons to keep the war going, and we got loads of cash. That's what I call a good day at the office!"

Once again, Anas mistook the shocked expression on my face for adulation. "What can I say, dude," he boasted, "I guess I've figured it all out. The only business that's better than drugs and prostitution is the business of war. And if you can combine them all, you're golden! Sex and drugs and bombs, baby!"

Just then, Abdullah returned. "Man, those are some slim pickings at Jules Bar this evening," he said to Anas in mock exasperation. Before Anas could answer, the waiter materialized with another glass of vodka and then proceeded to refill our wineglasses.

"It's early," Anas consoled his friend. "The good ones start closer to midnight."

"You're right," Abdullah said as he took a sip of his iced vodka. His alcohol tolerance was remarkable.

"Tell me, *habibi*," Anas said to Abdullah. "How's your family? How's Omar, and how are your beautiful daughters?"

"Omar's fine, *alhamdulillah*," Abdullah replied. "Not the smartest kid, as you know, but okay. What can you do? Allah decided to give the brains and the good looks to my daughters, so Omar will inherit my money. It all evens out."

Both men chuckled. "Your daughters are really gorgeous," Anas said.

"Thank you, *habibi*. God has richly rewarded me with them. And they are also so smart. Gentle, beautiful flowers."

"*Mashallah*," Anas said warmly. "You are really blessed."

"Anyway," Abdullah said abruptly, "the standards at Jules are really dropping. Nothing bangable there tonight. I did not see one single girl there that was more than a four and a half. A five, max!" Abdullah was completely oblivious to the stark contrast between his crude assessment of the young women at Jules Bar and the affectionate, loving tone in which he talked about his own daughters. It was as if he were referring to two different species.

"I told you, Abu Omar," Anas said, "the good ones arrive later."

"Not sure I can wait that long. I have a flight to catch tonight."

"Want me to arrange something for you?"

Abdullah nodded. Neither man seemed to mind the fact that I was witnessing their transaction.

"What package? Bonus? Jackpot?" Anas asked.

Abdullah shook his head. "No, just something simple. I can't afford your expensive packages, Abu Sayid; they're becoming too costly for me. With the oil price dropping, we've got to be more frugal."

Both men howled.

"How about the one you had last time?" Anas asked. "You know— Tiffany, from Homs. She's hot, I'd say at least a nine!"

"She'd be a nine if she didn't cry so much," Abdullah said. "Those tears get on my damn nerves. You've got to deduct a point for that pity party. But an eight will do. It's better than anything at Jules right now."

"Sounds good," Anas said. "Same place as usual?"

"Same place as usual. Put it on my tab, please." As Abdullah stood up, I discerned a smirk on his face, as if he had no intention of ever paying off his tab. It could have been the consequence of Anas's overkissing gaffe when Abdullah had arrived at our table, or it could have simply been their way of interacting, but at that moment I was sure that deep down Abdullah felt contempt for Anas. "Pleasure meeting you, Dee," he said to me, then kissed Anas deliberately once on each cheek.

As soon as Abdullah had left, I realized that my breathing was accelerating, and I took a sip of wine. The exchange between Anas and Abdullah about the girls had brought back that same sense of claustrophobia and suffocation I had felt when Loubna showed me the pictures of her battered sister. I was relieved that my hands remained steady and prayed that my demeanor would not reveal the turmoil inside me. I had a moment to regain my composure while Anas walked a few paces with Abdullah. Before he came back to the table, he made a short call.

"Sorry about that," Anas said as he sat down. "It's rude to mix business and pleasure, I know, even when it's the pleasure business. But Abu Omar's a good dude, one of my best customers."

I was at a loss for words and only managed to mutter, "It's all right." I was still trying to digest the revolting scene that had just unfolded.

"Anyway, let's have some more wine," Anas said. "I've got to return to Syria tomorrow, so let's enjoy this good stuff. Every dinner before I fly back to Syria feels like the Last Supper."

The last time I had heard a reference to the Last Supper was out of Huby's mouth over dinner at Marius et Janette in Paris. Perhaps this was a sign, and my only opening, to find out something about Paul Blocher. "What's it like in Syria?" I asked. "I hear that life in Damascus is pretty normal—as normal as can be in a war. But what's it like in other parts of the country? In the north? In Aleppo and the other cities?"

Anas took a long sip of wine. "Man, it's brutal out there. The worst is in the northeast, in places like Raqqah, where those crazy ISIS motherfuckers are. Those dudes are off their rocker to begin with, but feed them some Captagon, and they completely lose their motherfucking minds."

I felt like my heart had skipped several beats at the mention of Captagon. I took a few sips of wine to hide my excitement.

"But it's completely nuts all over the country, or whatever's left of the country," Anas continued. "The north, Aleppo, is destroyed. Whenever I travel there, I am almost tempted to become religious and pray. That's how bad it is."

This was my chance to probe. I decided to amp up the flattery and at the same time belittle myself, which would aggrandize him even more. Hopefully, Anas would brag to a point where he would reveal some information about Paul Blocher. But I had to be careful. If I overdid it, he might smell something fishy. "I've got to hand it to you, Anas,"

I began, "I don't know how you do it! I'd never have the guts to go to Syria and move around the country. I'd be scared to death. I mean, any mistake could be my last mistake. How do you do it? Where do you find the courage?"

Bull's-eye—Anas gleamed like a little boy who had just won his first sports trophy. He pulled a cigar out of his bag, bit off the tip, and spat it out in a large arc. "Do you mind if I smoke?" he asked, puffing like mad as he lit the cigar. "I feel like I need a Black Dragon. Did you know that this Gurkha Black Dragon is the most expensive cigar you can get? Great stuff!"

Given his taste in T-shirts and jeans, it figured that he would only smoke the most expensive cigar on the market. Thankfully, he did not offer me one. After being on the receiving end of his contempt for my wimpy no-meat-eating self, I wouldn't have dared tell Anas that I didn't smoke and knew next to nothing about cigars. "Enjoy it," I said quietly.

"Mmm," Anas moaned as he exhaled the thick smoke, "this is almost as good as sex."

"So tell me," I said, trying to steer the conversation back to Syria, "aren't you ever scared when you travel in Syria? How do you stay safe when you are there?"

"It's dangerous," Anas replied, "I'm not going to lie to you. And people know me there. I'm a big deal in Syria, not just here in Dubai. I'd be a trophy for any kidnapper or bounty hunter. Yeah, there's a target on these sculpted pecs. But I rely on these two beauties," he said as he flexed, then kissed his biceps. "And on this," he added, pointing to his head.

"Still, I admire your nerve, your fearlessness," I said. "What if you got caught by any of those gangs roaming the country?"

Anas laughed. "You're forgetting that the major ones are all my clients," he said, puffing away. "I supply them all—government, opposition, Nusra, ISIS, the Free Syrian Army, Ahrar al-Sham, Suqour al-Sham, or any other fucking al-Sham out there—you name it. I provide them with everything they need—drugs to boost their desire to fight, weapons to fight with, and girls to relax with after they fight. They all need me. On top of that, I have so much dirt on the politicians, on the policemen, on the intelligence agents, that they will do anything for me. You see, I've figured it all out. If you want to be safe, you have to rule. And if you want to rule, you have to know how to make people believe."

"Believe?"

"Yes, believe." Anas was suddenly serious now. "Those who are with you—make them believe in your loyalty, believe that you will take care of them. And those who are against you—make them believe in your cruelty, that you will destroy them."

"I see."

"So trust me, my friend, I am safer, more protected than Bashar."

Anas was smart enough to understand that he could be both strong and vulnerable at the same time. His awareness of danger, his caution, made him a more formidable criminal and ultimately even more power-ful. As he spoke, I realized how absurd even contemplating my original plan C had been. There would have been no way to threaten or intimi-date Anas into giving me any information on Paul Blocher. Anas would, in the best of cases, have laughed me out of the restaurant had I tried to strong-arm him.

"Wow," I said admiringly. "I suppose you really *are* as protected as the president."

"I said *more* protected," Anas corrected me quickly.

"You're right, *more* protected," I continued. "But that's just you. You are obviously a special person. But anyone else . . . I mean, why would anyone travel to Syria? It amazes me that you still have people who risk their lives traveling to Syria. I realize that most Syrians are stuck there and have no choice. But why in the world do others, especially Westerners, take that risk? It's like a death wish!"

Anas nodded. "No kidding. I wonder about that myself. My guys keep getting asked to take people into Syria, usually from Turkey, and sometimes also from Lebanon and Jordan."

The flattery trap was set; it was time to go for it. "What kind of people?" I asked. "Journalists? Doctors? I can't imagine even the most adventurous soul would think of this as an enticing experience, right?"

"Funny you should say that," Anas replied. "Just recently, one of our Kurdish smugglers tried to bring in some dude. But I fucked him up big-time."

My heart sank. I felt like I might pass out. "What do you mean?" I asked apathetically.

"Oh, just one of our couriers trying to develop a side business of his own, some pocket money," Anas said. "I had to teach him a lesson."

"What happened?"

Anas lit up his cigar again. The flame almost singed his eyebrows. "Holy shit, that was close!" he said as he quickly pulled the cigar out of his mouth and exhaled the thick smoke. "Well, what happened is that I have a network of Kurdish smugglers and couriers in the north, mainly in the area between Aleppo and a place near the Turkish border, which you've probably never heard of. A shithole called Kobane. In any event, the job of this particular courier is to take Captagon and some other drugs out of Syria into Turkey and to return with cash. That's it. Nothing else. Simple enough, right? No people-smuggling in that area—much too hot. We do that elsewhere, and never with the Kurdish couriers. All these one-trick ponies are supposed to smuggle is drugs. But apparently someone introduced this courier, a Kurdish dude called Alan, to another dude who wanted to travel to Syria. Some lost creature, a crazy motherfucker called Paul, who said he was looking for something, trying to trace a friend who had died or some kind of shit like that."

Hearing Anas utter Paul's name took my breath away. I tried to regain my composure but was not sure whether my heart could take any more of this.

"I mean, anyone who comes to Syria for sentimental reasons or to find some higher purpose in life or because of some jackass self-discovery, new-age stuff is probably too damn stupid to survive. Doesn't really deserve to live, if you know what I mean," Anas declared flippantly. "But I didn't give a damn about this Paul dude. My problem was with my courier Alan, who had decided to freelance and defied my clear orders never to smuggle people into Syria. It's too risky, and there's no upside— they pay for shit, plus there are way more smugglers than travelers, which means that supply is crushing demand—not exactly my preferred business model. So I decided to teach him a lesson."

"What did you do?"

"My homeboys had arranged to meet Alan in a city called Manbij, somewhere between Kobane and Aleppo, to receive his cash and supply him with a new load of drugs to take to Turkey. When Alan showed up with this Paul dude, they called me immediately. Luckily, I happened to be near Aleppo at the time, so I was there in less than two hours. My first instinct was to beat the shit out of Alan, but by the time I arrived in Manbij I had a better idea. I decided to sell the two men to Nusra. Trust me, that's a lot worse than getting the shit beaten out of you, even by a powerful dude like me! This way, word would get out to the other couriers who work for me. Don't mess with Anas! If you fuck with Mr. Big Time, you're the one who'll get fucked!"

I was shattered. I knew what being held by Nusra meant—daily beatings, torture, starvation, and mock executions until the day the execution was no longer staged but real. "So you sold them both to Nusra fighters?" I asked, hoping against all odds that Anas would tell me how in the last moment he had decided not to go through with his brutal plan.

Anas immediately crushed my foolish hopes. He nodded with a wide grin, clearly very proud of himself.

"I get it that you wanted to teach your smuggler a lesson," I continued delicately. "But why also sell this Paul fellow?"

"Collateral damage," Anas replied. "I considered killing him and blaming it on Nusra to make the whole thing more believable, but in fact this dude got me a higher price than my Kurdish courier. They actually paid me good money for this Westerner. The Kurd turd ended up being my freebie, just to sweeten the deal."

I considered asking him how much he had received for Paul but did not want to push my luck by seeming too inquisitive. "So what happened?" I was filled with dread.

"I dropped off Alan and his lily-white friend, who was scared shitless, at a safe house on the way to Aleppo," Anas replied. "The dude was shaking like a leaf. Then I called one of my dealer contacts at Nusra and told him where he could pick up his cargo. It all went very smoothly."

Being captured by Nusra was one of the worst possible scenarios for Paul. I was suddenly overcome by a wave of fury and thought of reaching over and smashing Anas's face into the table, bulging biceps and all. This monster had just described how he had delivered two people into an unspeakable hell just to teach one of them a lesson and make a little extra money. I could not stop myself from thinking about the agony that Paul Blocher must have been in—the abject terror he must have felt the moment he realized what was happening to him and the pain and torment he was now enduring in captivity. But I still did not know the full story and had to goad Anas as nonchalantly as possible into divulging the rest.

"So then what happened to those two? Did Nusra kill them?" I asked, steeling myself for the answer.

"No." Anas sounded exasperated. "You still don't seem to understand the principles of a war economy. As I tried to explain to you, it's all about business, about making loads of money. And when it comes to business, as I preach to my guys, you never, ever allow your money to get mad! Understand?"

I nodded.

"Besides," Anas continued, "why would Nusra buy these two dudes just in order to kill them?"

"Out of hate?"

Anas laughed. "You really don't get it, do you? This is not some ideological war, Dee! These Islamist fighters, whether with Nusra or ISIS or some other group, they don't really hate the West or other religions, just as they don't really give a hoot about Islam or the Quran. To them, al-Baghdadi's sermons* are just background noise, entertainment. Elevator music. Most of these fighters are completely unknowledgeable about the Quran, especially the ISIS guys. These are a bunch of derelicts. Ask them to recite a *surah*, and they'll draw a blank. Some of these assholes don't even know the Shahada."

"In that case, what did Nusra do with these two prisoners?" I asked.

"Well, it's all just business, remember? So first, they tried to sell them on to some of the other militias—especially the Westerner, this Paul dude. But they only received puny, laughable offers. The best price came from ISIS, but that one, too, was a joke. Some of the Alawi militias actually told the Nusra handler that they would only take the prisoners if Nusra paid them—like a garbage disposal fee."

"Why did these prisoners have so little value?" I asked. "I thought that the trade of prisoners in Syria was pretty lucrative."

"Normally, yes," Anas explained. "But this case was different. First of all, my Kurdish courier has no value to them because his family is dirt poor, so there's nobody who can pay for his release. No bidders mean zero value. As to this Paul dude, well, ordinarily these Westerners *are* worth something. But only if their government or their families or the

---

* Abu Bakr al-Baghdadi, born Ibrahim Awad Ibrahim Ali al-Badri al-Samarrai, was the Iraqi leader of ISIS from 2014 until his death in October 2019. Upon the declaration of a worldwide caliphate, al-Baghdadi was named its first caliph and referred to by his followers as "Caliph Ibrahim." In addition to the atrocities committed by ISIS under his command, al-Baghdadi was a serial rapist who claimed several sex slaves, including the American hostage Kayla Mueller who was murdered in February 2015.

organizations that sent them—you know, newspapers, TV networks, charities—only if they ask about these missing people, try to find them, and try to negotiate their release. In this case, however, nobody asked about this Paul dude. Not a family member, not an organization, not even his government. I know for a fact that Nusra put out word to this dude's country through their representatives in Beirut, letting everyone know that they were open for business. All they got was a big blank yawn."

"So what did Nusra do, what happened next?" I sounded breathless. I realized that my eagerness and anxiety were becoming apparent and that it could turn into a serious problem if I didn't manage to get a grip on myself.

"They called me a week later and blamed me for selling them damaged, worthless goods," Anas said. "It was a classic case of buyer's remorse. I thought of telling them that this was not my problem and that next time they should not buy goods sight unseen."

"If you had said that, they would have probably killed them both, right?"

"Probably. So what? Shit happens, not every sale ends up with a happy buyer."

"But you didn't tell them that, right?"

"No. I decided to buy back these two clowns. At a steep discount, of course, so that I still made a nice net profit. Tax-free," he added with a laugh.

"Why?"

Anas looked at me in surprise. "Because I always make a profit. What do you think—these cigars pay for themselves?"

"That's not what I meant," I clarified. "Why did you decide to buy these two back, to take them off Nusra's hands?"

Anas lit his cigar again. "Because the Nusra dudes have been excellent customers for my goods, and I did not want them to be unhappy and look for other suppliers. It was a small price to pay for the sake of good client relations. Especially considering the fact," he reminded me with a grin, "that I still made a nice little profit."

"So these two were released?" I asked, praying this was good news for Paul.

"It's actually a hilarious story," Anas said. He was shrouded by billows of cigar smoke. "One of my guys picked them up at the arranged location close to Aleppo and started driving north toward Kobane, where I had instructed him to drop them off. My Kurdish courier, this Alan dude, would never again ignore my instructions or try to cross me, so setting him free made good business sense. Otherwise, I would have just had him shot. It was hysterical, because this Kurdish idiot was convinced that he would be executed for having defied my orders, so at first he refused to get in the car. He got in only when the other guy, the Westerner, begged him to come along. My driver was speeding, driving like a maniac, because he still had to return to Aleppo to pick up some merchandise and bring it to Homs that night. Lots of driving. Two hours to Kobane, two hours back to Aleppo, and then another two hours to Homs. And he had to get there before sunrise. So he was in a huge rush. Those roads are not well lit and full of giant potholes. A few kilometers outside Aleppo he drove off the road trying to avoid one of these ditches. The car was totaled."

My heart stopped. "What happened to them?"

"By some miracle, my driver only had minor wounds," Anas said. "Lucky son of a bitch."

I waited for Anas to tell me what had happened to Paul and Alan, but he just picked up his glass and swirled the wine with a satisfied grin.

"What about the other two?" I finally blurted out when Anas showed no intention of sharing what had happened to those passengers whose fate I was actually interested in.

"Who?" he asked, preoccupied with the wine and his cigar.

"You know—your Kurdish courier and the Westerner."

"Oh, those two," Anas said. "They died."

I felt like I had been hit in the face with a sledgehammer. I wanted to ask him how it was possible that they had died and his guy had survived, but the words were stuck in my throat. "How?" I finally sputtered.

"I suppose God wanted my driver to live." Anas chuckled. "He probably knew that I was running a little short on good employees, so he made sure my guy survived."

Just when I thought Anas could not be any more repulsive, he managed to prove me wrong. "But why did the other two die?" I was no longer worried about seeming too inquisitive.

"How? Why?" Anas mimicked me in a mocking tone. "Who gives a shit! They were sitting on the right side of the car, which is where the car landed after it flipped over. Alan and this Paul dude just got crushed. Talk about being at the wrong place at the wrong time!" His obnoxious giggle morphed into a coughing fit as he inhaled the cigar smoke.

The waiter came with a glass of water, which Anas drank eagerly. "That's better," he said without acknowledging the waiter. "You know, it really cracks me up, I mean this Paul dude comes to Syria, manages to survive in the nastiest war zone, survives captivity with Nusra—he survives all that just to die in an ordinary car accident. That's some funny shit, man! I'll drink to that!"

Even though Anas expected me to raise my glass with him, I couldn't bring myself to do it. "It really is extraordinary," I said. "I wonder what last thoughts were going through his mind as the car was tumbling through the air."

"Probably 'Oh shit, I'm fucked'!" Anas said with an awful, dirty laugh. "Actually, my driver sent me some pictures of the car wreck while he was waiting to be picked up by another one of my guys. Look."

Anas scrolled on his phone until he found the picture of the car. He handed me his phone. The car had really landed on its right side, which was completely destroyed. It was evident that anyone sitting on that side of the car could not have survived the crash. I struggled to look at the image and handed the phone back to Anas.

"Wait, I think he also sent me a picture of this Paul dude," Anas said, scrolling through the photos. "Ah, here it is." He handed me his phone again.

I found myself staring at a picture of Paul Blocher, who was staring right back at me with his wide-open blue eyes. There was no doubt—this was unmistakably Paul, with that same shoulder-length blond hair. His head was tilted oddly to the side, almost disjointed from his neck, which must have been broken. Just above the edge of an uneven, reddish beard, a small trickle of blood rolled from his mouth over his cheek toward his ear.

"What happened to the two bodies?" I asked as I handed the phone back to Anas.

"I had someone call the Kurdish guy's family in Kobane to let them know." He wiped some ashes off his T-shirt with an irritated gesture. "I assume they were picked up and buried the same day. Well, this Paul dude did want to experience Syria, didn't he? Now he can stay there forever."

I WAS DONE in. I was trying to come up with an inconspicuous excuse to leave when two middle-aged men and a young woman stopped by our table. Anas gave both men a bear hug, then kissed the woman on the hand in an exaggerated gesture of chivalry. "Dee, I would like you to meet my friends," he said, loud enough for everyone to hear. "This is Mick from London, and this is his brother William. And this is William's stunning girlfriend, Chiara. Chiara is from Rome. She's the next big thing in the modeling world." Pointing to me, he added, "Guys, this is my old friend Dee."

Mick, William, and Chiara sat down. Anas summoned the waiter and ordered several appetizers and a new bottle of wine. "Time for some food," he said boisterously. "You are all my guests."

I decided to bolt. The new arrivals presented a perfect escape opportunity, especially as Anas seemed to be completely absorbed by Chiara. "Please excuse me," I said. "It's been a long day. I don't wish to be rude, but I need to get some sleep. Thanks for the wine, Anas."

"Sure thing. See you around, Dee," Anas mumbled, too busy ogling Chiara to care that I was leaving. The others waved goodbye.

I left the table and walked toward the taxi stand. Fortunately, there was no one in the queue, no one to notice the tears in my eyes.

TWELVE

THE DRIVE BACK to the hotel was a blur. As soon as I got in the taxi, I stopped the recording and reconnected my phone to the cellular network. Immediately, the phone buzzed wildly with notifications for voice and text messages. I was too exhausted to bother with them. The night lights of Dubai flickered by like rapid fire but could not erase Paul Blocher's dead, wide-eyed stare in the photograph Anas had showed me. For weeks, I had been searching for information on Paul, knowing all along that the chances of his survival were very slim. Yet now that I had finally uncovered the evidence of what had happened to him, I was crushed. I had never given up hope of finding proof of life, and instead I got proof of death. As much as I tried to convince myself that I had done everything in my power and that there was nothing I could have done to save Paul, I felt like I had failed. I barely managed to get out of the taxi when we arrived at the hotel. Dragging myself through the lobby, I ignored the on-duty manager who greeted me warmly.

Back in my room, I texted Khalid to let him know that I had found the answer to our question and that Paul was dead. Khalid called me immediately.

"I'm so very sorry, *habibi*," he said in a tender voice. "Have you informed your friend Hubertus?"

"Not yet. I'm dreading it. It will be a difficult conversation."

I told Khalid about the meeting with Anas and about Paul's bizarre journey and tragic, freakish death in the car accident.

When I finished, Khalid was quiet. "Strange," he finally said. "His death is so senseless, even by the standards of this senseless Syrian tragedy. The whole thing is almost as absurd as it is sad. It reminds me of the way Camus died.

"Who?" I was completely lost.

"Camus. You know, Albert Camus, the French writer. He, too, had been through so much hardship in his life, only to have it end in a weird, random traffic accident. Did you know that about him?"

"No, not really." My mind was elsewhere, still stuck on the image of Paul in that car wreck, and I was not in the mood for Khalid's literary musings, even though I knew that he was just trying to distract me.

"Yes, Camus suffered a great deal, even endured several awful bouts of tuberculosis. He'd had a very poor and difficult childhood in French Algeria. Then his experiments with Marxism and communism, then atheism, never quite finding his footing, not unlike Paul Blocher and the quests that doomed him. And then, shortly after Camus is finally recognized as the brilliant writer and thinker that he is by getting the Nobel Prize in Literature, after being nominated twice before and not winning, after all that, he dies in a car accident, as senseless as Paul Blocher's death. Though I suppose all car accidents and fatalities are senseless, aren't they? Their lives and deaths—Camus's and Blocher's—are like an existentialist story Camus himself could have written. Poor Paul Blocher! It's so dreadful, such an unimaginable story.

"I'm really sorry for the way it all turned out. But remember that the world of evil—the devil—is just an illusion. And the only way the devil loses his powers of illusion is if we realize that he does not exist. The truth will set us free, if you pardon the biblical reference. And whatever the truth does not destroy, the truth can heal, *habibi*. I hope that your friend Hubertus and Paul Blocher's father can find some solace and closure in the certainty, in the truth. May God bless them both and give them strength!"

I thanked Khalid for everything he had done to help me uncover Paul Blocher's fate and asked him to thank the Sheikh and Jamil on my behalf. We agreed to meet four weeks later in Istanbul to discuss an upcoming foundation project.

It was time now to call Huby and relay the sad news. I sent him a message and asked him whether he was available. Ten seconds later, Huby was on the line.

"I was expecting to hear from you today," he said.

"You were?"

"Yes," Huby answered in a sad voice. "Last night I had an awful dream about Paul. When I woke up, I knew that I would hear from you. He's no longer alive, right?"

I swallowed. "I'm afraid that's correct."

The line went quiet. After a minute, I heard Huby inhale and exhale slowly. "Was he executed?" he finally asked.

"No," I said. "He did not die in captivity. He died in a car accident, close to the Turkish border. He passed away instantly and did not suffer. The family of the Kurdish man who died with Paul buried him, too."

Again, the line went quiet. "Thank you for all that you have done," Huby said, speaking slowly and deliberately. "As painful as the news is, it is better than not knowing."

"I'm so sorry." I was close to tears.

"You've gone above and beyond, Daniel," Huby said. "You did everything you could to find my Baloo. I will never forget that."

"Huby, it goes—"

"How do I tell Paul's father that his son is dead?" he said, cutting me off. "That perhaps he is buried somewhere in Syrian no-man's-land, in an unmarked grave dug by strangers? Strangers who had no reason to be gentle with his body when they threw him into the pit. A grave Paul's father will never be able to visit. And how do I tell my Rose? My Rose." His voice trailed off. "How?"

"I am so sorry," was all I could say again. I heard Huby sobbing. "Huby?" I asked when the crying quietened.

"Yes?"

"Forgive this question, please, but would you mind telling me about your dream?"

"I dreamed that Paul was in a car that fell off a cliff and kept falling and falling and falling," Huby said. "When I woke up, there was no doubt in my mind. My Rose told me that I had let out a scream in my sleep. Why do you ask?"

Huby's words sent a shiver down my spine. His dream and my dream of jumping off a swing and falling forever, seeing Paul's face and his wide-open, terrified eyes, were so similar.

"Why do you ask?" Huby repeated his question.

"No reason," I said. "I just wondered."

Huby thanked me once more and hung up. I sat still for fifteen minutes. I remembered that I needed to let my prosecutor friend know that I was all right, so that he would not dispatch a search party to look for me. I sent him a short text message, and he replied instantly with a thumbs-up emoji. Then I attended to all the voice and text messages I had received while my phone was in flight mode at Casa Mia. One message was from Laura, letting me know that everything at home was fine and that the kids were at school. I replied that I would check in later.

I sat on the edge of my bed staring into space. I felt no satisfaction at having discovered what had happened to Paul Blocher, no gratification for having helped Huby reach some kind of closure. I no longer even felt any pain or sorrow for the loss of a young life. I just felt numb, empty. Nothing.

I decided to leave Dubai early the next morning. I craved my home, dinner banter with my family, long walks with our dog. But skipping town also felt selfish: after learning the details of Paul Blocher's death and witnessing the misery of Reem, Samar, and other young women, I was overcome with pangs of guilt at the prospect of returning to my normal life. Or perhaps it was just a case of postpartum blues after all the excitement of the past three weeks.

I picked up my phone and sent a text message to the local number from which Reem had contacted me when she let me know that Anas was back in Dubai: "Met A at cm, got answer to my question. Thank you for everything. D."

To my surprise, I received a reply just a few seconds later: "Glad you found what you were looking for. R."

Suddenly I felt a strong urge to thank Reem in person before I left Dubai. It was exactly midnight, so perhaps too late, but I still suggested a meeting: "Any chance we can meet just for a few minutes? D."

Reem did not reply immediately, and I worried that I had pushed too hard and scared her away. Finally, after three agonizing minutes: "Come to this location in 20 min, coffee shop next to it, if i don't show up leave after 10 min." Only then did I realize that Reem might have to take a serious risk just to break away and meet me. I was mortified that my request might place her in danger. I was about to send a message suggesting we cancel the meeting when I received another message from Reem with a location link. My caution evaporated before I even had a chance to feel selfish. With some luck, I would make it in time. I rushed out the door, down the elevator, and out to the taxi line. The doorman looked at me in surprise. Less than an hour earlier, he had helped me out of a taxi and watched me drag my sorry self into the hotel. Now I was skipping steps and racing down the ramp toward the waiting taxis.

Fifteen minutes later, I arrived at the coffee shop Reem had specified. There was nobody there other than a tired-looking waiter. I was wondering whether I had gone to the wrong place when I saw Reem and her sister nearing the entrance. I stood up and opened the door for them. They walked past me without a word and sat at a table in the far corner at an angle that hid them from anyone on the outside glancing through the window. I followed them and sat down.

"Thank you for agreeing to see me," I said.

Reem nodded. Samar sat impassively next to her. She was holding her headless doll.

"I really appreciate everything you have done for me. Without your help, I would never have been able to find—"

"Please don't mention A's name," Reem said, cutting me off. "Samar freaks out every time she hears it. She still has nightmares about him, still has visions of him ripping the head off her doll. All the other girls in the apartment know to avoid his name in her presence."

I nodded. "Without your help, I never would have been able to find out what happened to the person I was looking for."

The waiter arrived to take our orders. Reem ordered two Cokes for herself and Samar, and I asked for a cup of coffee.

"You're welcome," she said when the waiter left. "I am glad you were able to find out what happened to your friend. Though I assume what you learned from A is that your friend is dead."

"How did you know?" I asked.

"Because most people who enter A's orbit end up dead."

"My goodness, you really are wise beyond your years," I said.

"One learns real fast when one loses everything. And when you are forced, as I was this morning, to witness the death of a pregnant friend because they botched an abortion, wisdom kicks in rather quickly, right after the bitterness. I suppose it's all about survival, isn't it?"

I was chastened, too crestfallen to say anything. The waiter arrived with our beverages, and Samar immediately started to drink her Coke through a straw that she clutched with her left hand.

"I have no words," I finally said. "There are no words."

Reem looked at Samar for a while, then back at me. She had a distant, hazy gaze. "Samar and I were joyful, carefree girls. Our early years in Qatana were happy, though I'm no longer sure what happiness really is, other than a fleeting moment that passes immediately. Or is it a lifetime trying to remember and relive that short moment? Who cares—it doesn't really matter. In Qatana, we had friends who were Christians and Muslims, Sunni and Alawi. Then one day, it all changed. We went from happy, carefree kids to being sex slaves. So when you say that I am wise beyond my years, I don't really know what you are talking about. It sure doesn't feel like a compliment. Samar and I had our years stolen from us. I'd rather have my childhood back than my wisdom."

"I understand," I said.

Reem seemed to be elsewhere, but her words never lost their intense clarity. "I did not ask to grow up so fast. And I will never get to be a child again. But, yes, I did learn to think on my own. Funny, isn't it, how being raped every night has a way of sharpening a girl's mind?"

I struggled to meet her eyes. Samar finished her Coke, and Reem moved her own bottle in front of Samar, who immediately placed her straw in it and started to drink. She never let go of her doll.

"I apologize for my harsh words," Reem said after a pause. "I only pray for one thing—that this nightmare will end soon, one way or another."

"*Inshallah,*" I said. "God willing."

Reem's look was piercing. "God willing?" she shot back. "Which god do you mean?"

I froze instantly, transported back to the meeting with the Sheikh in Beirut. He had asked me that exact same question, with the exact same inflection.

"The god who left me or the god whom I left?" Reem continued in a cutting tone. I did not respond.

"The god who created this world or the god who destroyed it?" she asked.

"The god you pray to," I whispered.

"Oh, *that* god," Reem said sardonically. "You mean the god who doesn't listen to our prayers, who abandoned us, the *cruel* god."

"Perhaps." I hesitated before continuing. "But I suppose we are appealing to his more compassionate side when we pray."

Reem seemed to be mulling over my words. "I think human beings are too stupid and too selfish to pray for the right things. We don't need God's compassion to give us what we pray for. We need God's compassion so that he can help us pray for what we really need, not for what we want."

I stared at this seventeen-year-old young woman in awe and disbelief. In addition to her innate intelligence, she had a depth of wisdom and understanding, born of immense pain and suffering, that I would never be able to fathom. "Is there anything I can do to help you and Samar?" I finally said.

Reem looked at me for a long time. "We are the forgotten ones. For us, silence is violence. I don't want to be a statistic. That evil man told me I was nobody. But I am somebody. I don't want to be forgotten. If you want to help us, then tell our story."

I looked at Reem and Samar, who had finished her second Coke. "I will," I said. "I promise."

Reem stood up and motioned for Samar to follow her. "Thank you," she said. As they walked to the door, Samar turned around and looked at me. I hoped to detect a smile, some spark or emotion, but all I saw was that same blank expression. The waiter brought me the bill, and when I lifted my head again Reem and Samar were gone.

OUTSIDE THE COFFEE shop, I hailed a taxi and asked the driver to take me to Shoufi Mafi, one of my favorite spots in Dubai—a Jumeirah restaurant with a tranquil atmosphere, where I could sit outside in the pleasant breeze. I knew it would still be open at this hour. The twenty-minute drive through Dubai's night was a blur. I didn't see the skyscrapers. I didn't see the giant malls and restaurants. I didn't see the fancy cars. I didn't see the construction cranes. I didn't see the oversize advertisements and billboards with the sheikhs' images. All I saw were streaks of red and white lights.

THE MANAGER AT Shoufi Mafi greeted me cordially and led me to a quiet table. The restaurant was still surprisingly full of locals despite the late hour. I ordered some Moroccan mint tea and asked for a few sheets of paper and a pen. The *shisha* waiter came by for a friendly chat, but I waved him off.

A waitress brought me the tea and the pen and paper, and I started to write.

EPILOGUE*

I MET KHALID one month later at our regular spot in the Kempinski hotel in Istanbul. Even though he was his usual jovial self, I sensed that there was something he wasn't telling me. Toward the end of the evening, I found out what it was. Sheepishly, Khalid asked me whether I remembered our conversation about Jamil and the French intelligence officer who was his biological father. I did indeed. Khalid then asked me whether I also remembered our conversation about the former French intelligence officer who was Huby's friend. I told him that I recalled that, too. I was pretty sure where Khalid was going even before he informed me with a mischievous smile that Jamil had asked him to inquire whether I could find out if these two French agents happened to be one and the same. I replied that I would do so gladly. I reminded Khalid how he had suggested at the time that he would get more chips in his basket by waiting until Jamil asked for this information. But what really impressed me, I now told Khalid, was how he had managed to cash in Jamil's chips with this request rather than his own. Khalid laughed. "I taught you well," he said warmly. Suddenly he turned serious. "*Habibi*, we have to deal with Anas and his crew. If we allow them to continue in

---

* In this epilogue, I have relied on the accounts of Jamil, conveyed via Khalid, with respect to what happened to Bassel and on the accounts of Loubna as they relate to her and her daughter. With respect to Reem and Samar, I witnessed some of the events described in person, in particular the interactions with the two social workers. I have also spoken to Reem's schoolteacher who fully corroborated her narrative. With respect to the events and conversations for which I was not present, I have fully relied on Reem's account for everything she and her sister experienced. I trust her unequivocally. She has never yet uttered a single untrue word to me.

their evil ways, we will be enablers. Never forget what your own sages teach you: he who is compassionate to the cruel will end up being cruel to the compassionate."

AT HIS KIOSK in Beirut one evening, Bassel received a call from his sister in Damascus. In between sobs, she told him that the doctors had given their mother only a few days to live, possibly even just a few hours. Her lung cancer had metastasized to the brain and from there all over her body, and she was heavily sedated, moving in and out of consciousness. Bassel's sister implored him to come to Damascus to sit by their mother's bedside, at least for one night. Disregarding Jamil's plea not to make this dangerous trip, Bassel traveled to Syria in the middle of the night. His plan was to see his mother one last time and then return that same night to Beirut.

A friend from his former intelligence IT unit picked him up on the other side of the border and drove him to Damascus. In the apartment, his sister was waiting for him with tears in her eyes. Their mother, she told him, had passed away earlier that evening. She had tried to reach Bassel, but he had turned off his phone for the journey and removed the battery to prevent any GPS tracking device from following his movements. He had missed his mother by just two hours. Bassel was devastated. He begged his sister to come back with him to Beirut, but she told him that she needed to stay in Syria. Her boyfriend had gone missing, and she would not leave before she found him or at least learned what had happened to him. They parted after a long, tearful embrace.

Bassel's friend was waiting downstairs to drive him back to the Lebanese border before sunrise. As Bassel left the building, two men stepped out of a car and approached them. One of the men called Bassel's name. When Bassel turned around to face him, the other man fired two shots from a handgun with a silencer. The first shot hit Bassel in the chest. As he fell to the ground, the assassin stepped over him and fired another shot into the back of his head. Without another word, the men calmly stepped into the car and drove away. The whole thing had taken no more than fifteen seconds. Bassel's friend stood there paralyzed in fear and shock before running into the building to find Bassel's sister.

The killers were never found.

LOUBNA AND HER daughter made their way to a western European country. She was able to establish legal residence based on a sizable investment in a local community and was promised citizenship for herself and her daughter within three years. She has had tremendous success providing private clients with beauty and fashion advice, and the commissions earned from referrals to cosmetic surgeons haven't hurt. At nights and on weekends, Loubna volunteered in two immigration centers, helping Muslim women in their transition from the refugee camps they left behind.

One Friday evening, three weeks after Loubna and her daughter had arrived in their new home, one of the immigration centers was fire-bombed by right-wing agitators. Nobody got hurt, but the psychological damage was great. Loubna's daughter happened to be with Loubna at the center that evening. From that moment on, she refused to leave Loubna's side, even accompanying her mother to every business appointment. It forced Loubna to take her out of school and have her tutored at home.

One month after the firebombing incident, Loubna and her daughter were shopping at the local supermarket. As she placed her items on the conveyor belt, she asked her daughter in Arabic to get another carton of milk. The woman behind the checkout counter uttered a racist slur, telling Loubna that she and her daughter were dirty Arab terrorists who should go back to their country and blow themselves up there rather than infest this Christian town. Before Loubna could react, a man who was standing behind her gently put his hand on her shoulder and said, "Allow me, please." He then moved past Loubna so that he was facing the woman directly. "First of all, this lady and her daughter might not have a country to go back to," he said in a calm but firm voice. "Second, I would much rather have people like her in our community than ignorant, hateful people like you. And third, you don't even begin to comprehend the meaning of what it means to be a Christian."

He then stepped back behind Loubna without saying another word. Loubna smiled and mouthed a grateful "thank you." The cashier didn't say a word and continued to check out her items in total silence, including the additional carton of milk that Loubna's daughter had just placed on the counter. As Loubna and her daughter left the supermarket with their grocery bags, the cashier ran up to them. Loubna braced herself for another confrontation. Instead, the woman stretched out her hand and said, "I'm very sorry for the way I behaved. I apologize to you and your daughter." Loubna nodded and shook her hand.

The following week, Loubna's daughter agreed to go back to school.

REEM AND SAMAR left Dubai in a painstakingly planned and executed operation. Since Anas and his thugs had confiscated their identification papers, they first had to obtain emergency UN-issued laissez-passer documents with the help of a friendly consular official in Dubai, whose wife happened to work at the UN offices in Geneva. To be on the safe side, this official also issued two temporary emergency passports, just in case the laissez-passer documents ended up being contested by some overzealous immigration officer—"belts and suspenders," as the cautious official put it. The main challenge was to get Reem and Samar to the consulate in Dubai without their absence being noticed by Anas's men. Reem planned every step meticulously. She asked one of the other girls in the apartment to cover for her and Samar by telling their guard that they were ill. When the guard started to shout and demanded to see Reem and Samar, the girl coolly told him that she was happy to get them but that their cough seemed to be contagious. In fact, the girl added, it might be wise for him to arrange a hospital visit for the two in order to keep everyone else in the apartment from catching whatever they had. The guard handed the girl five hundred dirhams and ordered her to put Reem and Samar in a taxi to the hospital to be examined immediately and not to return without a clean bill of health. In this way, Reem and Samar were handed not only the perfect excuse for their absence but also the money for the taxi to the consulate.

Once they arrived at the consulate, they were received by the friendly consular official who showed them the safe room in the building in which they would spend the night. The next morning, their travel documents arrived along with one-way airline tickets to the consul's home country. That night, they left Dubai, together with a chaperone who accompanied them through check-in, passport control, and security. At the gate, he handed them over to another chaperone who boarded the plane with them.

As the plane took off and ascended into the sky, Reem and Samar looked out the window and watched the bright lights of Dubai fade away. They sat for over an hour in complete silence. Finally, Samar looked at Reem and smiled. It was her first real smile since they had been taken from their home in Qatana. Reem stared at her little sister in disbelief. She had been sure that she would never again see that beautiful smile on Samar's face. Reem's lower lip quivered before the floodgates finally opened and tears streamed down her face. A flight attendant rushed over and asked if she was okay. Reem nodded as she wiped the tears out of her eyes. Samar grabbed her hand and did not let go until they landed six hours later.

Three days after their arrival in their new home in Europe, and having received new identities, Reem and Samar were examined and assessed by two social workers to determine whether they would be able to join the local school after a two-month intensive language course. Reem blew the social workers away with her intelligence, and they concluded that she could skip a year and enter twelfth grade as soon as her language skills were adequate. Samar, on the other hand, refused to speak with the social workers, leaving them no choice but to recommend further counseling and homeschooling. Reem committed to helping out by teaching Samar herself in the evenings.

The social workers offered to place Reem and Samar with a family of Iraqi descent in order to provide an Arabic-speaking environment, but Reem turned down their offer and instead asked for a local family that did not speak a word of Arabic. When the social workers asked Reem why she preferred such a harsh and abrupt transition, she was analytical, almost clinical in her reply—first, because it would leave her and her sister no choice but to learn the local language and, second, because it preserved a language in which she and Samar could converse without being understood by their hosts. When one of the social workers asked Reem to reconsider so that she and Samar would have an environment that allowed them to maintain some continuity to their home and friends back in Syria, Reem glowered at her and replied that they had neither a home nor any friends left in Syria and that the door to their past was closed forever.

The social workers looked at each other in amazement. They did not have the heart to tell these two Syrian girls that they had actually contacted their family through the consul in Dubai in order to offer the parents a reunion with their daughters at a secret location. The father replied that the girls' mother never spoke to him again and died of heartbreak a month after the girls were taken away and that his daughters were dead to him because they had dishonored the family by becoming prostitutes. He then hung up before the dumbfounded consul had a chance to say anything.

Reem thrived in school, and within three months she was the top student in her grade. One day, the teacher asked the students to talk about their background and identity. Most students mentioned their country, their language, their religion, their family, the sports team they rooted for, even their preferred comfort food. When it was Reem's turn, she stood up and calmly proclaimed that she no longer had an identity. When the teacher asked her to explain, she said that only a person who had spent a lifetime walking on a straight road could maintain an identity. For her, there had been too many abrupt forks in the road, too many twists and turns, and too many dead ends. When she looked back on her path, she was unable to see her point of origin, unlike her fellow classmates who always knew where they came from. And that meant that she had lost her identity. Reem spoke these words deliberately, even serenely, with perfect diction in her new language. When she finished, the entire classroom sat in stunned silence.

For Samar, the transition was a little more difficult. Every day, she waited for Reem to come home from school. Before they would go over Samar's syllabus together, their daily routine included a walk in the park: first one round on the periphery and then a stop at the playground, watching mothers and nannies play with their little children. There was one tall, handsome boy around Samar's age, with beautiful, melancholy eyes, who was always there with his little sister. Reem noticed that Samar would watch him intently as he tapped his sister gently on the swings or bounced her on the seesaw, pushing off carefully so that she would not lose her balance. A tiny, faint smile crept up on Samar's face as she watched the boy play with his sister.

One day, four weeks after their first walk in the park, the boy and his sister failed to show up at the playground. Samar asked Reem if she knew where the boy was and remained uncharacteristically agitated for the rest of the afternoon and evening. When he was back with his sister the next afternoon, Reem encouraged Samar to say hello. At first, Samar refused. But once the boy and his sister were about to leave, she closed her eyes, mumbled a prayer under her breath, and walked up to him. Reem stayed on the bench and watched the scene unfold from a distance. At first, the interaction seemed stiff and awkward, but after ten minutes, she saw something astounding—Samar was laughing. When the boy finally took his little sister by the hand and left, Samar returned to Reem with an impish smile. She told Reem that the boy's name was Alex and his sister was Tatyana. Their parents were Russian Jewish immigrants who had moved to this country in the late 1980s. Samar asked Reem whether she would be willing to watch Tatyana at the playground the following afternoon so that she and Alex could go eat some ice cream together.

It turned out that Alex and Samar were the same age—Samar was exactly one week older than Alex. Three weeks after their first ice cream date, he persuaded Samar to come to school with him. Reem checked in with the social workers, and they agreed to give it a try, especially since Samar and Alex were in the same grade. The first month was difficult for Samar, but Alex happened to be the school's star athlete and captain of the soccer team, which meant that all his teammates took turns as her guardian angel. Reem knew that her little sister had finally turned the corner the day she noticed that Samar did not pack the headless doll in her school bag.

A few months into the school year, Reem's class read Anne Frank's *The Diary of a Young Girl*. The book had a profound effect on her, and she started to ask herself what she wanted to do with her life, now that she—unlike Anne Frank—had a chance at creating her own future. Her aspirations ran from writer to psychologist to doctor, but she felt unsatisfied. About three weeks after finishing Anne Frank's diary, she was contemplating these career options while watching little Tatyana on the playground. Alex and Samar were off on one of their ice cream excursions. Unexpectedly, Tatyana's mother showed up. The woman had been very kind and embracing to the two sisters and was grateful to Reem for minding Tatyana whenever Alex and Samar stole some time for themselves. She waved warmly to Reem from the bench as she watched her play with Tatyana.

When Alex and Samar returned, Reem joined the mother on the bench. After some chitchat, she playfully told Reem that, now that Alex and Samar had found each other, the time had come for Reem to find the perfect man for herself. "Show me a perfect man, and I'll show you a liar," Reem responded sharply. They both sat quietly for a few minutes, until the mother changed the topic and asked Reem whether she had given any thought to what she wanted to study at university. Reem replied that she hadn't committed to anything yet and asked the mother in return what she had studied. The mother told her that it had been her dream to study law and become a criminal defense lawyer, but after she left Moscow when the Soviet Union collapsed, she never regained her footing or the confidence she had had as a young girl. And then, after Alex was born, she sacrificed her career plans in order to raise her son and then Tatyana.

That night, Reem stayed up late as she researched the field of law and the criminal justice system. By the time she switched off her computer at three in the morning, she had made up her mind. She would study law and become a public prosecutor.

ANAS HAS BEEN retired.

POSTSCRIPT

MARCH 2021

THESE DAYS, CONVENTIONAL wisdom holds that the conflict in Syria has been decided. The war is over. Bashar al-Assad and his regime won with the help of Iran, Russia, and Hezbollah; the opposition, the Kurds, and ISIS were defeated. Sure, some nasty things did happen, but it's time to move on and rebuild the country.

Turns out, conventional wisdom is not particularly wise. This war is not over. The killings have not stopped. The chemical gassings, the cluster bombs, the executions, the torture, the human trafficking, the annihilation of entire villages—they all continue. For millions of trapped Syrians, the nightmare never ends. For others, however, this war has been a godsend. A small group of privileged men connected to the regime through family or business have amassed unimaginable fortunes as they control the war economy, trading everything—food, medicine, fuel, heating oil, drugs, weapons, prisoners, young girls—and looting the destroyed cities for scrap metal, copper, steel, and anything of value. Like in all wars, the only ones left are a few extremely rich individuals and many extremely poor people. Everyone in between has been wiped out. Yes, the war economy is alive and well, and this war will last as long as that remains the case.

MOST CONVERSATIONS ABOUT the war—policy debates, comments to news reports, pleas for help or intervention—tend to trigger those same disinterested, bored reactions: Can we please talk about something else? There's nothing we can do, and besides, that's just the way things are in the Middle East. Savages killing savages. Why is that *our* problem? And what about Yemen? Libya? Afghanistan? Chechnya? Congo? Why keep talking about Syria?

Usually I walk away from these discussions. But once in a while I persist, and in those moments I invariably hear those two dreadful words: Who cares?

Let's see if I can take a stab at answering that question.

Umm Majed, whose husband was tortured to death—she cares. Said, whose wife, four children, parents, and mother-in-law were killed in a cluster bomb—he cares. Manal, whose father and brother were executed and whose decapitated torsos were returned to her only after the payment of a huge bribe—she cares. Rima, whose husband and two children were burned to death when they were trapped in their car after it hit a land mine—she cares. Mohammed, whose wife and daughter were raped and then executed—he cares. Aisha, whose husband committed suicide in prison after being told that his wife had been raped and shot— she cares. Omar and Laila, who were told to pick up the mutilated bodies of their twin sons in a dumpster behind the police station—they care. Hana, whose husband's testicles were stuffed into his mouth after he was executed—she cares. Hussein and Amira, whose fourteen-year-old son's heart stopped beating after twelve hours of continuous pounding and whipping—they care. Umm Farook, whose husband was taken in the middle of the night in October 2012 and who has been showing up at the police headquarters every morning and evening to ask about him, just to be laughed away by the guards—she cares. Nabil, whose parents were shot before his eyes and whose sister was taken and shipped to a brothel in Dubai—he cares. Owiss and Nana, whose twelve-year-old son was captured spraying FREE SYRIA on a wall in the schoolyard and was beaten to death in the police van—they care. Abdullah, whose wife was caught giving water to a wounded protester and who swallowed acid after being raped for twenty straight days in prison—he cares. Abeer, whose infant twins died in her arms gasping for air after a chemical gas attack—she cares. Mimo (Mohammed), whose wife and six children died in a building that collapsed after a bomb raid—he cares. Ibrahim and Jamila, whose only child was killed by a stray bullet as she sat by the window—they care. Fatima, whose daughter died of an overdose when the packet of drugs she was forced to swallow in a transport for a drug gang tore in her stomach—she cares. Aliya and Rashid, whose daughter killed herself by jumping out a window in Dubai after three weeks of sex slavery—they care. Abu Sultan and Nadia, who could not recognize their sons' faces when their bodies were returned to their home—they care. Zahra, whose teenage son was picked up on his way to school and beaten so badly that half his face was missing and his chest was caved in—she cares. Umm Ali, whose husband and two sons were lined up together with twenty other villagers, forced to dig their own graves, and shredded by machine-gun fire—she cares. Mubarak and Yara, whose infant twins froze to death in their arms after their home was pulverized in a mortar attack—they care. Maher, whose seventy-year-old mother was forced to kneel before her executioner and beg for mercy, just to be casually shot in the back of the head—he cares. Amira and Suhail, whose two-year-old daughter died of an ear infection because their city was under siege and had run out of antibiotics—they care. Haya, who has been waiting for her husband and three sons to return ever since they disappeared without a trace in January 2013—she cares.

That's who cares.

THANKS

MANY PEOPLE HELPED me along the way. I wish I could list them all, but some continue to be in harm's way and might suffer grave consequences if I mentioned their names. To all these brave women and men, thank you from my heart.

Thank you, Khalid. You were at times my teacher, at times my guardian angel, at times my brother, and always my companion. You showed me the beauty in Eustache Deschamps's words: "Friends are relatives you make for yourself."

Thank you, Ali, Fatima, Hamdan, Mohammed, Noor, Rashid, Saif, and Salah, for keeping me safe and helping Reem and Samar get out.

Thank you, Manal, Masa, Majed, Renal, and Renwa, for your friendship and hospitality throughout these twenty days and beyond.

Thank you to my friends and colleagues for your critical comments, edits, and encouragement: Karin Beck, Ofer Becker, Ian Eisterer, Doris Frick, David Giampaolo, Helga Hagen, Doug Jaffe, Anita Lowenstein Dent, Oyama Mabandla, Andrew Miller, Adi Nir, Stefano Quadrio Curzio, Karan Rampal, Carrie Strauch, and Sonja Zwerger.

Thank you, Amy Gash, my fantastic editor. The moment I walked into your Algonquin offices in downtown New York, I had arrived home. I loved, loved, loved our editing sessions, even if I hid it well. You immediately "got" the book and helped make every character come alive, even that recalcitrant narrator. At times, you knew my voice better than I did, because you have the rare ability to appreciate the difference between knowledge and understanding. Thank you, Brunson Hoole, for shepherding the book so expertly through the production process while keeping so many balls in the air. Thank you, Michael McKenzie, for overseeing the marketing and publicity campaign with such skill and fervor. Thank you, Randy Lotowycz, for spearheading all on-the-ground marketing, and thank you, Amanda Dissinger, for handling all things media. Thank you, Debra Linn, for your online marketing guidance.

Thank you, Becky Sweren, my wonderful agent, for never wavering in your belief in this book. You worked magic, always with a smile and one step ahead of your surroundings, graciously effacing your own ego while radiating confidence in mine. There was not a single moment when working with you did not feel like a true partnership—you are everything I could have wished for in an agent. And you found the perfect home for this book! Thank you, Allison Warren, for your enthusiasm and wisdom in making the film deal happen, and thank you, Nan Thornton and Shenel Ekici-Moling, for supporting this process so expertly. Thank you, Chelsey Heller and Erin Files, for your efforts in selling the foreign rights.

Thank you, Mum, for not holding it against me that you had to find all this out from a book. Just as your love for me would have made you try everything in your power to stop me, my love for you made me hide it from you.

And thank you, my beloved Laura, Noa, and Ben, for putting up with me, for humoring me with all my odd accents and non-Americanisms. Hopefully this book will help explain why I can be a little cranky when I come home from these trips—though I'm afraid you're still left wondering what exactly it is that I do for a living. For that, I must continue to beg your indulgence.

In loving memory of my father
ZEV LEVIN (1927–2018)